The Force of
*The Umbrella Academy*

# The Force of *The Umbrella Academy*

## Essays on Voices and Violence in the Comics and Netflix Series

Edited by LISANN ANDERS

McFarland & Company, Inc., Publishers
*Jefferson, North Carolina*

*This book has undergone peer review.*

ISBN (print) 978-1-4766-8200-6
ISBN (ebook) 978-1-4766-4423-3

LIBRARY OF CONGRESS AND BRITISH LIBRARY
CATALOGUING DATA ARE AVAILABLE

Library of Congress Control Number 2021044702

© 2021 Lisann Anders. All rights reserved

*No part of this book may be reproduced or transmitted in any form or by any means, electronic or mechanical, including photocopying or recording, or by any information storage and retrieval system, without permission in writing from the publisher.*

Front cover images © 2021 Shutterstock

Printed in the United States of America

*McFarland & Company, Inc., Publishers
Box 611, Jefferson, North Carolina 28640
www.mcfarlandpub.com*

To Silja
"Yay sisters!"

# Table of Contents

*Introduction*
    LISANN ANDERS                                                                                   1

### Part 1: Forces of Identity

Gothic Academy: Horror and Crookedness in a Haunted Household
    KATHLEEN SHAUGHNESSY                                                                10

Liminal Spaces: Being Alone in a House That Isn't Home
    MIRANDA JOHNSEN                                                                          32

Superheroes, Transnational Adoption, and Hegelian Estrangement
    FERNANDO GABRIEL PAGNONI BERNS                                            49

### Part 2: Forces of Otherness

Artifice and the Superheroes of the 21st Century: Post-Cinematic Reflections on Constructedness
    MORGANE A. GHILARDI                                                                    70

Extraordinary Bodies and the Language of Pain: Disability in *Apocalypse Suite* and *Dallas*
    DANA FORE                                                                                          88

### Part 3: Forces of Violence

Domestic Abuse: Normative Violence and Child-Superheroes
    ALOKPARNA SEN                                                                              108

Crystal Moments: Sites of Music and Violence
    LISANN ANDERS                                                                                127

Dissonance: Striking a Chord Through the Silencing
    of Women's Voices
        J.E. HORNSBY                                               147
*About the Contributors*                                           167
*Index*                                                            169

# Introduction

Lisann Anders

Superheroes and comics have long formed a symbiosis that has intrigued decades of readers. In academia, the importance of this visual-literary genre has only been initiated in the 1990s through the work of Scott McCloud's *Understanding Comics* (1994), which formed the basis for a serious academic discussion. In her article "Why Comics Studies?" from 2011, Angela Ndalianis focuses on this slow acceptance of comics within academia. She observes, "As a medium, comics are older than film, television, and video games, and yet there has been resistance from within the academy to the serious study and analysis of this medium" (113). The change came through the "graphic novel" with writers such as Frank Miller or Alan Moore, who redirected comics from a genre that was often deemed to be just for kids to one with a more adult audience (Ndalianis 114; Gavaler). In one of the most recent works on comics and graphic novels, *The New Mutants* from 2016, Ramzi Fawaz even makes the claim that the themes of superhero comics, in particular, have never been solely for kids since, from the very beginning, superhero comics can be seen as "world making," i.e., allegorical devices to discuss social and political issues: "World making describes instances when cultural products facilitate a space of public debate where dissenting voices can reshape the production and circulation of culture and, in turn, publicize counternarratives to dominant ideologies" (Fawaz 14). It is, perhaps, this figurative presentation that makes superhero comics so appealing to filmmakers. While McCloud still saw a clear difference in comics and film in terms of storytelling, scholars have pointed out that they are quite similar in their narrative nature (Pratt 114). It is, therefore, not surprising that film and comic book culture have influenced each other and will, most likely, continue to do so (cf. Ndalianis 114).

While McCloud still made a resolute distinction between film and comics, this point of view has shifted over the past two decades. Drawing on Ng Suat Tong, Pratt explains in his article on narrative in comics, "the types of narrative transitions that McCloud finds to occur between panels are not unique to comics at all. Film excels at portraying the next moment in time in a narrative sequence, but a film can also easily shift between multiple temporal and spatial locations" (114). This volume does not, therefore, make large narratological claims about comics and film by an in-depth analysis of the differences between these forms of media. In contrast, comics and audio-visual adaptations are treated equally. That is to say, form—be it comic-style or film-specific—is always looked at in combination with content as to gain a better understanding of the inter-dependence between the two.

Today, comic book adaptations are no longer a marginalized genre but can be considered mainstream. Their most recent surge in popularity began with the *X-Men* film series, which started in 2000, and was taken to a new level with Christopher Nolan's *The Dark Knight* trilogy (2005, 2008, and 2012). *Iron Man* (2008) followed by *The Avengers* series (starting in 2012), hit home and culminated in *Avengers: Endgame* (2019), one of the highest grossing films of all time. While movie theaters saw a rise in the popularity of comic book adaptations, cable networks followed by releasing television shows such as *Arrow* (2012–2020) or *The Flash* (2014– ), and Netflix ensured the rights to Marvel series adaptations, resulting in shows such as *Jessica Jones* (2015–2019) or *Daredevil* (2015–2018). While DC and Marvel were already known and enjoyed popularity in their comic book publications, their filmic adaptations helped lesser-known comics and comic companies to generate interest from a broader audience. Thus, the general interest in other comic book adaptations started to grow (Rauscher 35). One of these comic book adaptions is the Netflix series *The Umbrella Academy* (2019– ). The original comic book series was released in 2008 but it only received attention from a wider audience once Netflix released the show. It is, therefore, not surprising that *The Umbrella Academy* has not caught the attention of academia, yet. The goal of this volume is to change that, as the series is a rich source for literary, cultural and societal discussions. In that, the show follows a tradition of comic book superheroes, such as "*The Silver Surfer* (1968), *The X-Men* (1974) or *The New Mutants* (1981)" that can be read "as visual allegories for racial, gendered, and sexual minorities. Though socially outcast by a bigoted humankind for their monstrous biology and alien lineages, benevolent mutant superheroes […] were celebrated in comic books as figures who sought alliances on the basis of shared ethical goals rather than national or ethnoracial identity" (Fawaz 5). Even though the series of *The Umbrella Academy* seems to focus more on the brokenness of the individual superheroes and the family as a whole, it is, perhaps, because of the social and political issues we are facing at the moment that the comic book series was adapted at this point in time, in order to become an active part of the ongoing discussions on race, gender, and sexuality. After all, the show not only displays universal themes such as violence in various forms, but it also raises awareness to current issues such as the inclusion of female voices.

*The Umbrella Academy* tells the story of a group of former teenage superheroes who reunite after their father's death. Having grown up, they still have their superpowers, but they have grown apart over the course of the past 13 years, and they are far from being heroes. Trying to define what it means to be a hero, what it means to have powers, what it means to be human, and what it means to be a family, they need to start over. Their identity crises were already made clear in their individual names as their adoptive father, Reginald Hargreeves, did not give them proper names but referred to them by numbers, creating a distance between him and his children. Through the names their robot nanny Grace, whom the siblings call "Mom," has given them, they receive an identity that is linked to their country of origin—a fact that is never referred to directly but becomes clearer in the second season when Vanya is held captive by the FBI and thought to be a communist spy, *inter alia*, because of her name. The comic book series adds another layer that complicates the identity of the siblings, namely their superhero names that show characteristics of the children's powers. Thus, Klaus, who can communicate with the dead is called "The Séance" and Allison, who can manipulate people into doing her bidding is called "The Rumor." The dichotomy between superhero identity and private identity is challenged prominently in the Netflix adaptation especially, as Klaus and Allison do not want to fully embrace their powers. Each one of the seven siblings (including the deceased Number 6, Ben, who is present only as a ghost and only visible to Klaus) needs to overcome their own individual struggles by means of their family to be a family once again.

The comic book series *The Umbrella Academy* by Gerard Way gives superhero stories a new twist as the narrative revolves more around identity quests and the acceptance of powers, or the lack thereof, within a dysfunctional family environment. Moreover, the comic has found a powerful new medium in its Netflix serial format. Here, the power struggles are foregrounded as they are more than just diegetic expressions of character development; they are a reflection of today's society, in which people who are different are still excluded, in which women are still trying to gain a voice, and in which violence is omnipresent. The series discusses these issues and tries to give a voice to individuals who struggle to be listened to—even though they are heard but often ignored. On a narratological level, the show also experiments with different forms of narration as it foregrounds

## 4    Introduction

aural senses in its choice of music, linking violence with voice. Since "comics are a silent medium and when we read a comic we never actually hear anything" (Hague 63), the problem of gaining a voice and being heard is even more apparent in the comics. The comics play with sensory effects by including music, which, of course, remains silent on the actual page. Therefore, no voices can be actively heard; however, the struggle can be seen in the comics' visuality. An example for how the Netflix show deals with the silencing of voices can be found in the character Allison Hargreeves, "The Rumor." She can manipulate people by telling them what to do, meaning her powers make people listen to her. However, when she does not use her supernatural powers but only her human strength, which is, for instance the case when she tells her brothers (in written form) to not harm their sister, her brothers disregard her voice and follow their own agenda, not listening to her. The same muting of voices and her struggle for recognition is, then, intensified in the show's second season where civil rights and sexuality are even more pressing and thus foregrounded in the narrative.

In doing so, the series plays with the notion of memories and points in time. Media science and film scholar Andreas Rauscher points out that many comic book adaptations gained a certain topicality and thus overcame the stereotype of nostalgic childhood memories often associated with superheroes and comics (Rauscher 36). While this is true for most movie adaptations of comic books, *The Umbrella Academy* intentionally plays with the notion of nostalgia and childhood memories, which makes it particularly intriguing for an audience familiar with the 1980s and 1990s. While in the Netflix show, the siblings were born in 1989 and are shown as adults in their late 20s or early 30s, meaning that the story takes place in the 2010s (2019 to be precise), the aesthetic of the show is still reminiscent of the end of the 20th century. This is especially visible in the lack of advanced technology—none of the siblings have cell phones but they use phone booths, they have records instead of CDs or Mp3 files (even hinting to decades before the 1980s), and their CCTV system works with video tapes. The latter probably makes the most sense, since the siblings grew up in the 1990s when VHS was still prevalent. On top of the lack of cell phones, the music choice on the show adds another layer of nostalgia, as the most dominant songs chosen range from the 1960s to 1990s (with a few minor exceptions from the 2010s). The merging and reimagining of time, then, is also displayed in the content of the show and the comics alike through the theme of time traveling. On the one hand, we jump between different historic periods, such as the Vietnam War and the apocalyptic future, on the other hand, time is erased and rewritten as the episodes "The Day That Wasn't" and "The Day That Was" most prominently demonstrate. The second season of the show plays in a different time altogether as the siblings travel back to 1963.

The heterochronic nature of the show, i.e., the setting of it inside and outside of time, is then also mirrored in its heterotopic spaces and the dystopian quality of the comics and the show. The apocalypse is probably the most striking heterochrony and heterotopia of the show. Yet, the childhood home is also positioned as a space of deviation, a space that is different from the norm. This is, of course, shown in the siblings' superpowers, which are controlled and refined in the childhood home but also in the violence the space triggers. This violence is again typical of superhero narratives, which emphasize and discuss violence in various forms through an aestheticization of it (Ahrens 125). This aestheticization is often expressed in the form of self-reflexive artificiality, as Hillary Chute explains in "Comics as Literature? Reading Graphic Narrative." She outlines that "[a] comics page offers a rich temporal map configured as much by what isn't drawn as by what is: it is highly conscious of the artificiality of its selective borders, which diagram the page into an arrangement of encapsulated moment" (Chute 455). In that, the Netflix show pays tribute to the comic books in its artificiality, as it is highly aware of its own medium, which can be seen in the aestheticization of violence and of personal developments. This aestheticization is most prominent in the musical accompaniment of violent scenes and scenes of family bonding in the Netflix show, as is outlined in the chapter "Crystal Moments: Sites of Music and Violence." While the aspect of "physically violent coercion plays a role in all superhero stories; it is practically a genre convention" (Klock 41). In her essay "Domestic Abuse: Normative Violence and Child-Superheroes," Alokparna Sen looks at a more specific violence, namely violence in the home, by outlining different forms of child abuse in the narrative. Moreover, Dana Fore examines the abnormal, i.e., the deviation from the norm, through bodily difference in his essay on disabilities in *The Umbrella Academy*. Hence, from home invasions to child abuse to physical deviations from the norm, the home is transformed into an uncanny space with Gothic qualities due to its moldering architecture and its dark color scheme. Moreover, despite being placed in a city, the house seems isolated and outdated.

It is this uncanny frame of the narrative, this play with familiarity and estrangement, which creates its fascinating suspense, and which is elaborated on in Kathleen Shaughnessy's essay on the Gothic aspects of *The Umbrella Academy*. This is then further highlighted through the framing of the individual characters and their relationship to their own powers. We are taken on a journey to their true selves, but it remains open what the true self is here: the public superhero persona or the private character. This is reminiscent of many superhero narratives, such as *Batman* or *Green*

*Arrow*. Often, the identity quest is closely linked to the space of the city as it presents an ideal frame to explore the characters' psyche as it mirrors the streets of the city and, on a meta-level, the frames of comics (Anders 1). While, originally, each picture is supposed to fit into a frame, this primary layout of comics has long been deconstructed. As we all know, comics show frames that are all but tidy. They are fragmented and blur into each other, often across pages. American cities are structured in a similar way to a grid that is supposed to give the city some structure, often neatly indicated by numerical signs, e.g., the streets and avenues are numbered. While the grid is confining, in the space of comics, and analogously the city, the corruption of the space can be liberating. In fact, when combining comics and cities, it can be seen that cities *in* comics are in fact often represented as confining and liberating at the same time on a metaphorical level. They promise opportunity and prospect, but this "American Dream" comes at a cost. This can be the loss of family and friends due to crimes, an overwhelming anonymity, or the loss the self. Cultural scientist André Suhr sums up this aspect of the city in Jörn Ahrens' and Arno Meteling's groundbreaking edited volume *Comics and the City* by outlining that "[o]n the one hand it [the city] liberates the individual to concentrate on him- or herself […]; on the other hand this very liberation may produce loneliness and isolation. In an atmosphere of general indifference it gets harder and harder to be recognized as an individual. So, according to Simmel, individuality in the modern city becomes a staged production of superficial effects" (240–241). The same holds true for the home of the Umbrella Academy, which is even shown as a cross-section image in the first episode of the Netflix show, highlighting the different rooms as if they were frames in a comic that are divided by the walls, the grid of the house.

Moreover, the performative aspect of individuality, mentioned by Suhr, is predominantly emphasized in superhero comics, in which the hero is dressing up in order to take on the persona of "hero" and/or "vigilante." Since the Umbrella Academy uses uniforms and masks—at least when they are children—their staged persona is stressed. Yet, even as adults, they cannot completely shed these masks, which is substantiated by their names. As mentioned earlier, their individual superhero persona is identified by means of the number they are given instead of a name, whereas their private persona is shown through their actual name. Moreover, the comic books add a third layer as here, we distinguish between the superhero persona through superhero names such as "The Horror," "The Rumor," or "The Séance," which shows an identification through the individual powers, the childhood persona, which can be seen in the numbers given to them by their father, and their names, which mark them as individual adult people. This dichotomy between public and private persona is discussed in this volume by Miranda Johnsen as she connects the different personae with different spaces. Fernando Gabriel Pagnoni Berns focuses primarily on the private personae of the characters as he discusses their estrangement from their own selves through their position as adoptive children. Estrangement is then also touched upon by Morgane A. Ghilardi, who discusses otherness through artificiality and applies the latter to the constructedness of the narrative, offering a post-cinematic reflection and reading of superheroes.

Since the protagonists try to gain a voice within their own home, the notion of space, in general, and the domestic space, in particular, is an important point of discussion. Foucault's concept of space is especially useful when defining the home of the academy, which frames the action of the TV show, as a "crisis heterotopia," a space separated from society in which individual developments take place. In contrast, a "heterotopia of deviation" encompasses institutions where individuals are placed whose behavior is outside the norm (Foucault 24–25). Interestingly enough, the academy combines both directions of heterotopias and presents the consequences of this combination for the individual protagonists. The home, as a Gothic space in which the homely and the unhomely merge into the Freudian Uncanny, is the central force in *The Umbrella Academy* since it is the site of child abuse, the site of coming-of-age, the site of emancipation, and the site of voice. The unheard voices are made heard in this volume, especially the voices of women, as is explored in J.E. Hornsby's piece, which serves as the closing essay to this volume. These paradoxes of confinement and freedom, joy and violence, silencing of voices and enabling them, make the home sublime in the sense that it bears potential for growth and destruction, beauty and horror. While the domestic space, traditionally speaking, has female connotations, the home of the academy is male dominated. Female voices are most of the time suppressed and actively muted here, however, with dire consequences. An example for this would be when Vanya is locked into a soundproof vault by her brothers, but her pleas and screams remain silent.

This collection thus seeks to carve out the different cultural and social forces at work within *The Umbrella Academy*, to explore different questions and forces on identity, individualism, family, and feminism addressed by the show within the space of the home and the narrative. This volume outlines how the series examines, challenges, and potentially reinforces stereotypes of the home as uncanny and destructive as well as of women as untrustworthy gossips or women to be silenced out of fear. This book thus sets out to introduce the comic book series and its Netflix adaptation to the canon of academic discourse in order to finally give it a voice.

## Works Cited

Ahrens, Jörn. "*A History of Violence*: David Cronenberg, die Graphic Novel und die Repräsentation der Gewalt." *Comic. Film. Helden: Heldenkonzepte und medienwissenschaftliche Analysen*, edited by Barbara Kainz, Löcker, 2009, pp. 125–137.

Anders, Lisann. "Seeing the Invisible: Batman's Gotham and Green Arrow's Star City Unmasked." *PopMeC Research Blog*, July 2020, pp. 1–10.

Chute, Hillary. "Comics as Literature? Reading Graphic Narrative." *PMLA*, vol. 123, no. 2, 2008, pp. 452–465.

Fawaz, Ramzi. *The New Mutants: Superheroes and the Radical Imagination of American Comics*. New York University Press, 2016.

Foucault, Michel, and Jay Miskowiec. "Of Other Spaces." *Diacritics*, vol. 16, no. 1, 1986, pp. 22–27.

Gavaler, Chris. *Superhero Comics*. Bloomsbury, 2018.

Hague, Ian. *Comics and the Senses: A Multisensory Approach to Comics and Graphic Novels*. Routledge, 2014.

Klock, Geoff. *How to Read Superhero Comics and Why*. Continuum, 2002.

McCloud, Scott. *Understanding Comics: The Invisible Art*. HarperCollins, 1994.

Ndalianis, Angela. "Why Comics Studies?" *Cinema Journal*, vol. 50, no. 3, 2011, pp. 113–117.

Pratt, Henry John. "The Poetics, Aesthetics, and Philosophy of Narrative." *The Journal of Aesthetics and Arts Criticism*, vol. 67, no. 1, 2009, pp. 107–117.

Rauscher, Andreas. "Von Gotham nach Sin City: (Anti-)Heldenkonzepte in Graphic Novel-Verfilmungen." *Comic. Film. Helden: Heldenkonzepte und medienwissenschaftliche Analysen*, edited by Barbara Kainz, Löcker, 2009, pp. 35–49.

Suhr, André. "Seeing the City Through a Frame: Marc-Antoine Mathieu's Acquefacques Comics." *Comics and the City. Urban Space in Print, Picture and Sequence*, edited by Jörn Ahrens and Arno Meteling, Continuum, 2010, pp. 231–246.

*The Umbrella Academy*. Created by Steve Blackman and Jeremy Slater, Netflix, 2019–2020.

Way, Gerard, and Gabriel Bá. *The Umbrella Academy: Apocalypse Suite*. Dark Horse Comics, 2008.

# Part 1

# Forces of Identity

# Gothic Academy

*Horror and Crookedness in a Haunted Household*

KATHLEEN SHAUGHNESSY

In a single moment of fortune, dozens of magical children are born all over the world; some of them will save the world, and at least one of them will try to destroy it. *The Umbrella Academy*'s near-mythic origins are built on these spontaneous, inexplicable, and un-inseminated live births by dozens of women worldwide—the cycle of creation has been somehow warped to bend time, resulting in nearly fifty simultaneous births of this nature. Both the show and comic book series indicate that there have already been cracks in the origin story for a destined superhero family—the mysterious adoptive father Reginald Hargreeves only acquires a very small percentage of the magical children, and their powers, while exceptional, are usually only seen as effective on a large scale when they work together. In addition to various external villains and unfortunate events, the plot's action is inevitably influenced by (and often brought about as a direct result of) both the warped family structure and the dark, emotionally crippling childhoods of the characters; I would like to argue that the Hargreeves siblings Klaus, Ben, and Vanya (per Hargreeves, these are Numbers 4, 6, and 7, respectively) show a range of classic Gothic characteristics and sibling dynamics. The Hargreeves siblings adhere to unstable but foundational tenets of Gothic literature and present a warped, dark vision of *Bildungsroman* that results in cathartic freedom from a traumatic childhood and the Gothic version of a happy ending.

In this essay, the first television season of *The Umbrella Academy* will be read alongside the first volume of *The Umbrella Academy* comics, which consists of six issues collected under the name *Apocalypse Suite*. As the second season has recently been released on Netflix, this essay will also briefly reference some of the season's elements and draw on some relevant themes from the second volume of the comics, *Dallas*, insofar as they relate to the

Hargreeves siblings' growth in the narrative as Gothic children who have struggled to come of age only to travel back in time. This essay does not specifically delve into the formal intricacies of how the media and modalities function and impact the larger story, and focuses instead on treating the television show and comic as texts to analyze closely. For every Hargreeves sibling focused on in the essay, the following concerns will be examined: the specific traits that make the character a Gothic child, how the character finds resolution in their plotline and in their place in a Gothic household, and the gap between the comic and television series portrayal that arguably create a doubled self. The characters themselves will be examined through Dr. Margarita Georgieva's framework of the Gothic child as seen in literature.

Georgieva conducts her study using first-wave Gothic and devotes much of the text to 18th- and 19th-century models, but the first-wave Gothic can be applied effectively to the more modern Umbrella Academy children, as she notes that "Both the first-wave gothic and contemporary cinema focus on the child as a receptacle, an object that can be influenced and manipulated (metaphorically filled with the soul of an adult) or employed by higher powers to become the hero or anti-hero of new creation/destruction myths" (Georgieva 186). The Gothic Hargreeves children who have been raised to save the world struggle to define themselves outside their childhood trauma and original purpose by forging their own futures outside of the planned path the family patriarch envisions for them, and taking more autonomous roles in fulfilling or avoiding good and evil destinies that may arise. Georgieva works with novels, but as the television series is based on a written story, namely the *Umbrella Academy* comic book, both can be read as parallel texts. The form and theme lend themselves to this, as Julia Round notes that "horror and comics have a long and intertwined history [...]. Gothic's revivalist tendencies means that Gothic stories frequently retell old or traditional tales" (Round 7), connecting well with the referential quality of comics, which often build on traditional types and plots.

In Georgieva's scholarly work *The Gothic Child,* her concept of Gothic childhood finds its origins in early Gothic novels of the 18th and early 19th century, rather than in the modern-day narrative of the Umbrella Academy's adventures, but her flexible definition of why someone in gothic stories would be called a "child" can be applied to all of the Hargreeves siblings at one point or another in the television show and comic:

> it is a mark of filiation; it denotes states of dependency (affective or financial); it is applied to persons of unstable perception and understanding as well as to characters of both sexes lacking affective maturity; to those who are vulnerable or helpless; to those who are under legal guardianship; and to those subjected to parental will and authority regardless of their age ... most gothic heroes and

heroines remain children until that moment of inexorable certainty when they are forced to look at a parent's dead body [Georgieva 2].

Hargreeves' untimely death and funeral bring the Gothic children back to the family home, and thus they can finally begin to grow up, a journey that will be discussed later in the essay. It is worth noting there is a certain gothic sibling not present in this analysis—Number Five, also simply known as "The Boy," is a prime candidate for further analysis as a Gothic child, but this study focuses on Hargreeves siblings who show Gothic child qualities and have grown up in this household. Five vanishes at a young age in both the television show and comic, and only reappears when his siblings are adults and his father is dead; he therefore misses out on many sibling experiences, even more so than the doomed Ben, who lingers after death by Klaus' side and vicariously experiences his coming of age.

The lingering impact of their childhood haunts each Gothic Hargreeves sibling and constantly pokes into deeper issues that resonate in today's culture. The Academy comic is part of a specifically modern moment combining the two elements of Gothic and comics that produce the superpowered individuals we see in the show: "in the late twentieth century, Grittiness, realism and violence returned to comics and, although the superhero still loomed large, he was a more conflicted figure" (Round 39). At the core of the plot, these are imperfectly formed and fundamentally insecure adult children returning to the patriarchal seat to confront ghosts from their youth as well as each other, and wrestling with superhuman powers along the way. Although people of all ages have watched the show and read the comic book, it is important to consider, in light of the characters' ages throughout the series, that "recent Gothic fictions for young people mobilise ghostly children to critique or remedy adult actions, often expressing distrust in adults as authority figures. The dead or ghostly children in these works do not unsettle other characters or the reader as they do in many ghost stories, but instead expose the serious harms posed to children by selfish or evil adults" (Smith 192). This implies that Hargreeves is at least somewhat responsible for Ben's death.

Reginald Hargreeves' adoption of seven children (only six of whom are publicly acknowledged) participates in but ultimately is independent of "the 1764–1824 Gothic tradition of depicting heroines who hide, protect or adopt lost or abandoned children and villains who capture and carry away stolen babies" (Georgieva 187). Hargreeves' assurance to curious reporters that the biological parents of the spontaneous infants "were suitably compensated" for giving up their children is chillingly unsatisfying for the audience to hear as an answer ("We Only See Each Other at Weddings and Funerals"). Although Hargreeves is meant to be a parent to the adopted children, his statement and subsequent parenting techniques indicate that he clearly sees parenthood as clinically transactional in nature. Hargreeves' adoption process is unique, as it is probable that the spontaneous and mysterious quality of the pregnancies (and possibly Hargreeves' offer to compensate them) act to knock out the middle (wo)men of biological parenthood from wanting to participate in bringing up the children. It is likely that few or none of the women who gave birth that day under unexplained circumstances woke up that morning wanting to become pregnant, or at least certainly not under those conditions. The audience is not enlightened about the biological mothers' feelings on the matter, but arguably the shock and chaos of these unexplained births make it possible for an eccentric old man with a checkbook to offer a quick and well-paid solution to their confusion, and thus Hargreeves cannot be fully categorized as either heroic adopter or villainous kidnapper.

However, it is both notable (and to date, unexplored) that the numbers do not add up: of the dozens of children born through these spontaneous pregnancies, Hargreeves is only able to acquire a small percentage of the infants. The narratives of both the show and the comic do not explore why this is or what happened to most of the uncollected children (although the show's second season introduces the character Lila Pitts as one of them), and thus the fates of the rest (and their families) are unknown ... for now. In a July 2020 interview, Gerard Way, the mind behind *The Umbrella Academy*, shared a tantalizing hint relating to this: "the writer/musician revealed that Vol. 4 of the mainstream series will be entitled 'Sparrow Academy'" (Weiss). In the last moments of the second television season, the siblings return from the past to find that Reginald Hargreeves is not only alive, but he does not seem to know the Umbrella Academy and states this is actually the "Sparrow Academy"; a character who looks very much like Ben is present, as well as other shadowy figures, and the Hargreeves siblings of the Umbrella Academy utter a collective curse at this ("The End of Something"). For the comic, Way promises in his interview that

> [It] deals with a very big reveal in the Umbrella Academy universe, something that had been secret for a long time, and our siblings learn a lot about what was happening behind the scenes, as well as discovering the true nature of some characters that have been with them since the beginning.... The series finally starts to answer the question: "What about the other babies born on that day, in that moment?" The Umbrella Academy siblings are not alone in the world anymore [Weiss].

As the adoption proceedings that Hargreeves initiated—at least, for the Umbrella Academy—are all implied to be publicly known news in the story's universe, it is interesting to examine how the international nature of

Hargreeves' adoptions contrast with the older model of "kinship by design" adoption in the United States, which

> governed adoption from the 1920s up to the 1960s [...]. The norm that kinship by design aspired to was that of the biological family, meaning that adoptive parents and adoptees ideally resembled each other as closely as possibly in terms of physical features, intelligence, religion and class background [...]. Science was to ensure a perfect match by controlling and monitoring the adoption process [Andeweg and Zlosnik 69].

The adoptions themselves have nothing to do with this conceptualization of science, but the story is likely centered in the United States, and there are some possible science-fiction elements at work in the very conception of the children. The Umbrella Academy siblings could potentially all come from different countries and backgrounds and certainly possess very different abilities, and there has been no effort to model some uniform idea of the family; their only truly unifying qualities in this respect is that they are all of mysterious origin and grow up to have supernatural abilities. However, Hargreeves' erasure of their backgrounds leaves them Gothic children without stable pasts, biological ties, or knowledge of their biological parents. Although this family has been adopted and forced together under one roof, they still struggle with the nature of the relationships they develop with one another.

Hargreeves' adoption practice is reminiscent, in name if not in method, of a roughly contemporary approach: "From the post-war period onwards, the 'kinship-by-design' paradigm was challenged head-on by an alternative that may be called 'kinship by humanitarian vocation' [...]. The internationalization of adoption was inspired by religion rather than science" (Andeweg and Zlosnik 69). Although the inspiration and intentionality are clearly different, Hargreeves is arguably a quasi-humanitarian in that he acts to adopt with the express purpose of saving the world through his adopted children's efforts. Blithely brushing aside concerns about how his plans for the children will endanger them, Hargreeves is a Gothic parent in the sense that for his family, "The creation of children thus ensures continuity and transmission of the heritage but also brings death. The balance of these two secures the fragile equilibrium of the family and state in gothic. Therefore, births of gothic children might occur in unusual circumstances and are often accompanied by deaths" (Georgieva 197).

The first episode of the television series and first issue of the comic both alters and transfers the balance; although there is no death mentioned at the moment of their births, most of the adopted Hargreeves children grow up trained to kill and are surrounded by death in their crime-fighting ventures.[1] Hargreeves' death sparks a new beginning for all of them.

However, as a parent, Hargreeves is not mourned in the traditional sense. There is a distinct lack of grief and some definite awkwardness when the siblings assemble after Hargreeves' death at the beginning of the television series, showing a sense of duty rather than affection in their actions. The family's half-hearted version of a Gothic childhood staple, the "observation of public or private mourning or execution rituals," is comically fumbled; Klaus knocks over the urn containing his father's ashes, and the informal service ends in a brawl between Luther and Diego that destroys Ben's memorial statue (Georgieva 3).

As a supposedly non-superpowered child, Vanya was deliberately prevented from taking part in the Umbrella Academy's heroics, but she joins her siblings in the family home for Hargreeves' memorial, and later on is with them when their brother Five reappears in the present. Thus, she is a part of the mysteries connected to these events that some of her siblings investigate over the course of the story, regardless of her perceived lack of powers, and the audience accepts that she too must take on her own quest of growth and self-discovery. In the course of their first day as a reunited family, the Hargreeves siblings reluctantly mourn their patriarch's death and bemusedly welcome Five back home, and thus the metamorphosis of the Umbrella Academy may begin: "In the typical gothic birth-chambers and nurseries, there is always a skeleton in the cupboard behind the baby's crib, ultimately linking life and death if taken symbolically. The transformation of the gothic child into a hero or villain is a process triggered by successive rites of passage or quests" (Georgieva 67). The death of Reginald Hargreeves, a man who was the sculptor of his children's haunted lives, coincides with Five's reentry into the present, and with these seismic shifts come opportunities for the siblings to make changes in their stunted lives.

In the comics' first issue, the gifts and their connected issues that come to frame the children's futures are related to the reader through Hargreeves' listed observations. Each child's powers, as well as the clear damage caused by these powers and their upbringing, are rattled off in the quasi-objective and quirky tone of a mad scientist conducting an experiment. Ben is considered by his adoptive father to be "Gruesome but fascinating. Easily manipulated due to enthusiastic but naïve nature. Must learn to suppress my nausea in order to study further," and is treated as a Horror by Hargreeves, who also actively schemes to control him (*The Day the Eiffel Tower Went Berserk* 2). Klaus's report is reflective of his haunted character while also morbidly tongue-in-cheek: "Development of psychic abilities stunted by fretful, morbid temperament. Inexplicable resemblance to an Ingmar Bergman extra" (2). Finally, the unfortunate Vanya is briefly dismissed as mediocre among a list of superpowered siblings, showing "No discernable talents. Some enthusiasm for music, but mediocre skill—can hardly even hobble through a Paganini caprice. Utterly useless," which implies through omission that Hargreeves has tampered with his own research to avoid the issue of Vanya's real abilities altogether (2).

Within the house itself, the viewer guest gets the impression of a Gothic setting that mirrors its inhabitants' gloom and pain. As Georgieva notes in her work, "The duality of the gothic child's home is an extremely convenient means to convey the message that fear resides within the boundary of the *developing* mind [...]. Childhood experiences within the labyrinth of the gothic home are determined by increasing terror" (Georgieva 173, original emphasis), and this is echoed in the television show's Umbrella Academy headquarters by eerie play model pictures on the walls around the children's rooms that have gruesome actions and explanatory captions marking "knee, disarm, gouge" ("We Only See Each Other at Weddings and Funerals"). The scope of the looming mansion the children grow up in and later return to lends itself to an uncanny sense of emptiness, which is particularly notable when Vanya, having recently transformed into the tragic and villainous White Violin, quietly wanders the many rooms and dim halls in her destructive stroll.

This moment of structural focus echoes the first episode's dance number that zooms out to show the building as a dollhouse-like structure, with its inhabitants moving in an independent but simultaneous rhythm. However, in this scene Vanya now knows that she has powers and has come to realize her full history in the house after decades of suppression and drugging. Her trip down a haunted memory lane through the house echoes the memories of a stunted child that has heretofore been disregarded or mistreated: "The gothic child frequently grows up with the effort of remembering and this effort goes hand in hand with a fear of forgetting the past, or of having to deal with modified (falsified) accounts of the past" (Georgieva 109). Vanya's flashbacks of the many rejections she received from the family in each room precedes a physical explosion in that room as she slowly destroys the house from the inside out. Ultimately, she transforms what was once the Hargreeves family's home into the very definition of a Gothic ruin: "It is not a sign of what has been lost but of what remains. The gothic ruin is the memory of a place that has been and, as such, it becomes a vial foundation for the gothic child" (*ibid.*).

Vanya also destroys the home in the comic, but here she is standing outside. As in the television series, Pogo[2] is killed in the process, but the tone of the aftermath is significantly different from the show's reaction, where Vanya's shocked and fleeing siblings are in deep distress. At the end of the *Apocalypse Suite* comic, the siblings come home to find the wreckage of the mansion Vanya destroyed, and an unnamed speaker, ostensibly one of the siblings, muses on the implications of the moment: "This was, of course, ironic. But far from tragic. A house that held so many awful memories for us was gone. And we were fine with that," showing that instead of mourning the structure's ruin, the Gothic children experience a sense of relief that the ruins of their childhood are now reflected in the ruins of the academy that Hargreeves built (*Finale; Or, Brothers and Sisters, I am an Atomic Bomb* 21–22).

One Hargreeves in particular has developed these awful memories from experiences with both sides of the veil. It is evident that Klaus exists, both as a quasi-functional drug addict and as an adopted Hargreeves with the primary power of communing with the dead, in a perpetual fog of unreality. An eccentric man-child who happens to be a necromancer, Klaus is generally unstable—his introductory scenes show him overdosing, being revived, and then cheerfully greeting the paramedic—and clearly haunted by his powers. As Georgieva explains, "On numerous occasions gothic children are represented on the threshold of death, on the margin of society. They are between worlds (that of the child and that of the adult) and in hesitation between two states or emotions, while the twofold nature of the gothic world is expressed in constant confrontations between good and evil" (197); and as a Gothic child whose powers blur the boundaries between the worlds of the living and the dead, Klaus has grown to adulthood unable to fully participate in either of them.

In the world of the comic, Klaus is seen literally hovering around his siblings for much of the plot. This version of Klaus differs from his television counterpart in that he is simultaneously more disturbed and better at crime fighting and problem-solving. He is in control of his abilities and is confident in using them in a more active role within the superhero team, albeit along with his own particular brand of dark, pseudo-nihilistic sassiness. He maintains a droll if morbid and inappropriate sense of humor about his mental health that he nonchalantly shares during a dramatic and chaotic battle: "was better off at Shinyview—at least you get a sponge bath from a large ex-con. The papers all said I was cracked, but I checked myself in […] comatose ward […]. I preferred the company. Ever wonder what a vegetable thinks about?" (*Dr. Terminal's Answer* 13–14).

As indicated by the first television episode's title, "We Only See Each Other at Weddings and Funerals," at the start of *The Umbrella Academy*, Klaus is cut off from his living family. He is a voluntarily liminal member of the superhero team due to his eccentricity and unreliability, and the other living siblings usually ignore Klaus' contributions, except insofar as he might be useful. Unlike the other Gothic Hargreeves children who are either simply reluctant to or prevented from using their powers regularly due to various obstacles, Klaus is the one to actively and knowingly block his own abilities through drugs. The nature of the spirits that haunt him bring to mind Victorian understandings of death, as "A failure or refusal to memorialise contributed, among other things, to the concept of persecutory, haunting ghosts associated with the Gothic hero-villain who is often also a persecutor" (Davison 7). Klaus' attempts to block communing with traumatizing spirits also accidentally stall his ambivalent efforts to conjure his father for much of the series. The trauma of being forced to communicate with the dead as a child has followed Klaus into his adulthood: "I know you don't like to do it, but I need you to talk to Dad," Luther says to Klaus in the first episode, acknowledging the strain of Klaus's abilities ("We Only See Each Other at Weddings and Funerals").

Despite being estranged from his family, Klaus is also drawn back to the Umbrella Academy mansion by the death of family patriarch and superfamily ringmaster Reginald Hargreeves. For the Gothic and childlike Klaus, death should act as an impetus to grow up, as "Contemplation of parental death and the observation of public or private mourning or execution rituals constitute a rite of passage for the child and are thus encouraged" (Georgieva 3). Klaus is an almost overly wrought Gothic child whose rite of passage involves the deaths and afterdeaths of multiple family members and loved ones as well as absolute strangers. In the show, the audience witnesses a horrible memory from Klaus' childhood that has had a lasting impact: as a child of thirteen, Klaus was forced to spend extended time in a mausoleum as part of Reginald Hargreeves' efforts to make him accept and access his powers. In a brief onscreen glimpse into Hargreeves' notebook of observations, this coolly clinical experiment is indicative of his approach to teaching his children-pupils to manage their abilities. He writes, "I found that number four was simply not progressing in his abilities to conjure the non-living. He seems to not want to embrace this power. I sped up that ability tonight by locking him in the mausoleum overnight. Hypothetically he is seeing gore and death" ("The Day That Was").

As is seen in Klaus' flashback to his adolescence, he indeed communicated with horrifying spirits that night, which undoubtedly prompted him to avoid conjuring them again: "Etymologically, 'haunting' emerged in English in the early thirteenth century, meaning 'to practice habitually' [...]. Ideas about returning and obsession are implicit and retained in its modern usage" (Round 60). The spirits are haunting Klaus as they are always present; they are a constant reminder of the dead or rather ubiquitous dead and scenes of death around him that Klaus has previously avoided through the only obsessive constant in his life: drugs. This experience undoubtedly had serious repercussions for a Gothic child connected to the supernatural world, as "If there is one visual setting that has proved indispensable to Gothic visual expression, it is the graveyard, serving, simultaneously, as terminus, stage set and point of re-entry, resting-place and haunt of vengeful revenants" (Jones 20). At the start of the fifth issue of the comic, a note from Pogo's diary shows the process of how Klaus' traumatic childhood transformed his personality: "The Séance (00.04) worries me the most. There's no youth left in him at all. Hargreeves means well, and only wants to make him strong, but he can't see how he's breaking the boy. Séance can't respond in any emotional way anymore; the only reaction I get out of him is bewilderment. I think the boy is on drugs [...]" (*"Thank You for the Coffee"* 2).

In a scene in the television series where Klaus involuntarily sobers up—something he finds more torturous than the actual torture that he is being subjected to at the hands of Hazel and Cha-Cha—Ben urges Klaus to take control of his own life and abilities by actively remaining sober and choosing to see the ghosts around him instead of avoiding them; Ben points out, "You haven't been this sober since you were a teenager, since you decided to keep the ghosts at bay. This is your chance ... to control them" ("Extra Ordinary"). During the times that Klaus does commune with the dead in the television series, their spirits range from nightmarish to banal, including the eventual one-on-one conversation that Klaus has with Hargreeves while briefly in Heaven after sustaining a serious head injury. In their meeting at an otherworldly barbershop, the deceased patriarch barks, "What in God's name took you so long? I expected my son who can conjure the dead to have brought me forth days ago," showing that even in death he maintains exacting standards ("The Day That Was"). Despite the oddly touching father-son element of the scene, where Hargreeves gives the forever scruffy Klaus a shave, there is an underlying menace to the moment due to their history together as well as the knowledge that Klaus will have to wake up eventually to a host of other problems. As Georgieva notes, "The confrontation between the gothic child and the monstrosity of the male father figure entails a host of morally and philosophically complex issues," and here, both Hargreeves men excavate the deep cracks in their past as Klaus challenges his father's parenting model and Hargreeves counters with his own logic (Georgieva 177).

This encounter, coming shortly after Klaus' return from time traveling to the past, cements Klaus' *Bildungsroman* as effectively molding him into a more adult figure, albeit one with remaining quirks: "The purpose of the child's quests is to find the skeleton, discover the history of its presence there and keep on living after the terrible secret is out" (Georgieva 67). Klaus has confronted not only his own demons but his father after years of estrangement and the two have hammered out the core arguments of their relationship. Ironically, neither is fully wrong or right in their argument— Klaus addresses the harsh childhood that the patriarch enacted on his adopted children, but Hargreeves notes that, "You children like to blame everything on me," which ignores the trauma of the children's upbringing but does touch on the separate issues they have developed as adults ("The Day That Was"). In the second season, the time traveling siblings meet a Hargreeves who has no idea that he will one day adopt them; however, he still manages to give callous and effective advice that serves to both infuriate and inspire the siblings: "you're the special ones, aren't you? Why don't you band together and do something about it?" ("A Light Supper").

In the television show, Klaus not only crosses the boundaries of life and death, but also accidentally stumbles into a time-travel love affair that ends in blood and death but ultimately shifts the balance of his life. In escaping from Hazel and Cha-Cha, Klaus accidentally steals a briefcase that acts as a time portal when opened, and lands in the middle of an American soldiers' tent during the Vietnam War. Even Klaus' accidental time travel figures him as a Gothic child, as he finds his footing swiftly in this alternate life:

> we find in the gothic novel the beginning of attempts to create a child figure entering parallel worlds, travelling to places outside the immediate reach of known society, where the limits shift from adult-enforced taboos, imposed on the moral and physical existence of the child, to unlimited freedom. The children's role is to test its boundaries and delimit a world of comfortable existence for the adults they will become [Georgieva 198–199].

It is evident that Klaus' experience in the past has changed everything, regardless of how little time it occupied in the present. As an impromptu combatant fighting for the United States who falls in love with fellow soldier Dave, Klaus finally experiences a true death-linked rite of passage on the battlefield, the briefcase taking him back to his own time just after the violent death of his lover. Losing Dave finally triggers Klaus' rite of passage into adulthood, which transforms his behavior and actions. It is an older and more sober Klaus who returns, visibly matured to the extent that he can only weakly imitate his old personality as an extravagant persona around his family members.

Five's closing monologue at the very end of the *Apocalypse Suite* comic takes a moment to reflect admiringly on Klaus' abilities: "We all knew The Séance was capable of telekinesis, but no one knew he could halt a forty-thousand-ton chunk of the moon rocketing toward us. I suspect not even The Séance had known this" (*Finale; Or, Brothers and Sisters, I am an Atomic Bomb* 19). Although the growth of the Gothic children in the comics is not nearly as pronounced as in the television show, the shocked expression shown on the cartoon Klaus' usually blank or snarky face as he saves the world indicates he has accessed some genuine emotions along with strengthened abilities.

Despite many perils in the children's traumatic upbringing, it was sweet-natured brother Ben's death prior to the start of both the show and comics that ultimately led to the end of the superhero team and quasi-family. "There are worse things that can happen," Five assures his adoptive sister Vanya after she confides to him that their family hates her, and her response, "You mean like what happened to Ben?" is the show's first acknowledgment that Ben's absence from some of the later family portraits has a tragic story behind it ("We Only See Each Other at Weddings and Funerals"). "Was it bad?" Five asks quietly, to which Vanya gives an acknowledging nod, and the episode immediately cuts to Ben's memorial statue in the courtyard of the family home, which bears a vague but suggestive epitaph: "Ben Hargreeves: May the Darkness Within You Find Peace in the Light" ("We Only See Each Other at Weddings and Funerals"). During an argument, Klaus distractedly tells Ben, "I'm sorry, I know you weren't ready to die violently at a young age," both implying a painful death and still avoiding talking directly about it ("The Day That Was"). The family unit's collapse after this event can be explained by the Gothic understanding of death: "Death was notably and frequently represented in the early, classic Gothic as a destabilizing, disruptive force involving intergenerational, historical crimes/sins requiring exposure, recognition, and appeasement by way of mourning rituals and memorialization processes" (Davison 6). Ben is the most mature and kind-hearted sibling and is implied to have been the glue uniting the siblings; as Vanya notes in her book, "in the end, after our brother Ben had died, there was really nothing connecting us. We were just strangers living under the same roof, destined to be alone, starved for attention, damaged by our upbringing, and haunted by what might have been" ("Run Boy Run").

The first episode's bank robbery shows the first onscreen use of Ben's force—powerful Lovecraftian tentacles that emerge from his torso and are only roughly visible behind frosted glass. The boy reluctantly uses them to rip apart bank robbers before emerging with blood all over his uniform and timidly asking, "Can we go home now?" ("We Only See Each Other at Weddings and Funerals"). This depiction of Ben's abilities and reluctance to fight lines up with the description of teenage Ben as given by Pogo in the comic: a strange combination of monstrous power and childlike innocence. Klaus is somehow able to conjure the ghost of Ben consistently, even when high on drugs, but the Netflix series and comic show that even in life, Ben was a Gothic child; "I didn't sign up for this," he quietly states before reluctantly using his abilities to slaughter the criminals ("We Only See Each Other at Weddings and Funerals"). The mystery of how exactly the Horror died prior to the events of the comics and show is still ongoing to date, as comic creator Gerard Way admitted in an interview with Forbes upon the first season's release, in response to a question about what unresolved questions he has had to address in helping to develop the show: "Probably what happened to Ben, what happened to the Horror. I never really answered that. I originally just wrote the character to be dead, that was his function. I always knew I was going to resolve it. The thing about The Umbrella Academy, it's almost like improvisational jazz. You're just making it up as you go along" (Baltin).

If the show's costumers are following the same logic in dressing and indicating causes-of-death for other ghosts, Ben was dressed in all black at the time of his death as a young teen and appears to have no visible cause of death. Again, this feature about Ben ties in with the concept of the Gothic child: "Because of this dual nature, the child is often transformed into a sublime object—a creation that combines natural perfection and projections of parental terrors linked to uncertainty about the future and death. The child's sublimity is dependent on two factors: its timelessness and its omnipresence" (Georgieva 192). Ben voices this as a primary complaint to his brother Klaus, while watching the necromancer go into drug withdrawal: "You know what the worst part of being dead is? You're stuck. Nowhere to go. Nowhere to change. That's the real torture, if you gotta know. Watching your brother take for granted everything you lost and pissing it all away" ("Man on the Moon"). Ultimately, Ben has not been able to experience rites of passage either as a traumatized child or as a young man cut off in the bloom of burgeoning adulthood: "the gothic novel stages experiments with children abandoned by the old generation and left by themselves to build new domestic structures or to reinforce the old ones [...]. All adults in gothic fiction are former children who survived" (Georgieva 67). As Ben did not survive and died somewhere in the in-between period between Gothic childhood and adulthood, he is also arguably on a quest to experience his *Bildungsroman* in the series.

Way's comment about Ben's original purpose relates interestingly to conceptualizations of the Gothic child: "when looking for the gothic child within a text, it should be borne in mind that children who are not subjected to certain rites of passage function as gothic elements enhancing the portraits of other characters" (Georgieva 75). Viewing Ben through this lens, the Horror should technically be a Gothic element created to be a common and divisive memory for the siblings as well as Klaus' companion; supporting this is his first appearance as a young adult ghost in the first episode of the series, sitting quietly in the backseat of Diego's car and visible only to the chattering Klaus. For Gothic children, "Often, the child is a projection, an idea or a memory in the adult's mind" (Georgieva 3), and thus an audience who has been conditioned thus far to see Klaus as unstable and perpetually on drugs may question whether Ben is simply in Klaus' head and occupying the role of a Gothic element.

However, throughout the series Ben becomes increasingly more visible and active, encouraging Klaus to become sober and confront his fears, and he starts expressing more opinions and emotions. Ben's first corporeal action is to punch Klaus in the face in frustration after Klaus tauntingly tries to take pills, knocking them out of his mouth. He later becomes corporeal to pull his family to safety as their home collapses. Ben's only appearance to the rest of the siblings in the first season comes in the final moments of the series, as the Horror is unleashed through the Séance's necromancy. As Georgieva notes, "On the one hand, there are children [...] who play a role of supporting characters or are mere accessories contributing to the general atmosphere [...]. On the other hand, there are children who participate in the plot, contribute to the creation of suspense and take part in the actions, becoming the main characters of the story" (Georgieva 8). Ben's status as the formerly living superhero who is tethered by Klaus' powers makes him uniquely able to shift roles from an invisible and incorporeal spirit to an active fighter, finally willing and able to fight in the name of defending his family. During the second season, Ben is able to temporarily possess Klaus (with reluctant permission) and uses his time in a physical body to walk barefoot, smell flowers, eat fruit and flirt awkwardly with a crush ("Öga for Öga"). In the second season's penultimate episode, Ben appears in Vanya's mind as she panics, and calms her down; this costs him dearly, and as Ben Hargreeves finally fades, he asks Vanya to tell Klaus that he was never holding Ben back from going into the light, admitting that he was afraid to go himself. He reminds her that "I died 17 years ago. All the rest of this, these years with Klaus, it's all been gravy" ("743").

Throughout the comics, Ben's ghost does not appear at all, and instead there is only a monument near the house standing as a silent presence. In the second issue of the comic, Luther returns from the moon and lands next to Ben's statue, which shows a more superhero-esque figure modeled with eldritch tentacle power in action as opposed to the simple and youthful memorial depicted in the series (*We Only See Each Other at Weddings and Funerals* 4). When Allison makes her adult appearance in the comics, she also comes to stand near Ben's statue, and tells Luther, "It wasn't your fault, you know [...]. I know everyone blames you for what happened to Ben. But none of us know what really happened that day" (4). Ben's very absence outside of flashback is as eerie as the awkward conversation skirting the details of his life and death that Allison and Luther have standing in front of his memorial statue, and the spaces where the reader imagines him to be tell his story more effectively: "A gothic structure is [...] apparent in comics, as the narrative is presented in a non-linear manner where all moments co-exist on the page, recalling the gothic trope of haunting"

(Round 74). Pogo's diary musings on Ben show the reader a glimpse into the character, a gentle and fragile sounding Horror: "None of the children want to be heroes, and none less than The Horror (00.06). He's only trying to please Hargreeves and Spaceboy. I suppose this is normal enough for a teenage human, but he's not learning how to be an individual in his own right" (*"Thank You for the Coffee"* 2).

In a position that the future White Violin would be all too familiar with from her childhood, the essay concludes with Vanya. Perpetually and purposefully left out of everything from family portraits to superhero team tattoos during her childhood, Vanya Hargreeves has built a life of quiet, dulled resentment against her adoptive family that has manifested in a tell-all manuscript, *Extra Ordinary: My Life as Number 7*. In the television series, she is inspired to write this five years prior to the main events of the show, after seeing a sale window displaying a set of comics that were written about her siblings' superhero adventures ("Extra Ordinary"). Vanya has grown up in a unique situation—the only (seemingly) non-powered Hargreeves to be born in the same exceptional circumstances as her siblings but not to develop any supernatural abilities. As her siblings save hostages at the bank in their first superhero outing, the young Vanya longingly looks on and asks Hargreeves, "Why can't I go play with the others?" to which Hargreeves, unnecessarily blunt to the point of cruelty, replies, "I'm afraid there's just nothing special about you" ("We Only See Each Other at Weddings and Funerals"). Vanya's accidental quest for self-discovery (largely motivated by her treacherous boyfriend Leonard) is the most impactful for the story's trajectory and the growth of individual characters. In this respect, Vanya is the most truly Gothic of her siblings, as she undergoes an unconscious quest that peels away years of negligence to reveal an ugly family secret. In envisioning the circle of a Gothic tale, Georgieva describes how "Large gothic families produce growing numbers of children and heirs (the 'growing crescendo') [...] delve deeper and deeper into their past (a 'deepening recess') to uncover family secrets of hidden, lost, kidnapped children" (16). Vanya's destructive stroll through her childhood home, described earlier in the essay, breaks down the structure along the memories she associates with it, engaging in "what Fred Botting calls 'homely Gothic' [...] it brings horror home, situating it within the bosom of the nuclear family" (Andeweg and Zlosnik 66).

As the show gives equal space to each of the Hargreeves siblings, the realization that Vanya has indeed been disdained and disregarded to some extent by all of her brothers and sisters comes as a surprise, but one that is clearly a part of her Gothic childhood. Although the envious Vanya projects an excessive amount of arrogance and indifference onto her powered siblings, it becomes apparent that Hargreeves not only trained Vanya to feel powerless, but also influenced her siblings to view her in the same way. This makes it easy for the psychotic Leonard to isolate her and mold her perspective to create a narrative pitting the unempowered Vanya against the rest of the family: "As for the future gothic villains, authors have two solutions—the child is either the exact copy of an evil parent or is nothing like anyone in the family, the case of siblings to be opposed to one another" (Georgieva 23–24). Vanya comes to see herself as the victim, but not necessarily the villain. In the show, during one of the few moments where Hargreeves' notes are discussed aloud in the show, the patriarch writes that Vanya's powers are "unlimited, uncontrollable, and dangerous," and prescribes "mood altering medication to keep her sedated" ("The Day That Wasn't").

Vanya herself does not necessarily need to be the sum of her powers, and the audience must also question how much of Vanya's personality has been informed by her upbringing: "the guilt of children in gothic is sometimes an issue of doubt since they are depicted as susceptible to outside influences" (Georgieva 85). However, as a Gothic child full of anger, Vanya must necessarily be set against her siblings to create a complicated dichotomy of good and evil, albeit with blurry distinctions: "The evil twin motif gains ground in gothic with stories of sibling conflict and fratricide. The device is used to create heroes and anti-heroes who participate in the same plot, and enables the author to compare and contrast conflicting ethical ideologies and draw a moral conclusion from the story" (Georgieva 23–24).

Although figured as a quiet constant among her wild and gifted siblings, the supposedly "Extra Ordinary" sibling, Vanya is easily manipulated by the first show of affection in her life as offered by Leonard. She also does not have the perfect sweet-temperedness of a traditional heroine. Her actual personality has been so deeply suppressed for so long that it is jarring to see how swiftly a non-drugged Vanya snaps at her sister Allison after over a decade of not seeing her, and how little it takes to push Vanya into violence: "Children, adolescents and new generations are powerful symbols of rebirth and renewal, or inversely, of vengeance, destruction and ruin, which means that child figures are an extremely pliant, exploitable material when working with the gothic" (Georgieva 32). The "dulled" personality that Vanya shows comes from years of taking mood-altering medication that she believes helps with anxiety but actually suppresses her abilities; as Leonard excitedly explains to her, "Your ability is tied to your emotions ... when you feel a strong emotion, the sounds around you are somehow converted into energy" ("I Heard a Rumor"). It is during another flashback to childhood in the penultimate episode that a different Vanya is revealed. As a four year old, Vanya was already very powerful and aware of her abilities;

Hargreeves tested her away from the other children and seems to have been aware of not only the threat Vanya's powers posed to the world but also of a more sinister side to Vanya's personality.

Hargreeves' notes about the youthful Vanya seem generally clinical but indicate some fear of what Vanya might be capable of: "A controlled environment has proved ideal for the maximum impact of Number Seven's powers. But in the face of sure, uninvited chaos, she must be trained to locate control in another form" ("I Heard a Rumor"). More than anything else, the trouble with young Vanya's power was that like the child she was, she did not seem to prioritize controlling it for the sake of others. The children's mother figure Grace is a robot because as a toddler, Vanya killed multiple human nannies when they tried to make her eat her oatmeal. It is only once Vanya understood that she could not destroy Grace, and saw the briefly contorted form of the robot, that she ate her food obediently. Soon after realizing young Vanya's homicidal tendencies, Hargreeves decided to isolate Vanya from the other children with the excuse of "illness," ordered Allison to use her coercive power to make Vanya forget her abilities and started Vanya on medication to alter her moods. These actions have further pushed Vanya into becoming a Gothic child, as "Used for the generation of mystery and suspense, this absence of early memories is also taken as a sign that the child exists outside of time and is therefore timeless" (Georgieva 193). In the present, Vanya tells her siblings in anger that "I have been left out of everything for as long as I can remember," unaware that the reason she has been left out of superhero activities is the same reason she cannot remember having powers ("The Day That Wasn't"). After the oatmeal debacle, Vanya pleadingly told Hargreeves "it was an accident" ("I Heard a Rumor"). Little four-year-old Vanya may not have been aware of the real consequences of her actions, but she recognized that what she did was bad and tries to mitigate it, just as Hargreeves also tried to control the situation. Notably, Vanya was ahead of the curve as a villainous Gothic child in the traditional understanding: "Gothic novels dealing with young children who kill during their early childhood are rare during the period 1764–1824. However, countless numbers of books deal with childhood intentions and desires to kill a parent or a sibling, and depict adolescents killing their fathers or brothers" (Georgieva 31). It is only as a moody young child and as a grown adult with recovered memories of her childhood that Vanya is murderous.

Vanya learns about her power suppression from Allison after her sister comes searching for her, attempting to fulfill her own quest to find and guard her family and realizing some hidden family secrets in the process. Vanya immediately believes Allison's story, but also decides that Allison is threatened by her powers: "Secondary narrator reliability becomes a crucial issue in many novels. The gothic child is in perpetual danger of encountering altered versions of the past" (Georgieva 110). Her near-murderous attack on her sister is soon followed by another effort to rewrite the story: she desperately tells Leonard that "I didn't—I didn't mean to kill Allison," shortly before killing him in an argument ("Changes"). It is tempting to believe Vanya, a Gothic child who has been all but forced into her role. However, during her transformation into the White Violin after Luther imprisons her in the superhero equivalent of a dungeon, Vanya has visions of two of her childhood selves as a toddler and a pre-teen that suggest she has possibly been moving towards this path for years. In the vision, little Vanya tells adult Vanya, "They're afraid of us. Embrace who we are ... who we've been all along" ("Changes"). In endeavoring to prevent Vanya from becoming a Gothic villain during her childhood, Hargreeves has only forestalled the White Violin from becoming a Gothic villain in adulthood. As Ben tells Vanya in the second season's finale, "Dad treated you like a bomb before you ever were one" ("743"). Vanya's layers of neglect and trauma multiply to produce a Gothic villain in the vengeful White Violin.

In the *Apocalypse Suite* comics, Vanya is a far more straightforward villain, sour-faced and more hostile even under the influence of her mood-altering medication, who has not played her violin in years. Similar to the Hargreeves family of the television series, Vanya's siblings in the comic also disregard her as "Just a citizen. No one special," rather than family, as Diego tells the others after Vanya runs off (*Dr. Terminal's Answer* 19). Although she initially rejects the orchestra's plan to destroy the world, Vanya immediately changes her mind after Diego rejects her efforts to alert and help the Umbrella Academy. Her decision to audition for the Orchestra Verdammten at the Icarus Theatre, a group of psychotic musicians, is an active betrayal of her family rather than a series of accidental steps towards evil (*We Only See Each Other at Weddings and Funerals* 18–19). The evil orchestra acts as the Leonard figure in the comic to goad and reveal her secret abilities.

Having apologized to her brothers and sister and father in her last tortured moments of sanity as the Orchestra transforms her into the White Violin, the newly villainous Vanya addresses the orchestra as "Brothers and sisters, listen to me—! Gather your trumpets, your cellos, your harps—! Lend me your lives and prepare for demise—for tonight we end the Umbrella Academy—and tomorrow we end the world," fully embracing villainy (*Baby, I'll Be Your Frankenstein* 23). The flashbacks of the White Violin transformation are echoed in the staggered release of character exposition and development in the comics, as "embedded stories are supported by the comics medium. Layers are added to stories and characters, creating a narrative structure that echoes the textual strategies used by gothic texts such as *Frankenstein*, which contains multiple framed narratives" (Round 158), and Vanya's transformation reveals the underlying Gothic child's road to villainy that is hinted at in her flashbacks and the tell-all book.

As she begins the suite to destroy the world, Vanya suddenly abandons her plan entirely in order to confront "Hargreeves," who is really Klaus in disguise. Even as the White Violin destroys the world, her adopted father and the source of much of her pain has apparently appeared to distract Vanya by coolly telling her that she is losing the larger fight. When Diego tries to soothe Vanya's clearly hurt feelings, the White Violin—in a rather meta moment as a Gothic child—wryly inquires, "Is this the part where we all go home and act like a happy family?" (*Finale; Or, Brothers and Sisters, I Am an Atomic Bomb* 14). In the context of this study, we can see that "that 'perfect circle' is closed with the happy ending of every gothic novel, which presents to the reader's view a happily married couple. The child in gothic is a means to obtain retribution; it is the assurance that one will prevail; it also is an end and a final purpose in itself and has the simultaneous capacity to tangle or resolve every plot" (Georgieva 16). In a sense, this is accomplished by the final actions of both the television show's first season and the comic's first volume, albeit through different resolutions.

At the end of the first season's finale, Vanya is unconscious but still empowered, and still has the opportunity for redemption and the happy ending of the Gothic heroine. Five takes the family back in time, as "the apocalypse will always happen and Vanya will always be the cause unless we take her with us and fix her," effectively choosing to unmake the Gothic child and re-form her ("The White Violin"). The narrative that her siblings fight to create will act to reverse the *Bildungsroman* of a Gothic villain and give Vanya another chance: "the adults belong to a certain pre-established archetype (villain, legitimate heir and hero, persecuted female) and the adolescents merely possess certain propensities. This idea is central to gothic novels that contain complex, developing child characters" (Georgieva 31). In the comic series, Five shoots the distracted Vanya, who survives the injury but is no longer be able to play the violin, and Klaus saves the world through his heretofore underestimated power.

Amid the dramatic storms of their strange lives, the Gothic children press on and grow. Throughout *Dallas*, Vanya remains a bedridden amnesiac, even as Allison angrily tries to show her what she has done; in the second season of the television show, Vanya is also an amnesiac searching for her memories, which are finally triggered by traumatic torture and nearly as destructive as the first time around (*The Jungle* 16–17, "743"). However, later in *Dallas*, Allison is shown curled up with Vanya, clearly forgiving her during a sibling montage (*The World Is Big Enough Without You* 24). Likewise, by the end of the second season, Vanya willingly travels back to her own time with her family and restored memories ("The End of Something"). In terms of perfect circles, there is no happily married couple by the end of the story, despite the development of Luther and Allison's relationship; however, most of the living Umbrella Academy members do actively go home together at the end of the *Apocalypse Suite*, showing a somewhat restored family unit, and the first television series ends with the siblings standing in a complete circle while going back in time to save Vanya. Although the outcomes of both the current television series' and comic volume's storylines are cloudy and mysterious for Vanya, Klaus, and Ben, the tones of both versions of the story are optimistic, and the characters have still changed their lives to reflect their shifted, more adult values. The academy's pupils do not all survive growing up, but the Gothic children have nonetheless graduated to a brighter future.

## Notes

1. The first episode of the second season takes the audience through a tour of the Umbrella Academy siblings' abilities: Luthor is "Number 1," or "Spaceboy," and has super strength and hardiness. Diego is the brooding "Number 2," or "the Kraken," and is able to manipulate the movements of objects in air, most notably his knives. He additionally can hold his breath for an unnaturally long time in the comic. Allison is "Number 3," or "the Rumor," and can make things happen by preceding her desired outcome with "I heard a rumor…." Klaus is "Number 4," or "the Séance," and is able to communicate with, summon, and corporealize the dead. In the comic, Klaus has a number of additional abilities, such as telekinesis and possessing a television set. Number 5 does not have another name, although he is sometimes referred to as "the Boy," and is able to time travel and teleport. Ben is "Number 6," or "the Horror," and can summon eldritch tentacles out of his stomach. Vanya is "Number 7," or "the White Violin," who eventually discovers her ability to manipulate sound waves to devastating effect, although in the comic this is chiefly done through music (Elvy).

2. Pogo is Reginald Hargreeves' assistant in the Umbrella Academy, a highly intelligent, human-like chimpanzee who is considered part of the family ("We Only See Each Other at Weddings and Funerals").

## Works Cited

Andeweg, Agnes, and Sue Zlosnik. *Gothic Kinship*. Manchester University Press, 2013.
Baltin, Steve. "Gerard Way Talks Fulfilling Comic Book Dreams with Netflix Series 'The Umbrella Academy.'" *Forbes*. 15 Feb. 2019, https://www.forbes.com/sites/stevebaltin/2019/02/15/gerard-way-talks-fulfilling-comic-book-dreams-with-netflix-series-the-umbrella-academy/#56ba718e5e37. Accessed 21 Dec. 2019.
"Changes." *The Umbrella Academy*, written by Bob DeLaurentis and Eric W. Phillips, directed by Jeremy Webb, 2019.
Davison, Carol Margaret. "Introduction: The Corpse in the Closet: The Gothic, Death, and Modernity." *The Gothic and Death*, edited by Carol Margaret Davison, The International Gothic Series, Manchester University Press, 2017, pp. 1–17.
"The Day That Was." *The Umbrella Academy*, written by Ben Nedivi and Matt Wolpert, directed by Stephen Surjik, 2019.
"The Day That Wasn't." *The Umbrella Academy*, written by Sneha Koorse, directed by Stephen Surjik, 2019.

Elvy, Craig. "The Umbrella Academy: How the Hargreeves' Powers Are Different in the Comics." *Screenrant*, 11 January 2020, https://screenrant.com/umbrella-academy-netflix-hargreeves-powers-comic-comparison/. Accessed 3 October 2020.

"The End of Something." *The Umbrella Academy*, written by Jeremy Slater and Steve Blackman, directed by Jeremy Webb, 2020.

"Extra Ordinary." *The Umbrella Academy*, written by Ben Nedivi and Matt Wolpert, directed by Andrew Bernstein, 2019.

Georgieva, Margarita. *The Gothic Child*. Palgrave Gothic. Palgrave Macmillan, 2013.

"I Heard a Rumor." *The Umbrella Academy*, written by Lauren Schmidt Hissrich and Sneha Koorse, directed by Jeremy Webb, 2019.

Jones, David Annwn. *Gothic Effigy: A Guide to Dark Visibilities*. Manchester University Press, 2018.

"A Light Supper." *The Umbrella Academy*, written by Jeremy Slater and Steve Blackman, directed by Ellen Kuras, 2020.

"Man on the Moon." *The Umbrella Academy*, written by Lauren Schmidt Hissrich, directed by Ellen Kuras, 2019.

"Öga for Öga." *The Umbrella Academy*, written by Jeremy Slater and Steve Blackman, directed by Ellen Kuras, 2020.

Round, Julia. *Gothic in Comics and Graphic Novels*. McFarland, 2014.

"Run Boy Run." *The Umbrella Academy*, written by Jeremy Slater and Steve Blackman, directed by Andrew Bernstein, 2019.

"743." *The Umbrella Academy*, written by Jeremy Slater and Steve Blackman, directed by Amanda Marsalis, 2020.

Smith, Michelle J. "Dead and Ghostly Children in Contemporary Literature for Young People." *The Gothic and Death*, edited by Carol Margaret Davison, The International Gothic Series, Manchester University Press, 2017, pp. 191–203.

Trowbridge, Serena. "Past, Present, and Future in the Gothic Graveyard." *The Gothic and Death*, edited by Carol Margaret Davison, The International Gothic Series, Manchester University Press, 2017, pp. 22–33.

Way, Gerard. *Baby, I'll Be Your Frankenstein*. Art by Gabriel Bá. Colors by Dave Stewart. Letters by Blambot's Nate Piekos. Milwaukie, Dark Horse Books, 2007. Digital Edition. Issue 4 of *The Umbrella Academy: Apocalypse Suite*, Volume 1 of *The Umbrella Academy*.

\_\_\_\_\_. *The Day the Eiffel Tower Went Berserk*. Art by Gabriel Bá. Colors by Dave Stewart. Letters by Blambot's Nate Piekos. Milwaukie, Dark Horse Books, 2007. Digital Edition. Issue 1 of *The Umbrella Academy: Apocalypse Suite*, Volume 1 of *The Umbrella Academy*.

\_\_\_\_\_. *Dr. Terminal's Answer*. Art by Gabriel Bá. Colors by Dave Stewart. Letters by Blambot's Nate Piekos. Milwaukie, Dark Horse Books, 2007. Digital Edition. Issue 3 of *The Umbrella Academy: Apocalypse Suite*, Volume 1 of *The Umbrella Academy*.

\_\_\_\_\_. *Finale; Or, Brothers and Sisters, I Am an Atomic Bomb*. Art by Gabriel Bá. Colors by Dave Stewart. Letters by Blambot's Nate Piekos. Milwaukie, Dark Horse Books, 2008. Digital Edition. Issue 6 of *The Umbrella Academy: Apocalypse Suite*, Volume 1 of *The Umbrella Academy*.

\_\_\_\_\_. *The Jungle*. Art by Gabriel Bá. Colors by Dave Stewart. Letters by Blambot's Nate Piekos. Milwaukie, Dark Horse Books, 2008. Digital Edition. Issue 1 of *The Umbrella Academy: Dallas*, Volume 2 of *The Umbrella Academy*

\_\_\_\_\_. "Thank You for the Coffee." Art by Gabriel Bá. Colors by Dave Stewart. Letters by Blambot's Nate Piekos. Milwaukie, Dark Horse Books, 2008. Digital Edition. Issue 5 of *The Umbrella Academy: Apocalypse Suite*, Volume 1 of *The Umbrella Academy*.

\_\_\_\_\_. *We Only See Each Other at Weddings and Funerals*. Art by Gabriel Bá. Colors by Dave Stewart. Letters by Blambot's Nate Piekos. Milwaukie, Dark Horse Books, 2007. Digital Edition. Issue 2 of *The Umbrella Academy: Apocalypse Suite*, Volume 1 of *The Umbrella Academy*.

\_\_\_\_\_. *The World Is Big Enough Without You*. Art by Gabriel Bá. Colors by Dave Stewart. Letters by Blambot's Nate Piekos. Milwaukie, Dark Horse Books, 2009. Digital Edition. Issue 6 of *The Umbrella Academy: Dallas*, Volume 2 of *The Umbrella Academy*

"We Only See Each Other at Weddings and Funerals." *The Umbrella Academy*, written by Jeremy Slater and Steve Blackman, directed by Peter Hoar, 2019.

Weiss, Josh. "Gerard Way on Klaus's Hollywood Hijinks in 'Umbrella Academy' Spinoff

'You Look Like Death.'" *Forbes*, 29 July 2020, https://www.forbes.com/sites/joshweiss/2020/07/29/tales-from-the-umbrella-academy-you-look-like-death-gerard-way-exclusive/#20df741b3310. Accessed 3 October 2020.

"The White Violin." *The Umbrella Academy*, written by Jeremy Slater and Steve Blackman, directed by Peter Hoar, 2019.

# Liminal Spaces

*Being Alone in a House That Isn't Home*

MIRANDA JOHNSEN

The superhero genre centers itself on trauma—whether it be the suffering that creates a compassionate hero, or the relentless pain that drives ordinary people to villainy. *The Umbrella Academy* (2019) follows in the same suit, in fact, Steve Blackman's adaptation of Gerard Way and Gabriel Bá's eponymous comic puts the main characters' suffering on the forefront. Outside a few flashy action scenes that maintain the source material's quirky and dark sense of humor, *The Umbrella Academy* Netflix series focuses on the main characters' traumas touched on in the Eisner Award winning comic book. In the show and comics, the Umbrella Academy's suffering derives from their turbulent and abusive relationship with their adoptive father, Reginald Hargreeves. During the Umbrella Academy's childhood, Reginald creates a police state which leaves no room for disobedience and which lacks a safe environment for the children to express their emotions. While heroes like Batman or Superman have distinguished lines that separate their civilian and heroic lives, they also have a liminal space where the alter ego and the heroic identity can co-exist.

Liminal spaces in this context follow the mirror model Foucault uses in his essay *Of Other Spaces*, where the mirror exists in reality with the one who views the mirror. but the image reflected within the mirror remains "absolutely unreal" (Foucault 24). It is the interaction between the two real objects that exists within a reality that creates a liminal space which reflects the relationship between both objects. Whether a cave beneath a mansion or a fortress in the Arctic, these liminal spaces allow the heroes the room to rest and develop further as a character, unburdened by their mission or everyday responsibilities. In his essay *Genre and Super-Heroism: Batman in the New Millennium*, Vincent M. Gaine describes how the lack of such a liminal space can lead the hero to violent and oppressive behavior against the very people they attempt to protect, as the lack of a safe environment to express their emotions leads the hero to adopt unhealthy means by which to express their feelings. Without the liminal space, the mise-en-scène becomes the only place for the hero's internalized trauma to go. With regard to *The Umbrella Academy*, for two specific characters, namely Luther and Klaus Hargreeves, trauma displaces itself in the set's physical condition and lighting.

The perfect example for a liminal space can be found in Batman's Batcave as it lies secluded from both Bruce Wayne's and the Batman's lives, yet he can access both personas there. Every hero has a liminal space—whether physical, temporal, or through a person—to grow and develop as a well-rounded character rather than two separate halves (Gaine 122). However, in *The Umbrella Academy* the space that should have functioned in this capacity gets corrupted by Reginald Hargreeves through his emotional and physical abuse towards the Umbrella Academy. Reginald's abusive behavior towards his children takes place within a building that should have been their safe haven, a place where they could have developed their emotions safely. Each of Reginald's seven children experience abuse in their childhood home, and not one child has a space to allow for their alter ego and heroic identity to meld. The children are to remain inside the household, and they only vacate the premises for missions or public appearances as they are celebrated personas. When inside the Academy, they are subjected to endless training that extends the heroic aspect of their lives into the liminal space, in which Reginald leaves his adoptive children no room to grow on a private level. When he adopts the seven children, he gives them numbers instead of names, a rating system that denotes their placement within the team structure according to how useful he sees the children's powers rather than a personal identity. Due to Reginald's attempts to minimize each child's personalities, he instills the heroic persona as the primary persona, pushing the private persona into the role of the alter ego.

Without the tools given to the Umbrella Academy, they have to learn how to create their own liminal spaces and alter egos with varying levels of success. The liminal space then becomes a coping mechanism to deal with the personal trauma of losing their individuality, so only after they discover their alter ego can the Hargreeves children find the middle ground that would help them process their childhood trauma rather than compartmentalize it. Most of the Hargreeves children learned to accept the existence of their childhood trauma and the loss of their individuality, leading them to move forward and create new lives for themselves outside of the Academy. Luther and Klaus, however, struggle to acknowledge or detach themselves from their childhood trauma. It is through their resistance towards mourning the loss of their childhood and individuality that they turn to having their childhood trauma manifest through an unreal space ("Mourning and Melancholia" 244). The unreal space through which they project their trauma being the set and props or the lighting of a scene.

Luther, or Number Once, finds it difficult to obtain an alter ego or a liminal space that exists outside the Academy because he relies on his heroic identity to keep him safe from his father's abuse in his adolescence. Unlike Luther's siblings, he holds a unique advantage with his leadership role and placement as Number One. By naming Luther "Number One," Reginald displays unquestionable favoritism that Luther utilizes to gain a relationship with his father that does contain neither the torturous training, nor the neglect his other siblings go through. Luther puts his energy into becoming the perfect son who never talks back, never disobeys an order, and never rebels. Although he uses the name Luther rather than Number One, he sacrifices his alter ego to perfect himself as a leader and a weapon that his father can use. Luther succeeds in this, but he unknowingly isolates himself from the outside world as a result. He separates himself from his siblings and the world to the point where his father and the Academy are the only constants in his life. Whether he never saw the lengths his father went through to train his siblings, or he ignores the abuse because he could not admit to himself that his father would ever knowingly hurt them, Luther retains the belief that the Academy functions as an uncorrupted liminal space. In the beginning of the series, Luther remains unwilling to acknowledge Reginald's abusive nature, and he carries on with his heroic identity and a poisoned liminal space that did not exist between anything. For this reason, the Academy does not perturb Luther as it does with Allison, nor does it anger him like Diego. When Luther returns from his four-year-long mission on the moon, he experiences the residence from a nostalgic point of view that is tinted by his father's recent death. The faux liminal space that Reginald manufactured for Luther requires his presence to hold any true meaning for Luther, and with the air of mystery that surrounds Reginald's death, a void in Luther's life opens up.

With Reginald being dead, the only authority he obtains over Luther comes from the Academy where he trained him. Portraits with his disapproving stare haunt the house alongside artifacts and mementos from the Umbrella Academy's glory days—children's magazines, action figures, and comics—all locked inside glass cabinets. There are no photos that commemorate their childhoods, only a painting with the children in their uniforms and masks. The only sign that children once lived in the house comes from the macabre educational illustrations that line the hallways that lead to the children's rooms. Each depicts children as they attack each other in horrific ways. The Academy's design mirrors Luther's private alter ego in both his adolescence and adulthood. Throughout his childhood, he took all the immature or personal aspects to himself and repressed them. He becomes a part of the Academy like Reginald's decorations or his prizes. His warped sense of childhood appears in the Academy's decoration, for he views himself as a trophy, reminiscent of a piece of artwork on the wall that must maintain an outward appearance of either obedience or violence. He only knows how to express himself through the physical world around him, so Luther mimics the social cues that he learns through the images of children around him. The liminal space and alter ego blur until Luther can no longer distinguish himself from one of his father's possessions. Luther imprints his identity onto the Academy, becomes its personification, and vise-versa.

Foucault's mirror example explains that the reflection of the observer created in the mirror's "virtual space" (Foucault 24) allows an opportunity for the observer to "come back toward [themselves]" (24). In this way the liminal space merges with Luther's alter ego and reflects it back at him. His trauma then executes itself onto the mise-en-scène through the set's physical condition as the Academy represents Luther's mental state. Because Luther dedicates his developmental years towards his attempt to become the perfect son for Reginald, his alter ego and liminal space of the home hinge upon the fundamental fact that Reginald acted in Luther's best interests. Without that belief, the entire structure begins to collapse. When Hazel and Cha-Cha, two recent antagonists of the Academy, break into the house, the ruin they cause reveals Luther's genetically modified form and mirrors the destroyed walls that he has erected to save himself from his sibling's judgment. No longer can he hide behind an oversized trench coat; the experimentation that Reginald had subjected him to has been revealed to his siblings. With that newfound vulnerability, the façade that covers the liminal space breaks away as the truth about the abuses that Reginald put Luther through are revealed—even if Luther does not admit to himself that what his father subjected him to was wrong. Still, the corrupted liminal space begins to show itself and, as it emerges, Luther begins to see his warped alter ego. His personality and body had been molded by Reginald until it became synonymous with heroism, which is why he does not mourn his missing autonomy. Instead, he attempts to latch on even harder to the liminal space that his father created to try and comfort himself. He does this in vain as the alter ego that is aware that his father abused him begins to break through and the intrinsic relationship between the alter ego and the liminal space begins to sever.

The alter ego balances the heroic identity and puts the actions and decisions a hero makes into perspective, so without the alter ego, there can be no basis for how the hero should act (Gaine 113). The alter ego acts as the moral compass because most positive personal relationships and experiences are created by the alter ego. Unlike the heroic identity, the private self faces personal consequences from the hero's actions—for example, in Christopher Nolan's film *Batman Begins*, Batman investigates Henri

Ducard's plans to destroy Gotham, Ducard retaliates by burning down Wayne Manor. The alter ego's interactions provide emotional context for the heroic identity's relationships with criminals and victims; their regular interactions with the citizens they are meant to protect reminds them of the people they are trying to save. It is the same narrative tool used to create a greater sense of stakes for world-ending fights, such as, in Joss Whedon's *The Avengers*, where the film repeatedly returns to a single waitress. By adding a character who can act as a representative for humanity—someone who stands out against the masses of people that the hero saves—the hero can reflect that relationship on a larger group of people. Changes to the heroic identity and alter ego work with each other, providing both personal consequences to their hero work and an intimate connection to humanity. So, as their dichotomy changes and the heroic identity becomes the dominant persona, their vigilante work leads to a suppression of their emotions, which are then deflected onto the space around them. Because Luther lacks a defined private identity—separate from his life as a hero or from his father's control—his liminal space, the Academy, is not weighted against an aspect in his life that does not intend to commit harm against his person. Reginald knows that Luther's life as a hero had nothing to balance it, and he exploited that fact. After Reginald's death, his abuses are made public and therefore, the alter ego is able to slowly emerge. This allows for a greater balance between Luther's personal life and his superhero life. When a balance between the two aspects of Luther's life begins to arise, the liminal space's unhealthy nature makes itself known to Luther, for when his relationship to Reginald and the Academy is compared to the healthier relationships, like his relationship with Allison, build the corrupted nature of the Academy becomes clearer to him.

Over the first five episodes, Luther gains more agency and realizes that his father did not act in his best interest, however, he still retains faith in his father. The coping mechanism that he put into place had twenty-nine years to solidify, so its removal becomes a long and painful process exhibited through passive destruction towards the Academy. These moments of passive vandalism are not caused by Luther, but rather by a third party in conjecture with moments when his alter ego emerged. However, as the apocalypse approaches, Luther becomes an active member in the Academy's decimation. After the Umbrella Academy discovers that the apocalypse has begun, Luther attempts to find the correspondence he sent Reginald from the Moon to discover clues that would help prevent the apocalypse. Luther, at this point in the narrative, has already had the non-consensual experimentation he went through put on display, and Diego has forced him to critically think about why he stayed at the Academy. His long withstanding belief that the Academy acts as a healthy liminal space begins to crumble.

The Moon mission functions as the linchpin that holds together the fantasy that his father once treated him well, which is why he clings to the search for the letters with erratic desperation. He, with no third-party involvement, tears his father's bedroom, which would have once been a forbidden place for him, apart. Reginald's bedroom symbolizes his father in a more personal way than the study. In that room, Reginald occupied himself with mundane things, it is where he lost the inhuman façade of scientific experimentation as well as stern authority over his children. The bedroom represents Reginald the same way that the Umbrella Academy's rooms provide greater insight into their own personalities. Therefore, when Luther dismantles the room to find the letters, he begins to strip away the person that he regarded as his father, revealing his father's true nature. The brutality in which Luther's frantic hunt for answers destroys Reginald's once immaculate room depicts the idealized image of Reginald as it disintegrates in Luther's mind.

After Luther does not find answers in the dressers or bedside tables, he begins to pull up the floorboards. The bedroom at this point begins to represent two different people simultaneously, both Luther and Reginald. Because Luther associates himself with the Academy as a whole, and Reginald acts the most unfiltered in his bedroom, the floorboards' removal exposes both father and son. Here, Reginald gets exposed as the cruel, apathetic, cowardly man that he attempts to hide, and Luther removes the barrier he had placed between himself and the truth about his father. Once the choice to rip open the floorboards presents itself, it creates a Pandora's Box effect; either Luther can leave what he knows on a subconscious level will be the evidence that his father sent him to live in isolation for selfish reasons, or he can reveal the truth and leave himself vulnerable to the abuse that he had been put through. He decides to remove the floorboards and discovers the truth about his father through all the unopened observations, scientific findings, and personal messages that he had sent to his father. The artifice fades away. Luther believed that his placement as Number One had given him a deeper connection with Reginald and that they had a deeper bond, i.e., that they were equals in a way because he had a leadership position. Then, once he no longer can repress the knowledge that his father betrayed his trust, he is offered two options: to find a new liminal space that he can balance with a fully actualized alter ego, or he can attempt to reject the tainted liminal space and the connected alter ego along with it and become a radically different person.

The two ultimatums are presented in the episodes "The Day That Wasn't" and "The Day That Was." In both timelines, Allison becomes the only person who Luther allows himself to show vulnerability towards; he feels safe enough around her during his adolescence to allow his true personality and alter ego to emerge. In "The Day That Wasn't" he admits to her that his life and sense of self was a lie constructed by his father that he had been foolish enough to believe. She returns with him to the Academy's greenhouse where they had constructed a tent when they were children. The tent existed as a true, though small, safe space for Luther within the Academy where he could act as both Number One and the person he wanted to be, freed from his father's gaze—at least for a moment. The tent acts as a heterotopia for Luther, where he could experience the freedom and security that would hold a utopic quality in comparison to the Academy, but it still exists within the Academy's boundaries (Foucault 24). It is a space that Luther and Allison created as children; so, rather than having to project onto a liminal space to subconsciously express himself, Luther had an active and physical role in the creation of the tent. The tent resembles Luther's view of himself which stands in stark contrast with the hyper-masculine version of himself he displays for his father. The tent is covered in sheets with pastel sheets and has a blanket and pillows covering the floor, all of which provides a view at the gentler side of Luther that never got a chance to grow.

Had Luther been able to return to the greenhouse with Allison as he grew up, he could have freed his inner alter ego and seen that the liminal space the Academy provided could not sustain him on an emotional level. Though Luther had what remains of his personal identity and liminal space forced upon the Academy by his father to the extent that he lacks people skills and missed many steps in his development—moving out, rent, and holding down a job—the continued existence of the tent shows that he still has a personality outside the one that his father pushed onto him. The personal identity Luther has forsaken cannot disappear despite his attempts to simply be his father's soldier. The tent resembles the remnants of Luther's individuality that he had repressed and forgotten about. For many years, Luther has believed that Reginald took the tent down, which is why he moved on from the alter ego that it represents while it remains untouched, uncorrupted by his father. After the devastation Luther felt when he realized that his father had not cared for him, the return to the tent provides him with an alternative alter ego that he can build upon. Allison then takes on the symbolic role of the liminal space as she accepts both sides of him.

When this untouched alter ego takes hold, its effects are seen through Luther's perception as he moves further outside of the Academy's grasp. The string lights inside the fort that cast a warm glow on the scene can be seen as an enlightenment for Luther and a first step to accepting his new alter ego; he begins to associate the safety inherent within the liminal space with Allison. Therefore, he can project his emotions onto a setting should Allison be nearby; he is no longer bound by the physical borders of the Academy. After he asks Allison to dance with him—both a romantic gesture and acceptance that he has found a new liminal space and alter ego—his apprehension is turned into joy and finally commitment in this fantastical dance scene. This is taken even further when string lights drop down from the sky and are suddenly wrapped around physical objects in the park the scene where the dance is elevated into a quasi-dream sequence. Unlike the physical changes that happen to the mise-en-scène within the Academy, the string lights do not exist within the show's reality but within Allison's and Luther's minds. The Academy functions like a cage that Reginald traps Luther inside, which is why he cannot function in a non-heroic capacity outside the property because his sense of self ensnares with a physical place that does not promote individuality and social skills. Once Luther frees himself from the Academy with the help of Allison showing him the liberty in an actualized alter ego, the liminal space, while still attached to Allison, can move with him. This episode, "The Day That Wasn't," shows how the liminal space should function, not as a means to control the hero, but as a conduit for their emotional development.

However, in the episode "The Day That Was," Luther does not register a personal identity, nor does he discover a new liminal space; instead, he falls deeper into the heroic identity until he exploits his status as Number One and becomes an oppressive force that detriments the Umbrella Academy's goal to stop the Apocalypse. Without Allison, Luther never obtains an alternative to his heroic identity to fill the void caused by the alter ego's departure. The heroic identity only cares about the mission's completion and relies upon the liminal space to inform its decisions. In "The Day That Was," Luther never receives the opportunity to replace his alter ego and never learns that the tent remains in the greenhouse. While the greenhouse remains above the Academy, Luther travels further within the Academy's depths to the holding cells where his father locked away Vanya and removed the latter's powers—a secret he skillfully kept from his children. Luther eventually copies his father's actions when he betrays Vanya's trust and ignores the other Umbrella Academy members, who try to persuade him to release Vanya. The further Luther travels into the Academy and Reginald's secrets, the more physical distance he puts between himself and his true alter ego that takes corporeal residence on the rooftop. He pulls deeper into himself until he rejects the alter ego, and Allison's near-death experience caused by Vanya acts as the catalyst for his descent into becoming an oppressive hero. Luther's sub-conscious, however, still accepts Allison as the true liminal space. Hence, when Vanya endangers Allison's life, he reacts by retreating further into the Academy and thus his superimposed hero-ego. The further he leans on the Academy's liminal space's unstable remains, the more he unbalances himself until he can no longer reconcile himself with the person he has become, resulting in the fall of the entire Academy and the world alike.

Without the mission to keep his heroic side under control, or an alternative alter ego to accept into his life, Luther attempts to fill the void by his belief in his father. The replacement coping method that Luther adopts copies his brother Klaus' behavior, i.e., dulling emotions through drugs. In "The Day That Was," Luther starts by drinking the alcohol from Reginald's liquor cabinet to numb himself from the liminal space's abrupt departure. He continues to act in the ways that he had seen Klaus coping with his abilities since he turned thirteen because Klaus had severed his relationship to any physical place after he left the Academy. Luther believes that the only way to cope with his father's rejection would be to discard the Academy in an abrupt manner. He tells Klaus that he desires the freedom that his brother has, ignorant of the problems that Klaus faces, such as the repercussions of his drug addiction, trauma, and the show's implication that he did not gain a permanent residence after he left the Academy. He associates the pain from his corrupted childhood to the Academy and its liminal space in general, consequently turning to Klaus, who he believes separated himself from any concept that could be confused with a liminal space. Luther can only grasp the concept through a physical connection with his surroundings; hence, to live Klaus' life becomes the only viable solution. However, he later regrets his decision because Klaus' coping mechanisms resemble a liminal space that exhibits itself through ways unknown to Luther.

In the second season, Luther still lacks the means to create a new liminal space for himself, newly ripped away from his family and lost in the early 1960s. Due to being lost in a new city and time period, Luther attempts to create a new coping mechanism to deal with the trauma of his childhood and the events of the first season. However, because Luther has nothing familiar to connect his trauma to in this time period, as he did with the Academy or Allison, he resorts to using his body. Not unlike Luther's brief experimentation with drugs, his time participating in illegal fighting rings under Jack Ruby could not satisfy his need for a new way to cope without a liminal space. Only once he reunites with Allison in the episode "The Majestic 12," does Luther find a connection to his previous liminal space, as displayed by his reestablished ability to affect the physical set as the audience views it. When Allison first embraces Luther, he is uncertain how to reciprocate the embrace; only after they both accept the comfort of their company does Luther regain his liminal space. The customers and staff that once populated the restaurant all disappear, leaving Luther and Allison alone. Luther's ability to not only make the string lights descend from the sky in "The Day That Wasn't" to being able to make the customers vanish in "The Majestic 12" indicates that an environment with people who make him feel safe and unguarded has more influence on his physical surroundings.

Klaus Hargreeves, unlike the other Umbrella Academy members, does not have a single physical location that he can refer back to when he needs comfort or safety, nor does he have a non-judgmental, reciprocated relationship with another person. When it comes to Klaus' relationship with the heroic identity, he juxtaposes Luther and divorces himself from the superhero lifestyle. He avoids any reminder that his powers exist, and he severs his connection to them in any way that he can, mainly through illegal narcotics. Klaus begins to use drugs early in his life to avoid the constant noise and terror that his power surrounds him with every day, for the ghosts that he sees cling to him and shout at him to get his attention. From a young age, Klaus learns not to associate any place with safety because his power shows him dead spirits covered in gruesome, gory wounds at all times. Unlike his siblings, Klaus cannot control his power; it haunts him. The heroic aspect in his life dominates every moment in his day, but unlike Luther, he has never received any praise or comfort from his father when using his power. Hence, because Klaus' life becomes overtaken by his power, any liminal space that he may have been able to find in the Academy gets drowned out by the horrors he sees every day. In his adolescent years, Klaus discovers that drugs are an effective way to cut off his powers leading him to sustenance dependence. His addiction to drugs creates its own faux liminal space that simulates all the positive aspects that he should have obtained through a healthy mental balance, but the liminal space of the Academy does not have the strength to help him beyond momentary relief.

In contrast, the connection that Luther has with the liminal space and his alter ego binds itself in a physical sense because he understands the world in a physical way—his power connects itself to his physicality, and his only means to assert any control over the world comes through how he could overpower people in fights. Klaus, however, does not connect to the world through his body. His powers are mental, which allows him to view the world on a deeper level than his siblings, and, as he learns in the final episode, he has dominion over the world's spiritual aspects. Klaus' liminal space, for this reason, displaces itself onto the tangible world with lighting and color tone. With the unconscious power he has over the world—even when he self-medicates, he still has enough power to see his deceased brother, Ben—all his unspoken trauma affects the world in a manner his siblings have never perceived. When Klaus becomes the primary force that drives the scene, the tonal quality in the scene's lighting changes to reflect his mood and emotional state, such as, in the episode "The Day That Wasn't." These moments have intense blue or red overtones that are absent throughout most other scenes, and their saturation levels are unrealistic given the scene's natural light sources. Tonal quality and saturation are the main indicators that clue the audience in on Klaus' current mental state and relationship with the liminal space.

In majority, Klaus-centered scenes are cast in deep blue lighting or have blue-tinted overtones. When Klaus is first introduced at his rehab facility in "We Only See Each Other at Weddings and Funerals," the entire room has a warm, yellow tone to the lighting which creates detachment from the set's serious nature. A warm color scheme implies that the area feels like a safe place for Klaus, one where he can act as himself in a free manner and talk with people who only wish for him to recover. The show never indicates that anyone at the rehab facility knows about, or, at the very least, cares about his power and star-status. Klaus feels security in anonymity and apparent uselessness. Though he shows annoyance towards his siblings when they treat him as a hindrance, drugs allow Klaus to cut himself off from the suffocating role that his father put him in at a young age. Unlike Luther, Klaus does not have the illusion of a higher position to create what could have been misconstrued as a healthy relationship with his father. Reginald's pragmatism does not allow for any hesitation or fear; so, while Luther can grow as a superhero under Reginald's rule with his enhanced strength, Klaus's fear of his powers aggravates Reginald as Klaus' reluctance is viewed as laziness. Though much about Klaus' childhood training regime remains unknown, he does mention multiple times how Reginald would lock him in a mausoleum around the age of thirteen. The scene within the mausoleum has exaggerated low-key lighting and a blue tint that comes from an unnatural angle for the moon to make it, but the light that shines low on Reginald's body as he stands outside the mausoleum door, and his obstruction causes the light to cast the deep shadows that surround Klaus in a vignette. This moment marks the point when Klaus' powers become too horrifying for him to handle, which is why he eventually removes them from the equation. The color tones of the specific scenes thus mark Klaus' liminal spaces as paradoxes and chiasmic in their presentation; they are empowering and liberating, seen in the yellow of the rehab facility, or enclosing and suffocating, as in the dark colors of the mausoleum. The irony in this chiasmic dichotomy lies in the intent of these scenes: while the drug consumption is supposed to drown Klaus' fears, the rehab could enable him to be clean and thus trigger his powers while the mausoleum is supposed to enhance his powers but instead, it stops them altogether.

However, as plagued by ghosts and abusive people as he has been throughout his life, Klaus still connects his liminal space to people; thus, when he does not have any place or person to find safety in, he turns to drugs to substitute his liminal space. In the first episode, "We Only See

Each Other at Weddings and Funerals," Klaus overdoses almost immediately after he leaves rehab. The ambulance ride where the paramedic resuscitates him displays Klaus' effect on his surroundings and how he finds a diluted liminal space within drugs and death. An ambulance should contain bright LED lights to allow for the paramedics to have a clear view, but Klaus' presence turns the ambulance into a deep blue and low-key lighting that throws everything besides Klaus and the paramedic into shadow. Along with the blue light that symbolizes Klaus' absent liminal space, a pulsating red light also integrates with the blue to mimic the emergency lights on top the ambulance, but those lights would not have been within view inside the ambulance. The switch between the unnatural blue and red lighting represents the push and pull between a world without a liminal space and the temporary relief he finds when he removes himself from reality. Klaus not only uses drugs as a means to escape his father's torment, but he seeks out the peace and tranquility that the liminal space should provide. The liminal space should function as the bridge between a person split in two and allow a hero a reprieve from the stressful, and often painful, duties that they must carry out. Klaus does not have a place or person to grant him any safety; so, once he discovers that drugs could remove him from his reality, he associates the liminal space with their temporary relief. After he drugs himself—or even after he overdoses and dies since he views his own death as a relief—the warm color tone that should imply his arrival to the real liminal space only suggests that he has found momentary relief but not a constant one.

Avoidance becomes Klaus' main coping mechanism; but due to his trauma's prolonged nature, he can never evade the aspects in his life that causes him to develop serious post-traumatic stress. Though Klaus refuses to continue on with his heroic aspect, he does still act as a superhero for many years at his father's behest, and he never learns how to control his power without drugs. His life still has those two aspects: the alter ego and the heroic. Unlike Luther, Klaus never had Reginald's constant pressure to always act as a hero, for he had already marked Klaus off as a lost cause due to his unwillingness to master his powers. This allows for Klaus to have the space to develop an alter ego and reject his heroic identity, but he cannot turn off his power or ignore the rigorous training that traumatized him. The heroic aspect to his identity remains, but Klaus does whatever he can to avoid his heroic duties, even if that means that he would no longer have a stable income flow or a place to sleep. However, he uses drugs because he still requires the comfort that the (mental) liminal space provides. In the episode "Extra Ordinary," Klaus' powers cause him to have a panic attack, and he uses drugs to both find comfort in the liminal space while he also removes the heroic identity that his powers resurface. The red tones caused by his lighter when he uses it to light his marijuana marks how this coping method would grant him peace. The red light that emits from Klaus' lighter flickers and disappears after a few seconds, and his joint loses its red glow the second it leaves his lips because these are weaker liminal spaces than what Klaus requires to have a stable mental space. His true liminal space comes from loving relationships, as indicated by the faint yellow glow from the hallway outside the blue lit bathroom. The warmer glow in the hallway symbolizes that a healthy liminal space remains within reach for Klaus, but his addiction to drugs and their momentary relief isolates him from the people who could help him balance his psyche.

Klaus can only retain his true liminal space—healthy and loving relationships—when he is sent back in time to the Vietnam War in the episode "The Day That Wasn't," where he meets Dave, the soldier that he falls in love with. When Klaus first arrives in Vietnam, the blue hue follows him. The lanterns that give off yellow lighting only change the hue in their direct vicinity, when logically, the lanterns' warm light would change tonal quality in the tent and surrounding items. While the lanterns should create a rim light on Klaus' skin, it remains absent in most shots. The yellow rim light appears strongest when Klaus first looks at Dave—here, the yellow cuts his face in half with the other half still in shadow. The strong rim light foreshadows the important influence Dave's character will have on Klaus; already their wordless introduction affects Klaus enough to break through the dark anti-liminal space that he constructed. In the next scene, when Dave formally introduces himself to Klaus, the yellow lighting grows stronger as it fights against the cool tones that still cling to Klaus. In the personnel transport vehicle, unnatural yellow lighting shines through every window and cuts through the blue-green lighting already present in the truck. While Klaus' interaction with Dave appears simple, it has a profound enough impact on him to both convince him to stay in an active warzone and change the color tint that is associated with Klaus' absent liminal space. Rather than a blue interior with yellow light that cuts through, the vehicle's interior has a green hue. The color shift from blue to green shows how the distance from the Academy, recreational drugs, and the added presence of Dave has changed the way that Klaus perceives the world. Dark, strong blues in the scene are contaminated with the bright, yellow liminal space, which creates a green tint that shows Klaus' steady recovery process. The added yellow light beams then push forward the idea that Dave helps Klaus create a healthy liminal space, for the added warm lighting symbolizes how Klaus moves away from self-medication towards Dave's requited love.

As the relationship between Klaus and Dave continues to intensify, so does the color pallet as it shifts further into warm tones. In "The Day That Wasn't," Klaus and Dave go to a bar in Vietnam, and the lighting makes its full shift from blue to red tones. Dave's effect on Klaus appears everywhere within the bar from the red and orange lighting, to the yellow shirt that Klaus has on. Warm colors that carry the same saturation levels as blue hues appear for the first time as Klaus has begun to embrace his new life with Dave. His demeanor shifts, and his trauma no longer drowns him in dark and cool colors. The scene continues with intermittent shots where Klaus and Dave stand in a curtain behind a beaded curtain. The hallway that they stand in has a saturated red hue with a purple curtain to the side. Like the color green in the previous scene, the purple in the curtain shows the empty liminal space's steady dismantlement as Dave's presence continues to rebalance Klaus. While Klaus attempts to remove himself from his heroic identity, his power makes that impossible. He cannot turn it off; however, when Dave comes into Klaus' life, he provides the emotional support for the alter ego allowing Klaus to cope with his powers and begin to move away from drug use. This recreated balance fills in the space where there should have been a liminal space. As the cool colors get pushed to the side, Klaus and Dave become more intimate and move closer to the frame's center. Because the camera tracks towards Klaus and Dave, the purple curtain moves further out of frame as the warm tones take over the shot. This continues until Klaus and Dave kiss and the curtain turns white, a symbol that the empty liminal space has disappeared and a new liminal space has opened up for Klaus.

The new liminal space that Klaus builds does not have the strength to stand on its own, yet; like Luther's reconstructed balance, Klaus requires an external source to aid his recovery. Reminiscent to Allison leaving Luther and thus making Luther's new liminal space fall apart, Klaus' liminal space cannot survive after Dave's death. The scene when Dave dies begins with a saturated red shot as explosions go off in the distance. After the second explosion, the deep blue tint returns to the scene, the red lighting only remains in gunfire from the nearby soldiers. The lighting foreshadows Dave's death before Klaus has become aware that he has been injured. Although Klaus does not yet know that Dave is about to die, his power brings him closer to death and allows for his liminal space to react to Dave's passing before he can. The warm tones begin to fade away, only remaining in short bursts from gunfire as the newfound balance tries to stay alive along with Dave. As the scene progresses, the red flashes become further apart and reflect less on Klaus as he learns that Dave has been shot in the chest. The tentative balance that Klaus created through his relationship with Dave begins to fade out and the constant lighting provided by gunfire fades, replaced by sudden red bursts from explosions.

Dave's death echoes in the liminal space through those two light sources as they resemble his heart rate. The gunfire resembles how Dave's body attempts to keep itself alive, mimicking the fast beat of his heart as the adrenaline passes through him. However, as his heart rate slows down, so does the time between the liminal space's visual markers. The explosions take over for the rapid gunfire and more time passes between each red burst; however, the lighting is stronger as Dave's heart has to push harder to keep attempting to create oxidized blood. The liminal space has grown so dependent on Dave's survival that it begins to die at the same time as him. Nevertheless, the red explosions linger on after the viewers can see that Dave has died. While Dave no longer lives, Klaus still attempts to keep him awake and cannot reconcile with his death, which is why the liminal space lingers through the color code. Only once Klaus has broken down, realizing that Dave has passed away, do the red bursts fade away. The liminal space could still live along with the hope that Dave could recover, but when Klaus' hope fades away, the blue lighting that symbolizes an empty liminal space returns.

In the episode "Number Five," when Klaus comes back home after Dave's death, he has completely returned to the blue world that he had departed from. The only reminder that he found a stable liminal space appears on his hands, which are stained red from Dave's blood. Besides the allusions to Dave and the liminal space's apparent death, the red on Klaus' hands shows that Klaus' healthy liminal space still hangs on, even though it appears to have faded away. Klaus' ability grants him the power to commune with the deceased, so while Dave has died, he still remains available to Klaus. The liminal space that Klaus began to build with Dave has been weakened by his death, but he still has access not only to Dave's spirit but their emotional connection as well. The red on his hands and the fire that erupts from the time machine suitcase that Klaus destroys resembles the violence and rage that Klaus has either experienced or feels. The emotions that he has attempted to numb until he met and lost Dave are free to release themselves. By attempting to distance himself from the liminal space in this way, it had no choice but to react in turn. The fire from the suitcase and the blood on his hands display his rage through color tone, but it only lasts for a short time as the liminal space does not have the strength to prolong itself. His liminal space begins to appear when he remembers Dave and moves towards combatting his addiction that his father spurred on through his constant abuse. After Klaus falls unconscious in a nightclub, he enters the sphere of the afterlife, which the show portrays as a black and white world where the only color appears in Klaus' brightly colored shirt. The liminal space hangs on in the afterlife because Klaus anticipates his reunion with Dave, and they only disappear once his father places a black sheet over them. As Reginald covers Klaus' shirt, he brings forth the constant tension that Klaus experiences in regard to his liminal space.

When Klaus and Reginald talk in the barbershop in the episode "The Day That Was," the tension between Reginald's authority over Klaus and the newfound agency that Klaus has gained are at war with each other. Reginald's spirit assumes dominance over Klaus by removing the color that remains in the afterlife, consequently changing how Klaus views his surroundings. By eliminating color, Reginald morphs the liminal space of the afterlife from a peaceful place outside the color spectrum into one that resembles his black and white morality. He imposes his belief set onto Klaus by removing any deviance from his immaculate barbershop and gains power over his son by removing any sense of security. Reginald attempts to reason that his intentions to save the world counteract the trauma that he put the Umbrella Academy through as children, therefore, invalidating the depression and post-traumatic stress that Klaus experienced throughout his life. Reginald removes the liminal space because he wants Klaus to view himself as a tool, the same way that he does. In his eyes, Klaus and his siblings were never children with any agency or aspirations of their own, they were merely meant to save the world and nothing else. Reginald only ever saw them as heroes, so they never needed to have a liminal space. He removes the color from the room to emphasize how he believes that his children do not have their own agency or moral beliefs. Klaus, however, views the black and white color scheme in his own way. For him, the lack of a liminal space does not symbolize the alter ego's extinction but rather the opposite. Klaus views the space of the afterlife as the final departure from the heroic identity, and he takes solace in his reprieve from the disconnection between him and his heroic duties. However, the world where he can exist as himself with Dave shuts Klaus out, and he gets thrust back into the red and blue world to struggle once more to regain balance with his liminal space.

*The Umbrella Academy* focuses on the trauma that an individual raised as a superhero experiences when they attempt to balance their two identities. The liminal space creates security for a hero and provides a place for personal development and allows them to create relationships. For Klaus and Luther, who had separated themselves from healthy liminal spaces at their father's behest, their reconnection to the liminal space provides room for them to heal from their childhood traumas. For these two characters, who grew up in an abusive household that put little emphasis on the healthy expression of their feelings, the mise-en-scène provides a buffer zone until they find people that accept them as they are. As both the television show and the comic emphasize, the only way for these traumatized superhero characters to heal from their traumatic origins is to create balance in their lives and, by extension, their physical surroundings.

## Works Cited

*The Avengers.* Directed by Joss Whedon, Marvel Studios, 2012.
*Batman Begins.* Directed by Christopher Nolan, Warner Brothers, 2005.
Foucault, Michel, and Jay Miskowiec. "Of Other Spaces." *Diacritics*, vol. 16, no. 1, 1986, pp. 22–27. JSTOR, www.jstor.org/stable/464648. Accessed 22 Apr. 2020.
Freud, Sigmund. "The Interpretation of Dreams." *The Norton Anthology of Theory and Criticism*, edited by Vincent B. Leitch, translated by James Stratchey. W.W. Norton & Company, 2010, pp. 807–824.
\_\_\_\_\_. "Mourning and Melancholia." *The Standard Edition of the Complete Psychological Works of Sigmund Freud*. Vol 14. Translated and edited by James Strachey in collaboration with Anna Freud, assisted by Alix Stratchey and Alan Tyson. The Hogarth Press, 1981, pp. 234–258.
Gaine, Vincent M. "Genre and Super-Heroism: Batman in the New Millennium." *The 21st Century Superhero: Essays on Gender, Genre and Globalization in Film*, edited by Richard J. Gray and Betty Kaklamanidou. Jefferson, McFarland, 2011, pp. 111–128.
*The Umbrella Academy.* Created by Steve Blackman and Jeremy Slater, Netflix, 2019–2020.

# Superheroes, Transnational Adoption, and Hegelian Estrangement

FERNANDO GABRIEL PAGNONI BERNS

Science fiction has always been a perfect vehicle to channel real social and cultural anxieties and concerns. Through his theory of cognitive estrangement, Darko Suvin (1979) argued that by imagining strange events, worlds and people, we come to see our own conditions of life from a new and potentially revolutionary point of view. The familiar is fantastically transformed to offer the receiver a new understanding of the naturalized (but socially constructed) conditions of life. In his text *Positions and Presuppositions in Science Fiction* (1988), Suvin argues that

> The presuppositions, the ideological givens, are thus both logically prior and analytically posterior to the text: its emergence as well as its interpretation is impossible without them. They are crucial factors of the context; but they are also among the materials with which the writer has to work, the building bricks which he can manipulate in the text. Ideology is pre-eminently a compromise between the discursive and the non-discursive, a "representation" of the imaginary relationship between a subject and the situation in which it practically exists [Suvin *Positions* 64].

Ideology, culture and society are organizers of both the empirical daily life of the readers and the speculative world created by science fiction writers. Behind any science fiction text, analyzers may find, on the one hand, coherence between the used tropes and the story and, on the other hand, an intertext linking social and cultural context with the text.

With a story revolving around adopted siblings, superheroic feats, parenthood and doomsday, the TV show *The Umbrella Academy*, based on the graphic novel of the same title, seems to be polyvalent in meanings. Uniting science fiction with the superhero genre, the show offers rich and complex interpretations, varying from the role of superheroes and its marketization in our current society to issues related to trauma and body modification. Amidst these urgent topics, the TV show examines concerns on adoption and social estrangement, including variations of alienation and self-estrangement.

The show revolves around Sir Reginald Hargreeves (Colm Feore), a man who has adopted seven kids from all over the world and reunites them under his care. All of them have different backgrounds and powers, personal histories and identities. In consequence, all of them feel somehow estranged from their father as well as their brothers and sisters. It does not matter how important their identities as superheroes are: even under the "umbrella" of the Academy, their common ground, the siblings' prevalent feeling is that of deep estrangement. They mostly feel uneasiness, rather than belonging when engaging with any other member of the family. This estrangement, I argue, mirrors, through a fantastic lens, that felt by many adoptees, especially in transracial/transnational adoptions. As argued, "children of color adopted by white families may experience discomfort and a sense of alienation as they age, struggling to feel a sense of belonging within their cultures of origin" (Fedders 58). Our global scenario of transnational adoption increases the probabilities of intra-familiar estrangement. Accepting difference is important for parents who adopt foreign-born children; however, the building of a sense of national and familial belonging is not a simple task, as the family must inscribe difference within a nucleus.

But what does the term "estrangement" mean? The term itself is hard to define as it varies across disciplines. Philosophers, psychologists, sociologists and theologians differ not only in their definition of estrangement, but also in the implications the term carries, especially in its linkage with other, similar terms. We will follow philosopher Georg Wilhelm Friedrich Hegel here. For the author, there are four forms of estrangement: first of all, there is estrangement between people. This parallels the estrangement experienced by the brothers and sisters of *The Umbrella Academy*, who feel distanced from each other and from their father. Second, there is self-estrangement of an action or process. With the exception of Diego (David Castañeda), all the other siblings feel estranged from their super-powers. Third, there is a sense of self-estrangement when the subject feels alienated from herself or himself. The estrangement has been internalized, as it happens with Vanya (Elliot Page) and her sense of solitude and displacement. The fourth use for estrangement is what Hegel calls "spirit" self-estrangement. This refers to human culture and society and a sense of being and/or belonging. As each member of the family belongs to a different cultural background, the feeling of estrangement should increase; this intercultural clash, however, is downplayed through the series right up to the point of being invisible. This invisibility presents a positive note, as the show encourages diversity and acceptance of different ethnic backgrounds. Still, the diversity as staged in *The Umbrella Academy* could be read as a source of tensions between the siblings, thus asking for a close reading and unpacking of how the dynamics of estrangement work within this superhero nucleus, on the one hand, and how these dynamics connect with real issues of transnational adoption, on the other hand.

## Defining Transnational Adoption, Defining Estrangement

Transnational adoption has become increasingly common, as laws' newfound flexibility regarding adoption allowed for a more fluent, global net of circulation of families looking for babies and babies being longed for. Currently, "transnational adoption has been a topic of intense media attention and public discourse in Western cultures. Celebrities such as Madonna and Angelina Jolie and Brad Pitt have been both admired and maligned in the popular press for the motives and methods of their multiple adoptions from various nations" (Fogle 1), thus making the understanding and the visibility of transnational and transracial adoption even more urgent. Transnational adoption was historically initiated in the aftermath of the Korean War (1950–1953). This particular aftermath produced geopolitical effects across the globe, including positioning the Republic of Korea as the world's leader of global exchanges in transnational and transracial adoption. Transnational adoption arose from an effort to help Korean War orphans and became a multimillion industry. Korea, orphanages, adoption agencies and American immigration policy operate in conjunction with one another: "From their interwoven connections, the transnational adoption industrial complex (TAIC) emerged" (McKee 137). Thereafter, "transnational adoption increased steadily until it finally surpassed domestic adoption" (Hübinette and Tigervall 121) in countries such as Sweden and North Korea.

Transnational adoption can bring to light issues on race, ethnicity, identity, and cultural roots. The tensions between legal, adoptive relations and blood ties "become the tension between legal belongings and the pull toward a mother(land), culture, or native soil in a global context" (Yngvesson 8). According to Barbara Yngvesson, the uprooting of an adopted child manifests "the tensions between humanitarian ideals that are expressed in the figure of a generalized child who can be 'loved by anyone,'" but who must first be "freed of his or her preadoptive history to become adoptable" (*ibid.*), thus materializing hierarchies and inequalities inscribed in the body and identity of the adopted son/daughter. As argued, "transnational adoption has been marked by the geographies of unequal power, as children move from poorer countries and families to wealthier ones—and the forces that make a country rich and powerful are above all historical. In this sense, transnational adoption has been shaped by the forces of colonialism, the Cold War, and globalization" (Briggs 1–2). As adoptees living in America, the different siblings of the Umbrella Academy struggle to adapt their different personalities into the common goal of saving, helping, and serving one of the most powerful nations of the entire globe. The only child who may be coming from an equally powerful region (some unspecified place of Asia) is, ironically, dead as the series begins. It is noticeable that the TV series departs from the graphic novel in some of the siblings' identities: while in the comic the "Rumor" is white and Diego is blond-haired, the adaptation enhances the multicultural aspect. Rumor (Emmy Raver-Lampman, herself adopted as a newborn) is dark-skinned while Diego (David Castañeda) is a dark-haired Mexican American actor. Thus, the hierarchical structures of multiculturalism-within-America points to the subsuming (and subjugation) of the different kids into the American ethos, the latter including ideals of superheroism and vigilantism. Values attached to traditional hierarchies of superheroic power read the superhero as the ultimate savior, the man (and, in a lesser degree, woman) in charge of saving and representing the conservative values of capitalism, individualism, and freedom framing America. The different superpowered children are then blended into these social structures of power where their real voices are muted to serve seemingly superior purposes.

The maintenance of identity is important for any subject, but especially urgent for children and young adults. Being an adoptee may lead to a sense of uprooting or not-belonging and thus an increasing estrangement from the rest of the family (parents and siblings), the community (school), and even themselves (self-estrangement). If "natal alienation is a part of all adoptions" (Fogg-Davis 100), as children are materially transferred from their native families to a group of "strangers," this sense of estrangement increases in transnational, transracial adoptions—as the TV adaptation of the comic book series highlights. The kids are not just transferred from their families, but from their nation and, many times, from their ethnic culture, thus emphasizing the sense of being rootless. Relationships of exclusion and inclusion, belonging and alienness, signal a complicated position where the child may feel dislocated, his/her history obliterated in favor of a new, superimposed one. What is important in transnational adoption is "the culture question," meaning, how much and what kind of vernacular culture "do/should/can we incorporate into the child's and family's life?"

(Dorow 206). Even the parents may manifest a "sense of estrangement from their transracially adopted child" (Simon and Altstein 196).

At this point, how I understand estrangement in the context of *The Umbrella Academy* should be defined. As outlined before, the term is inextricably linked to the theoretical framework using it. For Marxist scholars it "is the belief that human individuals have become divided within and have lost touch with themselves" (Churchich 102), thus losing consciousness about themselves and the reality of capitalist exploitation that oppresses them. To somatic pathology, estrangement indicates a pathological feeling of isolation (Robinson 97) while for religious thinking, the term "is a problem of finding a public life in which structures relating persons allow for the humanity of one person to acknowledge, address, and respond to the humanity of others" (Cummings Neville 282). For frameworks such as postcolonialism, estrangement serves to analyze "the histories of movement of peoples across borders" (Ahmed 95) and how these shifts dislocate temporality and spatiality. In all these conceptions, estrangement is associated with "disaffection, hostility, and antipathy, but it can also describe a separation, split or breach" (Matthews 102). Many of these understandings of estrangement continue George Wilhelm Friedrich Hegel's ideas on the topic as expressed on *Phenomenology of the Spirit*, which the author wrote in 1807 and which became one of the most influential texts in the history of philosophy. Here, Hegel proposes a novel understanding of the relation of the mind to the world and of people to each other. To Hegel, issues related to sociability and the individual were urgent matters, as for the author, "individuals and societies are mutually interdependent; neither is more basic than the other" (Westphal xvi). Since living is an inter-subjective and therefore social experience, concepts such as estrangement were of ultimate importance to Hegel at the moment of analyzing human cognitive and practical capacities with reference to their social dimensions. Here, estrangement refers in the first place to how people feel about one another describing the affective tone of a relationship, or the direction in which its emotional content is shifting from empathy to enmity and/or discord. The basic sense of mutual estrangement refers to people regarding one another as strangers or enemies. This is the type of relationship that prevails among the different members that compose the group of adoptees in *The Umbrella Academy*.

In the next section, it will be discussed how some notions of Hegel's conception of estrangement, arguably, a watershed from which this concept descends into modern thought, can serve to unpack some issues on transnational adoption. This will include a discussion of the different episodes of *The Umbrella Academy* to highlight how different forms of estrangement are related and illustrated in the show. The aim is to show how all these ideas can be read as interrelated to each other, metaphorizing urgent issues related to global adoption through the superhero and science-fiction genre.

## Hegel's Estrangement

Hegel's ideas of estrangement received their full philosophical development in *The Phenomenology of the Spirit*. My focus is on how Hegel's theory of (spiritual and psychical) estrangement can be related to culture and social formations—central ideas for the author as the subjectivity of the "I" cannot exist without a background which it delineates itself from: "The inequality which takes place in consciousness between the I and the substance which is its object is their difference, the negative itself" (Hegel 23). In brief, the subject acquires consciousness of his/her existence and identity against a negative "Other": the reality outside him/her (being humans or objects). The existence of a reality outside the subject, however, can lead to feelings of estrangement.

Before dealing with self-consciousness, Hegel had expounded the elements of consciousness, including our perception of things. He claimed that in perception we establish a world in which thinghood (Hegel 69; 332; 334) consists of a negative basis: the properties and qualities of an object make it a determinate thing and not any other. Through needs and desires, the subjects in the world grasp objects not just as an external force foreign to them but as objects which, in turn, exclude them. Through the appropriation of the things, the subjects work to overcome the foreignness of things. In the process, the subjects acquire the sense of selfhood, and on the other hand, experience the independence of objects, their resistance to the self. Among external objects are other self-conscious beings, and towards these, the subject directs the need to receive the confirmation of the self from another active consciousness: certainty and recognition of the I. Self-identity is constructed by exclusion of every other from himself/herself: "Consciousness henceforth has a doubled object: The first, the immediate object, the object of sensuous-certainty and perception, which, however, is marked for it with the character of the negative; the second, namely, itself, which is the true essence and which at the outset is present only in opposition to the first" (Hegel 103). But the other subject with equal sense of self-consciousness is also an individual that excludes us: "Self-certainty can only rise to the level of truth if others confirm it" (Torrance 24); still, "others are neither able nor willing to grant recognition, simply by the fact that they are others" (*ibid.*).

Here, issues of interpersonal inequality (such as slavery) and estrangement first appear. According to Neuhouser, "It is important to note that even though every act of recognition involves some degree of reciprocity (since my seeking recognition from you implies that I regard you as sufficiently worthy for your recognition to count), reciprocal recognition need not be *equal*" (49, original emphasis). Each subject seeks the acceptation that the "I" holds more value than the "Other." There is a struggle for recognition as everyone wants to be recognized as a Self. Thus, rather than a plurality of inter-connected egos, a stratified community of subjectivities emerges in which self-consciousness is socially established but sustained in the downgrading (as human) of the Other. With this begins the most important section of the text: the master-slave dialectic. The one who takes the decision (the master, the father figure) and the one who obeys and places his/her subjectivity at the hands of some other. In tracing this dialectic, Hegel makes the first explicit reference to estrangement. For the author, the cause for estrangement taking place in the community is that individuals confront each other as foreigners, for example, through the dissolution of national identities. No doubt this occurs "mainly in cities where immigrants of many nationalities mingle" (Torrance 28), but this situation can be grafted onto the peculiarities of transnational adoption, when subjects from all over the world become rootless and converge in a foreign family and location (and, sometimes, race) through an abrupt process of dislocation. Even of a little baby, the subject is fragmented to "fit" into a new spatial and emotional landscape. Further, the receiver family also has to face a sense of estrangement when somebody desired but strange nevertheless comes to the home. The child confronts an alien cultural heritage; the family, a stranger that they ached for.

For Hegel, the idea of estrangement requires an analysis into abstract concepts such as history and human reason. What interests me in this essay, however, are Hegel's distinctions between four different kinds of estrangement taking place within the individual and with the subject and the community. This sense of estrangement is related, in turn, in the master-slave dialectic.

## First Form of Estrangement: Between Persons

First, there is estrangement between persons. Examples are the estrangement between master and slave, the latter serving the commands of his master rather than those of his own. The master's (a figure easily replaced by that of the father) ultimate achievement is that his self-conception as a self-sufficient subject is now recognized by another consciousness that, through its complete obedience, proves the authority (the "I") of the master's desires. An individual may treat the external reality or himself as alien in so far as he is in the power of a stranger, thus becoming a mere extension of the desires of somebody else's personality. The master's will and point of view will carry authority for the other subjects. This is the clearest example of estrangement between people.

*The Umbrella Academy*'s opening episode, "We Only See Each Other at Weddings and Funerals,"[1] is exemplary in this type of rift already from the episode's title, which implies a common kind of estrangement: of people who, albeit being part of a family, basically have drifted apart with time. What this kind of estrangement emphasizes is that family is not enough to keep a relationship running in a healthy way. Commonly, it is believed that being part of the same family (especially birth family with blood relation) means that people belonging should care for each other and, what is more important, love each other. Mostly, this thought answers social and cultural constructions that speak about what a family must be, obliterating and/or ignoring other possible relationships between members of the same family. This exigency may be read as a burden, rather than a form of solace. The pressure to conform to a type of family that behaves in a "normal" (i.e., caring) way may lead to further estrangement as people try to feel love, empathy, and sympathy but feel emotional distance instead.

Indeed, "We Only See Each Other at Weddings and Funerals" begins with the five surviving siblings (one is dead, another one missing) reluctantly reuniting together for the funeral of their father. Rather than warmth, care, or even hatred (a form of emotion that at least may indicate hurt feelings), the siblings feel awkward in the presence of each other. This estrangement is a sharp contrast to the episode's opening scene, depicting two young Russians trying to make eye contact and flirting to each other before the woman (miraculously) gives birth to Vanya. Unlike the opening scene, filled with warmth and the desire to interconnect amidst a repressive climate, the siblings arrive at the Umbrella mansion dispassionately and mostly unaffected by Hargreeves' death. When Allison Hargreeves (Emmy Raver-Lampman), a celebrity with the power to control minds, is making an appearance at the red carpet of a gala, the questions of all the reporters revolve around how much time has passed since she saw her father for the last time. Also, how long since she saw any of her brothers and sisters. The uneasiness in her face reveals that she feels uncomfortable with the questions about her family. It is clear that everyone knows that Allison has an estranged relationship with her family. Further, it is indicated that she does not understand why the questions come up in the first place, showing that the reporters know about Hargreeves' death before Allison does, a fact that emphasizes her estrangement and how distanced she is from her father and siblings. News about her family reach strangers first before they reach her. Furthermore, this scene establishes to viewers that she does not feel being completely part of the family even if she bears the surname, a sentiment shared by all her brothers and sisters. This lack of real belonging parallels the feelings shared by many families but may resonate especially strong in families with adoptee members as the urgency "to fit" and establish a bond of mutual care is stronger and, as such, can be an emotional burden.

The two first siblings to arrive at the mansion for the funeral are Allison and Vanya. After seeing each other in the main hall, they both welcome each other briefly, either with coldness (Allison) or shyness (Vanya). After a moment of awkward silence, they blend in an uncomfortable embrace. They embrace each other not because they want to do so, but because it is the right thing to do; it is more of a response to the pressure of cultural rites of familial behavior than real caring. Their mutual embrace is interrupted by Diego, who has no welcoming words for any of his sisters. In turn, when Diego sees his brother Luther (Tom Hopper), the former welcomes the latter dryly with mocking reference to Luther's new body size. Later in the episode, when Klaus (Robert Sheehan) meets Allison, he embraces her with fuzziness. His commitment, however, is motivated by greed as Allison is the richest of the siblings and Klaus is always short on cash. Allison, in turn, does not respond to his embrace (even if, later in the scene, she warms up to her brother's charming behavior). Besides the mutual grudges the family shares, there is a clear lack of real commitment in terms of mutual trust and care. When in "Run Boy Run" Vanya invites Number Five (Aidan Gallagher) to sleep at her apartment, the boy looks surprised, as if his sister's invitation is something completely out of character or foreign to him. In the same episode, Number Five must pay his brother Klaus money to get the latter's help finding clues about a glass eye. They all may be family, but they are strangers to each other as well.

Hegel's first form of estrangement, however, is best illustrated in the uneasy relationship the siblings shared with their deceased father. If for Hegel the first kind of estrangement is best illustrated by the dynamics taking place between a slave and his master, Hargreeves, more master than father, is the perfect allusion to this hierarchy. As legitimate adopter, Hargreeves is the father of all the seven adoptees. However, he was never able to develop a healthy relationship with his kids. Part of the fault resides in his determination to make superheroes out of the children, rather than make them feel like real brothers and sisters. Even if forming a group of superheroes to help people may be read as laudable, the brothers and sisters have little say in what they really want to do with their childhood and lives. They must obey the architectural plans their father created for them and apply to his designs. It is of little importance if they really want to help people or not, their voices are obliterated by their father's strong will. Following Hegel, John Torrance explains this dynamic as follows: "Thus the slave or the subject are estranged from their conditions of existence, and even from their own existence, in so far as they are self-conscious beings who see their lives surrounded and permeated by the will of the master or despot" (41). The law followed by the subject/slave does not have its ground in the will of the individual, but in the absolute pure will of the master. When Diego tells Luther that there is no foul play involved in the death of their father, he highlights his lack of commitment; it is not that Diego is sure that there was no murder. What prevails is his complete lack of interest in investigating the death of an "old man" (in Diego's words) who died alone in an empty house. Diego is a good person, but he feels no emotional attachment to his father. Likewise, Klaus does not feel any emotional attachment towards his father, either, right up to the point of celebrating his death. For Number Five, their father's death is just part of the cycle of life. When Luther reunites all his siblings to communicate his doubts about their father's death, no one is interested in investigating. They are so indifferent to it that they leave Luther alone in the middle of his explanation. Clearly, Hargreeves has been more of a "master" figure (as understood through the master-slave dynamics) to the adopted siblings than an embodiment of care, trust and union.

There is the possibility of "conformity," i.e., the slave accepting the rules and norms of the master as a way to survive—here, the children of an assembled family accepting without questioning the rules of the father as the best way to "fit" within the new surroundings without generating tensions. This kind of relationship, however, does not mean affective commitment, which is why the estrangement continues. For the slave, the new set of rules remains alien for him or her, only accepting it as a way to avoid further problems. Hargreeves never performed as a father with regard to emotionally caring for his children, but as a master, he is consequently able to shape relationships based on emotional detachment. For Hargreeves, all his children were just numbers ("One," "Five," etc.; the failure of giving the children an identity through names is one of the issues Diego repudiates most about his father). In the comic, the children have, at least, superhero code-names such as Kraken or Rumor. Emphasizing estrangement, the TV adaptation only gives them numbers. The children are just components of the oiled mechanism that the Umbrella Academy is (or was). Even Grace, or Mom, as the Umbrella children call her, a human-like AI, showed more warmth and desire of bonding with the adoptees. It was her who named each of the kids and gave them the love they were missing from their father. As told in a flashback, when their "mother" gathers the children to say goodnight to their father, he ignores them ("We Only See Each Other at

Weddings and Funerals"). They may be a family, but they were never really close to each other in the first place and thus destined to remain strangers with little in common. This estrangement between people, perfectly delineated through the dynamics taking place between slave and master, basically stages the first steps into self-estrangement.

## Second Form of Estrangement: To Actions

The second form is a kind of self-estrangement but referring to an action or process rather than a condition. It is thus not so much a feeling of self-alienation from all the people around him or her that the subject experiences, but also an alienation from the very actions and tasks he or she makes through the day and life. This is a continuation of the logic of the master and slave; not only is the slave answering his master's voice (estrangement between persons), but he is also performing what he is told to do (alienation from the tasks). The slave does what the master tells him/her to do, rather than doing what he/she (the slave) really wants to do. Thus, the slave's actions are foreign to him or her, as any action really comes from the master's will. Daily life becomes a set of performances which hold no real meaning for the slave, but which do for the master: "The whole therefore is, as is each singular moment, a self-alienated reality" (Hegel 283). For any child, obeying without really internalizing the father's rules (or rather the parental rules) may fall into the category of tyranny. For adoptee kids or teenagers, the rules of the adopter father/mother, especially in cases of transnational and/or transracial adoption, may read as especially alien since the man or woman in command is not even blood-related.

As John Torrance notes, however, this kind of estrangement is connected also to public life as individuals, even those free from servitude, must obey to norms, rules and orders dictated from someone "above" them (the law, the government, etc.). Hegel shows

> that the historical evolution of self-conscious reason would eventually lead modern man to know himself as the author of his social world and the source of the morality that sustains it. Men would then become conscious within themselves of being these individual independent beings through the fact that they surrender and sacrifice their particular individuality, and that this universal substance is their soul and essence—as this universal again is the action of themselves as individuals, and is the work and product of their own activity [Torrance 42].

The Umbrella Academy is a group formed to help people, but this ideological and pragmatic goal comes mostly from Hargreeves' will. The making of the collective order is sustained upon the renunciation of individual autonomy of each sibling, which has been overtaken by their father/master. In the Netflix series, the different members of the group help Americans (not the people of their native countries, apparently) using their superpowers. They are depicted as even having fun while doing it and when posing for the reporters ("We Only See Each Other at Weddings and Funerals"). Still, their actions follow exclusively Hargreeves' set of ideological and pragmatic rules. In the opening scene—a flashback—of "Run Boy Run," Number Five asks a question to his father during dinnertime. Hargreeves, however, is adamant in keeping up one of his rules: nobody talks during dinner. Number Five's siblings look nervously at the talking boy. They have the rule deeply internalized, even if they do not completely understand and/or accept it: a tracking movement of the camera reveals that almost everyone looks distracted and/or bored, scratching the chair with a knife (Klaus), casting furtive glances to each other (Allison and Luther) or reading at the table (Ben). They are detached from both their father sitting at the head of the table (estrangement from other people) and dinnertime (estrangement from actions). Number Five further emphasizes this estrangement from actions: he wants to know why he cannot travel through time and space even if he feels fully prepared to do so. Soon enough, a fight with his father begins. Number Five tries to interrupt the process of estrangement; he has a power that he wants to use but cannot. This impediment is not due to some lacking on his part but because his father prevents him from using it. Basically, he is castrated from reaching his full potential. Rather than being his own person, Number Five (like his siblings) is an extension of his father's desires. Hargreeves tells Number Five that traveling through space and time can have weird, unpredictable effects on the body of the young boy; thus, the father figure (the master) wants to control his son's will, mind, and body.

The group works based on designs and rules formulated by Hargreeves; the children have no voice in the decisions, as the conversation between Number Five and his father reveals. Nobody wanted to be shaped up as heroes and only Diego continues the superheroic feats in his life as an adult. In the first episode of season two, "Right Back Where We Started," Diego is the only one who, after traveling back in time, immediately starts to perform as a superhero, helping a woman who is being mugged. Through the series' first season, the siblings laugh at Diego behind his back, ridiculing and mocking him for still using a black superhero costume. To his siblings, Diego is still living a self-estranged life as his sense of identity is still attached to the designs of his master, his adoptive father. It is almost impossible to separate Diego's desires of being a superhero from the plans orchestrated by his father, one and the other conflating together undifferentiated. Ironically, Diego ridicules Luther for the exact same reason. Certainly, Luther's own body has been shaped by his father, his interest in investigating the patriarch's death, arguably, an extension of his "superhero" persona—the latter, grafted upon him by Hargreeves.

This estrangement from the acts of the everyday does not solely imply the interactions of the different siblings with the world of superheroism, but their lives as common people as well. In season one, episode three, "Extra Ordinary," Vanya becomes more and more estranged from her world as a musician. She has been struggling to become a great violin player, but she is always fading into the background. After a rehearsal, she approaches the best violin player of the group and applauds her mastery on music. Rather than appreciation for the compliment, she obtains a cold, disparaging reply from her: "How many years have you been stuck at third chair? At a certain point, it's not about practice. It's whether you've got something special. And maybe you just … don't." What is implied here is not so much that Vanya has no talent, but that playing the violin is not really something that fulfills and excites her enough: "You can put in your 10.000 hours or … you can go find something you're actually passionate about." Vanya has been practicing the violin, but she is actually estranged from her position, role, and identity as a musician. She plays the violin, but she is detached from the origin of her love for music, i.e., why she picked it up in the first place and why she is still playing it—if it is not for passion, it seems that the only explanation would be inertia. When Vanya actually picked up the violin for the first time is a key scene. Her father's placing of the violin and his facial expression when she starts feeling passionate about it, reveal that he planned (or, at least, hoped) for her to pick it up—especially because his deceased wife loved it so much ("The White Violin"). As an architect, Hargreeves has even designed this (allegedly personal) path for his daughter. While her siblings are estranged from the superheroic acts that supposedly shape and sustain their identities, Vanya (who actually never takes an active role within the superhero group) is nevertheless similarly estranged from ordinary daily life. It is her own desire to be "extraordinary," to fit in with her adoptive family what pushes her; Vanya's dreams of glory seem to stem from the lack of affection shown by her father, rather than coming from her own desires.

## *Third Form of Estrangement: Within Itself*

In this third case, "the subject adopts an attitude of estrangement towards an imaginary being, and also imagines himself adopting a reciprocal attitude of estrangement on behalf of that being, towards himself" (Torrance 44). In this stage, the previous senses of social estrangement have been internalized and the subject becomes estranged from himself or herself the same way he or she is estranged from others. With regard to this internalization process Hegel outlines, "The I is in that content as differentiated, as having taken a reflective turn into itself" (Hegel 460). This is a logical consequence of being estranged from other people and from the acts that the subject performs every day as routine. Children endure, routinely, the subjugation to rules and norms established completely by and for others, the figures of authority of the family. This feeling may be exacerbated in transnational adoption. Due to being transnationally adopted, children are alienated from their birth country, their culture and their birth family as well. This lack of recognition about what constitutes the new life may lead to self-alienation, as the "I" is severely dislocated. The kid is "in" the family and nation (one of "us") but feels "foreign" nevertheless. This produces self-estrangement as the kid is both the new son/daughter and the foreigner.

All the siblings of *The Umbrella Academy* feel estranged from themselves. Their roles as superheroes are something alien to their identities since the decision was never theirs to make. The most obvious cases of this self-estrangement are Vanya, Klaus and Luther. Vanya feels estranged from herself due her character as "common" or "extra ordinary." This estrangement is also deeply entrenched in the second form of estrangement that was outlined earlier, as it was Hargreeves who lied to Vanya and made her feel detached from her identity as a superheroine. In fact, Vanya is the most powerful of the siblings and the drugs she takes to keep her healthy are inhibitors that keep her controlled. Even after her father's death, she is still the product of her master rather than a "real" I, a whole Self. When her powers finally find a path to come out, they pour upon Allison, almost killing her. In "Changes" (episode 9), Vanya's sense of self-estrangement deepens: after almost killing Allison, Vanya is seemingly welcomed to the family home. There, Luther offers the suffering girl an embrace. Rather than friendship, Vanya finds more rejection as Luther chokes Vanya until she faints. Luther only wants to subject and imprison her into the mansion's basement. Thus, Vanya's self-estrangement increases her estrangement from all the others.

Klaus and Allison are also estranged from their powers. Allison has lost her daughter to her ex-husband in the divorce after she had broken her promise of never using her power to control her daughter's mind ("I Heard a Rumor"). Like Vanya, she has a strong superpower, but she is estranged from it since she does not use it anymore. Klaus, on the other hand, is free to use his powers to contact the deceased. His powers, however, come with a negative secondary effect: he is frequently haunted by visions and presences from the other side, including his deceased brother Ben. The only way to downplay the presences surrounding him is through the consumption of alcohol and drugs—an escape mechanism that has taken him to dark paths of self-destruction. His clashing, unreliable personality makes him especially difficult to deal with; thus, his sense of self-estrangement leads him to increasing estrangement from others, including his sexual and romantic life. He is the first to admit that his longest romantic relationship only lasted three months ("Run Boy Run"). Still, Vanya is the most estranged of the siblings, as she is completely unaware of her powers and thus, feels foreign in her "common" body.

The latter is a feeling she shares with Luther, who possesses an extremely strong body due to his ape-like physiology. After a failed mission, his father could only save him by injecting a special formula that partially transformed his body into the shape of a gorilla. Despite his super-strength, Luther is ashamed of his body. In the opening episode, when he presents himself with his new appearance to all his siblings, Luther's face reveals how much his body pains him. In episode 7, "The Day That Was," it is revealed that Luther is still a virgin. As a consequence of the feeling of estrangement that Luther feels towards his own corporeality, the leader of the Umbrella Academy finds it hard to get undressed and is thus vulnerable in a romantic or sexual relationship, which is why his sexual life is non-existent. The alienation Luther feels towards his own corporeality has led him to a deep estrangement since his relationships with people like Allison (whom he had been secretly in love with for years) are short-circuited due his lack of confidence. Furthermore, his conversion into an ape-like creature is a consequence of a decision taken by his master/father, Reginald Hargreeves. Again, Luther, like the rest of his siblings, has little to say with regard to his own identity, as he has been defined completely by a foreign will, namely that of his adoptive father.

## *Fourth Form of Estrangement: Culture*

The fourth and last form of estrangement in *The Umbrella Academy* is, paradoxically, mostly shown by its complete absence. The fourth use of estrangement is what Hegel calls "spirit self-estranged." This refers to the state of the human—in engagement with a concrete time and space—when not only the Self, but likewise society as a whole, is divided into mutually estranged parts. Consciousness now struggles to make itself feel "at home" in a world from which it feels essentially estranged. In the modern age, the human faces a set of binary oppositions between state (as government, as society) and the individual or the divine and the human that emphasizes the feeling of estrangement. The individual consciousness

> therefore develops not only a world, it also develops a doubled world, which is divided and opposed within itself. The world of ethical spirit is its own present time, and hence every power within it is in this unity [...]. Nothing signifies the negative of self-consciousness; even the departed spirit is present in the blood of his relatives, current in the self of the family, and the universal power of government is the will, the self of the people [Hegel 282].

This fourth form of estrangement marks the lack of (beautiful) concord between the human with the social and the cultural. Ethical formation is, indeed, something laudable; "This individuality culturally educates itself into what it is in itself and only as a result is it in itself, does it have actual existence. The more it has such cultural education, the more it has actuality and power" (Hegel 285). Yet, culture and society deepen the separation between the Self and Nature.

This fourth estrangement is inextricably linked to how society works. As explained by John Torrance, as social groups come into being divided by absence of a common purpose, "the social order resulting from their interaction would be one whose unity lay outside the collective self-consciousness of any of them" (45). The latter means an external purpose that gives them identity and transcends each subject's individuality: to being self-estranged is to call attention "to the extent to which society was not a self-conscious unit, so that people failed to recognise themselves and their intentions in the collective consequences of their deeds" (*ibid.*). It is for that reason that the main goal of the particular family of adoptees that forms the Umbrella Academy lies outside the unity (of the family): bring justice to the world. Doing this masks the fact that the family is shaped by different identities, cultures and backgrounds that are so diverse that the unit lacks coherence.

I have stated that this fourth form of estrangement is the most important and the most invisible in the TV show. Indeed, the different backgrounds of the siblings are never explicitly mentioned: even if the TV show, as mentioned, highlights multiculturalism, viewers never know what Allison feels as a black woman (albeit this topic is taken up in the second season more prominently), or how Diego feels as a Latino or Ben as an Asian young man living with white Western parents. They are completely different from each other and from their adopting country, but their differences are obliterated and supplanted with a common (external) goal: bring justice (to America). The lack of real unity within the family takes viewers to the cultural and social policies of transnational adoption. It may be argued that Hargreeves' main mistake was that of not taking into account the different individualities of his children. Rather than preserving their birth heritage, the father figure obliterates any difference through the imposition of his own will and the common (external) goal by means of which the kids should adapt to the structures of the United States of America. Like Hegel's idea of the self-estranged human (at odds with the structures of culture), Hargreeves has made it impossible for his children to feel at home. The siblings are happy to serve America (the state) and have a positive evaluation of their actions while, at the same time, resenting their subordination to the ruler and his designs. This "sci-fi" situation actually mirrors that of transnational adoption. As Sara Dorow suggests, adoptees' movements between geographical and temporal locations asserts that "difference matters materially, relationally, and experientially" (264). Local or global inequities can exacerbate adoptee's resentment about the receiver land. The family unit is in danger of instability when the kid is happy to conform while resenting the very act of conforming to a unity of strangers in a strange land.

## *Conclusion: Emotional Engagement*

One way to avoid the pitfall of estrangement in transnational adoption is through policies of emotional engagement. Through them, both the adoptees and the family choose to work hard on the building of affective liaisons while keeping intact the identity of each member of the new family. Politics of kinship must be erected to create a union where the common goal is not external to the family (= Hargreeves' mistake) but internal. Emphasizing the differences while, at the same time, celebrating the similitude may be a way to create this kinship: the adoptee retains his or her individuality while sharing some emotional bond with the adopters.

"We Only See Each Other at Weddings and Funerals," the opening chapter in the life of the siblings populating the Umbrella Academy, offers not only the first signs of estrangement (as studied above), but also some hints at the possibility of emotional bonding. Before the funeral (and before the sudden return of Number Five), Luther puts on Tiffany's "I Think We're Alone Now" at full volume. The song is heard through the mansion. Slowly but surely, each sibling cannot stop themselves from moving along to the beat. Luther starts to move first, following the rhythm. Each of the siblings starts to dance as well, in their own space. A wide shot shows the house as cut-by-the-half, each brother and sister dancing to the same song in different parts of the mansion, all of them united into a full-blown dance party separated by walls. However, every one of them retains his or her identity: Luther balancing with some style (and some difficulties) his huge body, Allison wearing a glamorous feather boa, Vanya timidly, Klaus looking for a partner (looking for affection?) between the objects of the house and Diego showing all his incredibly good movements (after all, he is the only "superhero" of the group). The song speaks of being oneself when we are all alone, nobody watching. After the song is interrupted by the arrival of Number Five (from the future), emotional walls are erected once again. Estrangement resumes. But the emotional bond was established; they have shared something, but, at this point, it remains to be seen if they are able to unify this common ground, this care they are too timid to share at the face of "strangers." The beautiful warmth of the moment, however, lingers. Outside from all the designs orchestrated by their father, they have found a bond to share, a moment through which their identities can shine in harmony with each other. It is a bonding that is related purely to the intimate space of the family.

In this sense, it should be noted that season two of *The Umbrella Academy* begins with all the siblings looking for each other and for support from each other after been divided temporally by the events of season one's conclusions. It seems that estrangement is starting to fade away when the family shapes itself on the cohesion of individual identities rather than upon unidirectional orders. Thus, this fantastic group gives some answers to the issues brought by transracial and transnational adoption when emphasizing the fact that parenthood must negotiate shared bonds without imposing a goal or downplaying individualities. As Number Five notes in "The Day That Wasn't," the siblings should not let themselves be defined by what Hargreeves thought of them and for them; they must (re)create their own identities, in relation with themselves and others. Only then, they can all be part of the Umbrella Academy family.

### Note

1. In the comic, the events of the first episode are told in the second issue, mostly following the same pattern of uneasiness and estrangement between siblings.

### Works Cited

Ahmed, Sara. *Strange Encounters: Embodied Others in Post-Coloniality*. Routledge, 2013.
Briggs, Laura, and Diana Marre. "Introduction: The Circulation of Children." *International Adoption: Global Inequalities and the Circulation of Children*, edited by Laura Briggs and Diana Marre, New York University Press, 2009, pp. 1–28.
Churchich, Nicholas. *Marxism and Alienation*. Fairleigh Dickinson University Press, 1990.
Cummings Neville, Robert. *God the Creator: On the Transcendence and Presence of God*. State University of New York Press, 1992.
Dorow, Sara. *Transnational Adoption: A Cultural Economy of Race, Gender, and Kinship*. New York University Press, 2006.
Fedders, Barbara. "Race and Market Values in Domestic Infant Adoption." *Race in Trans-

national and Transracial Adoption, edited by Vilna Bashi Treitler, Palgrave Macmillan, 2014, pp. 49–69.
Fogg-Davis, Hawley. *The Ethics of Transracial Adoption*. Cornell University Press, 2002.
Fogle, Lyn Wright. *Second Language Socialization and Learner Agency: Adoptive Family Talk*. Multilingual Matters, 2012.
Hegel, Georg Wilhelm Friedrich. *The Phenomenology of Spirit*. Cambridge University Press, 2018.
Hübinette, Tobias, and Carina Tigervall. "When Racism Becomes Individualised: Experiences of Racialisation Among Adult Adoptees and Adoptive Parents of Sweden." *Complying with Colonialism: Gender, Race and Ethnicity in the Nordic Region*, edited by Suvi Keskinen, Salla Tuori, Sari Irni and Diana Mulinari, Routledge, 2016, pp. 119–136.
Matthews, Sara. "Rethinking the Good in Good Global Citizenship: The Ethics of Cosmopolitan Pluralism." *The World Is My Classroom: International Learning and Canadian Higher Education*, edited by Joanne Benham Rennick and Michel Desjardins, University of Toronto Press, pp. 93–110.
McKee, Kimberley. "Monetary Flows and the Movements of Children: The Transnational Adoption Industrial Complex." *The Journal of Korean Studies*, vol. 21, no. 1, 2016, pp. 137–178.
Neuhouser, Frederick. "Desire, Recognition, and the Relation Between Bondsman and Lord." *The Blackwell Guide to Hegel's Phenomenology of Spirit*, edited by Ken Westphal, Blackwell, 2009, pp. 37–54.
Robinson, Douglas. *Estrangement and the Somatics of Literature: Tolstoy, Shklovsky, Brecht*. Johns Hopkins University Press, 2008.
Simon, Rita, and Howard Altstein. *Adoption, Race, and Identity: From Infancy to Young Adulthood*, 2d ed. Transaction Publishers, 2009.
Suvin, Darko. *Metamorphoses of Science Fiction. on the Poetics and History of a Literary Genre*. Yale University Press, 1979.
\_\_\_\_\_. *Positions and Presuppositions in Science Fiction*. Macmillan, 1988.
Torrance, John. *Estrangement, Alienation and Exploitation: A Sociological Approach to Historical Materialism*. Macmillan, 1977.
Westphal, Ken. "Introduction." *The Blackwell Guide to Hegel's Phenomenology of Spirit*, edited by Ken Westphal, Blackwell, 2009, pp. xvi–xxvii.
Yngvesson, Barbara. *Belonging in an Adopted World: Race, Identity, and Transnational Adoption*. University of Chicago Press, 2010.

# Part 2

# Forces of Otherness

# Artifice and the Superheroes of the 21st Century

## *Post-Cinematic Reflections on Constructedness*

### Morgane A. Ghilardi

It is difficult not to read *The Umbrella Academy* as a reaction to the overabundance of superhero tales that have flooded TV and silver screens in the past decade.[1] In many ways, it situates itself in the tradition of postmodern reflections on the figure of the vigilante crime fighter as a cypher for American individualism and power, presenting us with a particular if recognizable take on a strange family of superhumans. Early deconstructionist ventures of the genre tackled a rising sense of unease with the very concept of the superhero in the context of neoliberalism.[2] They were maybe most famously undertaken in the 1980s by Frank Miller in *The Dark Knight Returns*, which "so confidently and aggressively rebranded the Batman story as a violent operatic myth of eighties America" (Morrison 190), as well as Alan Moore and Dave Gibbons in *Watchmen*, a book which called upon superhero stories to "evolve or die" (195). J. Michael Straczynski's *Rising Stars* (1999–2005) or Brian Bendis's *Powers* (2000– ) were among those comic book series that heeded this call to reframe and reformulate the tale of the superhero, as both adopted noir tropes and aesthetics to explore the dark side of a world populated by superhumans with twisted politics and a propensity for murder. We can think of Straczynski and Bendis' work as a continuation of the questioning and reframing accomplished by Miller and Moore, bringing new aesthetic and political developments into play (e.g. as emerging from the neoconservatism that arose with the new millennium rather than a neoliberal context of the 1980s; or, the rise of the internet in the wake of MTV culture). Considering Grant Morrison endorsed *The Umbrella Academy* as "an ultraviolet psychedelic sherbet bomb of wit and ideas," claiming that "the superheroes of the 21st century are here at last" (*The Umbrella Academy: Apocalypse Suite*, cover copy), reflecting on the cultural moment from which *The Umbrella Academy* emerged—specifically, the 2019 Netflix adaptation of the comic book series—presents itself as a worthwhile pursuit.

The series has to be considered both in terms of its mode of mediation and its place within a genre that crosses media boundaries. In fact, rather than being overtly concerned with the political climate of its time (unlike HBO's *Watchmen* series, which came out later in 2019 and is highly political in its preoccupation with power and race), *The Umbrella Academy* can be read as an example of a self-reflexive examination of its genre's peculiarities in the post-cinematic age. The superhero's revival or reanimation on the screen is no small part due to the advancements in CGI technology, and has become a pillar of the current popular media landscape, embroiling its audiences in the long and layered—i.e., intertextual and palimpsestic—history of the genre. The Netflix series is intriguing precisely because of its palimpsestic or citational nature. On the one hand, it appropriates the trope of the dysfunctional patchwork family—familial loss and trauma remaining a mainstay, if not cliché, of the superhero origin story—maybe being most obviously reminiscent of *X-Men* as a story of young misfits who are sequestered in the home of an elderly, affluent father figure intending to mold them into a cohesive team of crime fighters. On the other hand, the aesthetic and narrative mode of the series (re)mediates a postmodern sensibility for irony, nostalgic pastiche, and fragmentation, which, I would argue, is translated into a concern with the notion of *constructedness* itself, i.e., the authored, mediated, or arranged nature of not only text/media, but of larger aesthetic and epistemic structures.

This concern relates not only to the nature of the image and its artifice in the era of post-cinematic modes of representation—i.e., those modes that are fundamentally shaped by digital media technologies and the shift towards television as the culturally dominant medium (Shaviro 1; Sobchack 135–6)—but arguably connects to apprehensions about the meaning of the figure and genre of the superhero. The characters of Grace, the robotic mother of the Umbrella brood, as well as Pogo, the "advanced" chimpanzee, are central representatives of constructedness and our precarious relationship to this concept in a time in which deep fakes are just one example of hyperreality's anxiety-inducing hold on society. Both are literal embodiments of artificiality not only on the diegetic level, having been technologically engineered to be what they are, but also in terms of their place within the media-technical and aesthetic framework of the show. With her 1950s garb and Stepfordian demeanor, Grace conveys a sense of gendered nostalgia that speaks to the inherent wistfulness of the superhero genre, while self-reflexively pointing to the citationality and artificiality that pervade post-cinematic modes of representation. Similarly, Pogo, who is entirely CGI-made and transposed unto the captured performances of two actors (this will be addressed below), manifests the paradoxes of hyperreality in the post-cinematic image, as we both recognize the artificiality of the image and are compelled to *feel* that it is real because of its role in the diegetic system. While both characters overtly indicate and articulate the complex imbrication of diegetic, aesthetic, and media-technical constructs, they are also central to the family melodrama, i.e., the narrative of familial dissolution and restoration that is so often at the center of the superhero tale, bringing us back to the question of generic formulae. Among other elements, it is in these artificial creatures that the series' affective power can be identified with, or, to put it differently, where we can locate conflicting dimensions of feeling about artifice and constructedness.

Media, as Vivian Sobchack points out, are technologies of perception as much as expression, affecting "our sense of ourselves" (135) and "transform[ing] us as embodied subjects" (136), holding the power of both mediation and constitution of our sense of self. Media and their technologies have the power to "unsettle" aesthetics and representations of the lived world, according to Sobchack, and thereby also unsettle and change values and perspectives. How, then, are we affected by this genre and its current (serial, digital) modes of mediation in our perception of ourselves and our reality? By looking at the show as "*expressive* [...] [of] a kind of ambient, free-floating sensibility that permeates our society today, although it cannot be attributed to any subject in particular," as Steven Shaviro puts it (2), the intent here is to explore Netflix's *The Umbrella Academy* and its post-cinematic modes of representation as what Shaviro calls "affective maps, which do not just passively trace or represent, but actively construct and perform, the social relations, flows, and feelings that they are ostensibly 'about'" (6). The central argument will be that the series' affective maps convey a concern with constructedness on both an aesthetic and narrative level, which is embedded in the superhero genre's contemporary emanations, and which speaks to the way in which we are unsettled in our sense of a world in which digital technologies of representation destabilize the perceiving subjects' sense of being-in-the-world.

What defines the genre of the superhero tale is the fact that it is so highly formulaic, which simultaneously accomplishes two things: firstly, it is based on a narrative dynamic of serial continuity and remediation, and, secondly, it is exactly by virtue of what we might call self-haunting that the superhero tale can reflect or channel the *zeitgeist* of a given era with great acuity. What I mean with the former is that the serial nature of the superhero tale and the existence of so-called universes, which hold their own discrete timelines, locals, and denizens and contain narrative axes that span from the creation of certain superheroes to today, makes the genre fundamentally citational and cyclical, especially considering that they are sometimes discarded, interrupted, and rewritten—or rebooted, as popular parlance would have it. Comic book readers are ever so often referred to earlier events (i.e., comic book issues), which creates a sense of both diegetic and real history. When these superhero tales then bridge transmedial gaps when they are adapted and transferred to television, film, or video games,[3] a new universe is produced that stands apart from the original text(s),[4] presenting a discrete version or retelling of a superhero's origin and life that can introduce a new audience to it, but which simultaneously counts on another kind of audience's recognition of and familiarity with the original.[5] These remediations are certainly symptoms of an "age of adaptation" that is the result of the emergence of new media and their techniques (Hutcheon 109); they hold a specific affective power by virtue of their citationality, inviting viewers (or, in the case of video game adaptations, players) to indulge in the pleasure of recognition or remembrance (111).[6] If its seriality and transmedial layerings make the superhero genre inherently citational and therefore also repetitive, it is in that repetition that lies its potential to provide an even surface for the reflection of contemporary sociopolitical or media-cultural concerns. The familiar formulae of the genre allow for any difference in the refiguration of the same old to stand out in a significant way. Changes of this nature have not only affected surface structures of the narrative (e.g., enemies might change faces with the times, so that Nazis were replaced with the Red Threat) but also deeper structures (e.g., the concept of an enemy Other being be replaced with the reality of internal social struggles like racism or the drug epidemic, for instance in issues 96–98 of Marvel's *Amazing Spider-Man*, or issues 85–86 of DC's *Green Lantern/Green Arrow*, published in 1971). The fact that postmodern and deconstructionist thought really took root in the world of the superhero in the late 1970s and 1980s, putting into question the very concept of the superhuman vigilante and its ideological implications, points to a desire to reexamine, reformulate, and revisit the foundation of the genre as well as the values in place at its heart. We might ask ourselves how such postmodern deconstructions affect the genre in the long term, especially considering that it has experienced a large-scale revival and expansion with Marvel and DC's launch of massive cinematic franchises (which also extend to serial formats for television and streaming platforms). Or, put differently, what do the genre's thematic and aesthetic emanations express or perform today if we consider its texts as having inherited a postmodern tendency for self-reflexive examination? And, how does this in turn affect texts that were created outside of these publisher's genre-dominating universes and franchises, both in terms of narrative and mediation?

Netflix's *The Umbrella Academy*, released in February 2019, is based on three limited comic book series published between 2007 and 2019 by Dark Horse Comics. The adaptation was said to be motivated by the "unique, visual, and stylized" quality of the comic book, according to Netflix executive Cindy Holland, as well as the fact that "these aren't the usual superheroes" (Wagmeister par. 7). It makes sense that the over-saturation of the superhero media market would make uniqueness and difference salient selling points, yet this statement might also prompt us to think about what a "usual superhero" is, i.e., in what way *The Umbrella Academy* presents us with a different kind of superhero story.

Like other comic book adaptations, the Netflix series self-consciously points to its status as an adaptation and the transmediality at play. For instance, season 1, episode one ("We Only See Each Other at Weddings and Funerals") centers on the homecoming of the disbanded Umbrella Academy's members. As they explore their childhood home, we see a comic book titled *The Umbrella Academy* (00:15:10) as well as magazines featuring pictures of the children displayed in the library. The suggestion seems to be that the superhero team's early ascendance was accompanied by a publicity and marketing campaign that included media coverage and merchandizing efforts (a fact that is later highlighted when we are also shown other collectables, a staple of the franchise-based economy of the comic book world, and the consequences of excessive fandom).[7] The comic book is especially interesting for several reasons: while the art is that of the comic book's co-creator Gabriel Bá, thereby connecting the adaptation and the original, the layout and look is reminiscent of Golden Era superhero comic books, which not only highlights the slightly anachronistic aesthetics of the show, but also evokes the history of its genre in what we might consider both an ironic and nostalgic gesture. The romantic irony that is at play signals self-awareness both of the text's generic roots and of its transference from one medium to another, while the nostalgia is the product of a conscious summoning of memory and desire for a past that is now inaccessible and stands in harsh contrast to the present (Hutcheon and Valdés 19–20). This nostalgia functions both on the metatextual and diegetic level, as it calls on the viewer's memory, while also implying that the characters of the show are experiencing a moment of longing for a past that cannot be recovered (and, as we soon learn, about which most feel more than a little ambivalent). Another way in which the series links to its original text is through a newspaper clipping in the background with the headline "EIFFEL POWER!" (00:18:29). This is a reference to events that take place in the first issue of comic book series ("The Day the Eiffel Tower Went Berserk"), when the young superheroes avert a catastrophic attack on Paris. However, this reference is aimed at a specific group of viewers, namely those familiar with the comic books. For those viewers, this is a moment of pleasurable recognition, as the text acknowledges their special knowledge. For some viewers, then, this bridging of the comic book and the series' diegesis or universe enables a (gratifying and media-crossing) conflation of the two, while merely providing color or the sense of a narrative history or diegetic depth to those viewers that are new to the universe established by the Netflix show and perceive it as discrete. Overall, the first episode sets the tone for the rest of the show, establishing a sense of tongue-in-cheek self-awareness but also of a nostalgia that is both sincere and playful, linking the viewer's intertextual memory and its affective power with the narrative's emotional arch about the confrontation of a superhero family's past trauma—which ranges from paternal disaffection and familial alienation to death—and its future survival.

When it comes to the issue of family, the series reworks a narrative trope that pervades comic book history, specifically the post–World War II superhero comic book: the story of a specific kind of family, constructed in a dynamic of dysfunction, dissolution, and reunion. As Ramzi Fawaz argues, superheroes in postwar comics transitioned from "symbols of national strength and U.S. citizenship" to freakish biological and cultural figures of difference, so that "superhero comics visually celebrated bodies whose physical instability deviated from social and political norms" and "produced the visual lexicon of alliances between a variety of 'inhuman' yet valorized subjects as a cultural corollary to the cosmopolitan worldviews of movements for international human rights, civil rights, and women's and gay liberation" (4). Part of this transition was an emphasis on "social communities and solidarities" that enabled "progressive social transformation" and critically reframed the notion of the heteronormative, consumerist hyper-individualism that emerged in cold-war America as potentially damaging to society (11). Superhero comic books thus became a production site for new social and familial modalities:

> Against this self-centered figure of liberal politics, superhero comics celebrated the production of implicitly queer and nonnormative affiliations that exceeded the bounds of traditional social arrangements such as the nuclear family and the national community. Whether willfully choosing alternative solidarities or unwittingly thrown into relation with a host of mutated or monstrous others, postwar superheroes produced complex and internally heterogeneous communities of fellow travelers—often brought together under the rubric of the superhero "team" of chosen "family"—who sought to use their powers for shaping a more egalitarian and democratic world. Like the bodies and identities of the superheroes, aliens, mutants, and outsiders that composed their ranks,

these alternative solidarities were depicted as being in constant flux, expanding, retracting, and transforming their stated values on the basis of unexpected encounters with a wider world [11–12].

These superhero comics, therefore, operated in two, parallel modes. On the one hand, they centered on the notion of family as a core structure of society, thereby reproducing traditional generic conventions of the family melodrama as an—often sentimental—examination of morality and values in which the family functions as a microcosmic reflection of larger societal structures. On the other hand, "alternative solidarities" introduced a new notion of family and emphasized differences which are often rooted in the body, and which allowed for a progressive push against cultural boundaries of gender, sex, race, and class, making them less solid and emphasizing the reality of and need for change. Fluidity, or as Fawaz calls it, "fluxability" (11) is a key aspect of the postwar superhero,[8] which suggests a tendency towards constant (de)construction and (re)constitution.

*The Umbrella Academy* incorporates this notion of alternative alliances and fluxability in many ways. At the center of the story are the seven adopted children of Sir Reginald Hargreeves, who were born on the same day and all possess special abilities. Hargreeves numbers the children rather than naming them—a fact that should already reveal why this group of superhumans might be considered a dysfunctional family—and trains them in order to turn them into a superhero team, thus forming the Umbrella Academy. The children grow up fighting crime as a unit until familial strife—caused by internal tensions but surely accelerated by the death of Number Six (a.k.a. Ben or The Horror) and the disappearance of Number Five—tears them apart, sending them on their own journey in the "wider world." The plot sets in long after the Umbrella Academy's glory days, after most of the children have long since left their home and pursued their individual paths, struggling with their own, though not necessarily unrelated troubles: Number One (a.k.a. Luther), who stayed loyal to his adoptive father, is on a solitary research mission on the moon; Number Two (a.k.a. Diego) remains a vigilante crime fighter, assisting a reluctant police detective; Number Three (a.k.a. Allison) is an actress and has started a family; Number Four (a.k.a. Klaus), who is plagued by visions of the dead, is addicted to drugs he takes in an attempt to suppress his abilities; and Number Seven (a.k.a. Vanya), who has never exhibited any special powers, is a violinist and has published a memoir about her life as the only non-gifted member of the Umbrella Academy, which led her to be permanently ostracized by her adoptive siblings and father. Each of them has suffered from both (familial) trauma and the consequences of their difference, exacerbated by their father's parental disaffection and investment not only in whatever abilities set them apart from regular humans, but also their internal differences (e.g., by numbering them according to their value,[9] or not giving Vanya the umbrella tattoo, setting her apart from her siblings). The central overarching plot is the reunion and reconciliation of the fragmented family whose dysfunction was preprogrammed. The five remaining members of the Umbrella Academy are brought together once more in their childhood home—welcomed back by their robotic mother, Grace, and their father's simian assistant, Pogo—after they receive news that their father has died. As mentioned before, the moment of their return is fraught with irony and nostalgic sentiment that links to the family's fragmented state, which comes to the fore in a musical interlude of sorts: as each of the siblings explore different parts of their childhood home, Number One/Luther puts on Tiffany's "I Think We're Alone Now" on his record player (00:30:32). As the song penetrates the space of the massive urban mansion, the siblings start dancing to the 1980s pop anthem, each on his or her own. In an "impossible," CGI-enabled extreme long shot, the mansion becomes a kind of diorama in which the characters can be seen dancing together but apart in the various corner of this house divided. If this highlights the fragmented state of the family, it also evokes a common trope of the genre, namely that differences can act both as a separating wedge and as a force of cohesion; they may have chosen to be apart, but nothing changes that they are different *together*. Soon enough, they are thrust on a mission that forces them to confront the ongoing tensions that have driven them apart, as space-and-time-traveling Number Five miraculously returns from the future, where he has been trapped for a lifetime, to announce that the apocalypse is imminent. In the course of the season, we also learn that Number Six/Ben, though dead, has stuck around as a ghost and can only be seen by Number Four/Klaus.

The plot follows two major intertwined arcs: humanity's salvation in the face of an unknown apocalyptic threat, and the healing of the fractured family that was never normative in the first place, that has always been in flux, has always been challenged by differences acting in- and outwardly, but whose reconstitution is as central as global survival. Their father's death not only prompts their reunion but also motivates Number One/Luther to investigate further, as he does not believe that he died of natural causes. As the ensuing investigation reveals, Hargreeves died at this own volition, knowing that it would be the necessary catalyzer for his children's reconciliation. At the same time, it is precisely this process of forced confrontation that leads to potentially apocalyptic events: Vanya is made more aware than ever that she has been ostracized by her siblings and her sense of powerlessness is compounded. Out of rising frustration—heightened by the influence of her new, unstable boyfriend—Vanya discovers that she does, in fact, wield a unique and overwhelmingly powerful ability that she can channel through her musical talents. It is revealed that she has always been the most powerful—and potentially destructive—of her siblings, a fact that her father became aware of early on and which led him to suppress her knowledge about her own capabilities. It is her trauma—the exclusion and rejection she suffered at the hand of her father and siblings—that turn her into the annihilating force that threatens to end the world. These developments build on self-reflexive and ironic tendencies: the father's self-staged suicide underlines the very notion of narrative construction, as he is effectively creating a mystery that is meant to reunite his children to address whatever impending doomsday event may present itself; yet, his grand plan is revealed to be a self-fulfilling prophecy, as it is his schemes and precautions that lead to Vanya's explosive and catastrophic self-actualization. Moreover, the threat of time-traveling assassins that work for the Commission, an agency that regulates timelines and wants the apocalypse to unfold unhindered, implies that history itself is a consciously authored chain of events over which various parties want to exert control. The power that is desired here, one may deduce, lies in the exertion of control over how a story will unfold, and yet it is elusive and struggling for it is a futile exercise. As a text that delivers commentary on its own genre in a postmodern fashion, Hargreeves can be read as an ironically unaware agent of generic prescription: he lays out a narrative path that ultimately reveals him to be not an operator but another cog in the narrative machine.

As a paternal instance, Hargreeves is an agent of construction in other ways, however, as he not only assembled the superhuman family, but also assumed the Promethean role of creator. It is arguably Pogo, a quasi-parental figure, as well as the siblings' robotic surrogate mother Grace, who are the family's most unusual constituents. While the first season of the adaptation does not address Pogo's creation,[10] he acts as both a valet to Hargreeves and as a caregiver to the Umbrella children. Grace, too, is one of his creations. A robot designed to look like a stereotypical 1950s housewife, Grace's role is to provide the emotional and parental care that Hargreeves does not give his children. However, as we learn later in the series, Hargreeves created her because Vanya's destructive powers proved to be deadly for the other, human caregivers he had hired, making Grace a solution for a problem that is fairly unique to the kind of family he had assembled. It is important to note that both Pogo and Grace are engineered and unreal on different levels.

Pogo represents a form of layering that relies on the simultaneous collision of real and unreal on the level of the image and the narrative. Pogo is a digitally rendered image that is based on the performances of two actors: Ken Hall played Pogo on set in a motion capture suit which recorded his physical performance, while Adam Godley's vocal and facial performance was added in post-production and melded with the first by the prolific visual-effects specialists at Weta Digital (Mele; Weta Digital; Seymour). The resulting image possesses a hyper-realistic quality—i.e., one that undermines the distinction between reality and simulation—not only in terms of lighting and textures, but also because they accomplish to render what can only be imagined, namely the bodily presence and movement of a chimpanzee-human hybrid. The hybridity of the image means that the spectator encounters both artifice (the final image) and realness (the original performances of Hall and Godley) in Pogo's image: we want to trust the image, and yet we know we cannot. Post-cinematic modes of representation, impacted by the collision of the real and the simulated, i.e., the digital alteration that adds layers of artifice to or wholly creates the image, position the viewer in a state of phenomenological tension. Visual effects (VFX) and animation can be prominently marked and be made recognizable because they not only represent something we know to be (physically) impossible but are also designed to be spectacular; other effects, however, are less ostentatious and do not draw attention to themselves as such, feigning realness, even, in the interest of artfulness. It is in the tolerance or acceptance of the impossible or spectacular image that the tension truly takes hold. The affective dimension of this tension is mirrored in the narrative role of the character, as Pogo is a structural keystone in terms of narrative tension. It is in the fifth episode ("Number Five"), at the very latest, that it becomes clear that Pogo is keeping vital information from the children, saying to Grace, "Do you understand that the children can never know?" (00:57:48). Fiercely loyal to Hargreeves and his grand plan, Pogo, together with Grace, has kept secrets which, upon their revelation, lead to catastrophe.

Grace inspires similar tension; yet, the question of artificiality connects to that of gender. Not only does the first episode already reveal that Grace is not a "real" woman, it plays with the very notion of woman being a construct. From the beginning, it is indicated that Grace is a little off or confused, being seemingly unaware that Hargreeves has died. The fact that she is very youthful-looking for the foster mother of the now-adult superchildren, as well as one of the many flashbacks that pervade the narrative structure in which she looks exactly the same as she does in the present, already let us know that she, too, might be inhuman in some way. How different she truly is, is revealed in an intriguing scene (00:47:15–00:48:19): Grace, wearing a black funeral gown and pearls, walks towards the gallery where she takes a seat and stares at various landscape paintings, which are shown in consecutive POV shots. Her gaze then lands on a portrait of a woman,[11] also seated and wearing black. Grace's face seems to betray a sense of longing that is hard to understand. Grace lays her hand on the armrest, adopting the same pose as the woman, when a shot from the back shows some kind of cable emerging from the back of Grace's seat, and approaching her head, before entering her ear canal. A medium-close up of Grace's face reveals her eyes and face suddenly glowing, so that it has become clear that she is a machine that has connected with its docking station to recharge. Her gaze remains fixed, just like the gaze of the woman in the portrait, whose image we return to in a counter-shot. Later, Grace says to her son Number Two/Diego, "What a wonderful world she lives in," speaking of the paintings that surround the portrait, adding, "Sometimes, I wonder if she's lonely." Not only does this point to her ability or willingness to view art(ifice) as constituting a space of phenomenological realness, it also suggests more explicitly that she identifies with the painted woman and her loneliness in a world made up of fragments of images. Connecting the image of (a) woman to this mechanical woman, the scene highlights the artifice and constructedness not only of this specific, robotic woman, but of the very notion of "woman." Both the painting and the robot are representations of a woman in the sense that they were made to reflect a living, real being in two different media—paint and plastic—yet Grace is animate and therefore capable of performing speech, gestures, and other acts that produce her gender in a very "real" way, even if this realness is inherently imbricated with the notion of artifice.[12]

As the narrative develops, the concern with Grace's "realness" is mediated through her role as a mother. She is not a mother in the biological sense, yet she performs the duties of a mother, most notably that of naming the children (as Number Two/Diego states in his father's scathing eulogy) and providing them with emotional care. A scene in episode three ("Extra Ordinary," 00:30:20–00:32:30) shows Grace fixing zippers, putting out literal fire, encouraging the children, and helping Number Two/Diego with his stutter. Nonetheless, some of her children are ambivalent about the authenticity of her motherly love, simultaneously harboring a desire to believe in her realness and the awareness that she was engineered to fulfill a function that their father did not want to assume. This ambivalence is intensified when Number Three/Allison and Number One/Luther find evidence that Grace might be responsible for their father's death:

> LUTHER: "I don't like this anymore than you do, but she's hiding something."
> ALLISON: "Hiding something? To me, she sounded confused."
> LUTHER: "Well, you saw the tape. Grace knew what she was doing."
> ALLISON: "'Grace'? This morning she was 'Mom.'"
> LUTHER: "She's a machine, Allison."
> ALLISON: "Who read to us, cleaned up after us, and put us to bed. And then we left her here, alone in this house for 13 years. I mean, no wonder she lost her mind. To be away from your kids?" [Episode 3, "Extra Ordinary," 00:13:08–00:13:36]

Number Three/Allison empathizes and (over)identifies with Grace as she herself has lost the custody battle for her daughter, from whom she is now separated. She does not question the "realness" of Grace's motherly acts, as she seems to either accept them as motivated by genuine parental instinct and devotion, or not to care about the motivation at all, emphasizing instead what it is that she has done for her children, regardless of whether or not she was programed to do so. When the other siblings learn about Grace's potential involvement in Hargreeves' death, it becomes clear that they do not all share this position:

> VANYA: "Do you ever wonder—all those moments with mom, the things she said—like, was it her, or was it really dad?"
> DIEGO: "What are you talking about?"
> VANYA: "Well, he built her. And he programmed her to be a mom—to be *our* mom. Sometimes when I look at her, I just see him."
> DIEGO: "Maybe that was true at first, but she evolved."
> VANYA: "Well, how do you know?"
> DIEGO: "Because dad only loved himself." [00:29:08–00:29:46]

On the one hand, then, Number Seven/Vanya's point of view highlights the recognition of her artificial nature, i.e., an awareness that she is constructed and programmed to fulfill parental functions, while Number Two/Diego's answer suggests faith in her evolution and, implicitly, a belief in the authenticity of her emotions and instincts, and thus an acknowledgment of some form of subjectivity. Yet, he begins to question this faith: when Grace states that "being your mother has been the greatest gift of my life," he asks her if it is truly her saying that, or whether it was their father speaking through her (00:32:40–00:33:30). On the other hand, Number Three/Allison subscribes to a Butlerian reading of the constructedness of sex/gender, acknowledging the performativity of Grace's woman-/motherhood: she is not only paying heed to the way she is called upon ("Grace"/"Mom") as a constituting act of interpellation, but also sees her mother as defined by repeated acts—acts through which "social agents constitute social reality through language, gesture and [...] symbolic social sign" (Butler, "Performative Acts," 519)—rather than biological status or the ontology of a natural essence (Butler, *GT*, 10). What these different perspectives foreground, then, is that the notion of "realness" is put into question, as the very concept is fundamentally destabilized.

While this destabilization affects the notion of sex/gender and motherhood in this context, it is also the "realness" of the post-cinematic image that is at stake. The specific tension that is at work when it comes to Grace is a combination of the affective dimension of narrative and image: while the story highlights the question of Grace's literal constructedness as the robot mother of the fragmented Umbrella family, the viewer also encounters her as a visual, aesthetic construct. Various types of VFX mark her as such, most notably at the end of the third episode, when Number Two/Diego deactivates her: he cuts open her arm, revealing the wiring inside which he then cuts through, before she and the eerie blue glow in her eyes and face slowly fade away (00:50:22–00:50:55). If we indeed find ourselves in the "the age of the animatic apparatus," as Deborah Levitt posits, which foregrounds notions of "appearance, metamorphosis, and affect" that reflect a shift in the "reigning cultural paradigms of life," we may consider the spectator's simultaneous confrontation with constructedness on the diegetic and visual level as indicative of our time's preoccupation with realness/artifice, i.e., bodies and their construction. As Levitt puts it, "the rise of animation and simulation, that is, their move from the margins to the very center of cultural production, has produced a key dimension of this shift, releasing images from actual and perceived ties to a real world as living bodies are increasingly untethered from determinations of biological vocations or destiny" (2).[13] Grace, then, who is recognized and accepted by her children as well as the viewer as a construct—as a character, a person, a woman, a mother, a body, and an image—functions in many ways as a representative of a paradigm of de-essentializing tendencies. There is ambivalence about but no definite mutual exclusion of her artificial body and her maternal vocation, nor between the artificiality of her image and her affective role within the narrative. In other words, she can be a robot and a mother, just as she can be a recognizably artificial, computer-generated (or rather computer-enhanced) image while being a vital and engrossing actor within the story's emotional arc. Yet, the underlying ambivalence (and possible discomfort) that is engendered by the narrative as well as the inherent qualities of post-cinematic aesthetics is a fundamental part of the spectator's relationship to this media text, so that the tension is never truly resolved.

It seems relevant that both Pogo and Grace are ultimately killed by Number Seven/Vanya. It is not only the discovery that her father suppressed her awesome powers for fear of their destructive potential that launches her into a murderous and world-ending fury, but ultimately also learning that Pogo and Grace assisted him in this endeavor. As addressed earlier, the secrets and ensuing mysteries that have reunited the family are also the catalyzer for the change she undergoes—from mousy outsider to unstoppable force—and, thus, for the apocalypse. While the Umbrella's siblings' attempts to prevent global annihilation turn out to be no more than a wild goose chase, they do achieve reconciliation and evolution. This, however, seems to be contingent on the transformations the siblings have undergone, enacting the "constant flux" Fawaz describes both in terms of their bodies and their mindsets: Number Three/Allison loses her voice and therefore her ability, but reconnects with her childhood love, Number

One/Luther; Number One/Luther, whose body was irreversibly altered by his father, seems to find some level of comfort with his gargantuan, apish shape; Number Four/Klaus is clean and has tapped the full potential of his power, being able to conjure his brother, Number Six/Ben; Number Two/Diego finds compassion, as he chooses not to kill in the name of revenge. The cycles of transformation the narrative undergoes hinge on the establishment, dissolution, and restoration of familial cohesion, the germane value of the story's melodramatic core being that of inclusion and connection in spite of differences. Once again, this story of individual and group "fluxability" points to its own teleological futility in terms of the narrative: a story with an ending that turns out to have been inevitable all along suggests not only a self-reflexive awareness of the narrative's status as a construct, but an awareness of the formulaic narrative constructs that pervade this genre, which is so prone to present us with grand and fantastic stories of a few, chosen individuals that must rally in the face of global or cosmic destruction. At the same time, the story thereby takes an ambivalent stance towards power itself, both on a diegetic and on a meta-level. As a group of superheroes, the Umbrella family is fairly ineffective, even as it goes through the motions of the melodramatic formula that is so popular in the genre. Number Seven/Vanya, ends up being the ultimate force of figurative and literal deconstruction as she violently kills Pogo, when she learns that he has been lying to her all her life. She also (passively) kills Grace when she destroys Hargreeves' mansion. As the story comes to its head, the season finale presents a spectacle of VFX that not only mark Number Seven/Vanya's otherness and might, but also emphasize the artifice at work, while the story comes to its conclusion, and, with a final, ironic gesture, points to its serial and self-reflexive nature by ending on a cliffhanger. Number Five, who can travel through space and time, opens a hole in the space-time continuum, positing that the only way forward is to start over and try again. The series already introduced the notion of winding back the tape, so to speak, as the events of an entire episode are erased when Number Five returns to an earlier point changing what we have already witnessed (Episode 6, "The Day That Was"). Number Five's plan, then, implies that everything we have seen will be undone. And, so, the Umbrella brood disappears into the past. At the end of season one, we do not know whether their journey through time was successful, but thanks to this potential and fantastical second chance at saving the world, we can rest assured that the series can be continued in a second season.

If I have said in the beginning that the intent of this reflection was to consider what this cultural product was expressive of in order to explore what its "affective maps, which do not just passively trace or represent, but actively construct and perform, the social relations, flows, and feelings that they are ostensibly 'about'" (6), in Shaviro's words, the question at hand is what *The Umbrella Academy* is about. Firstly, it is a product with strong postmodern tendencies, performing self-reflexive gestures that point to its status within a genre and media regime, i.e., of the superhero tale in the age of post-cinematic modes of representation, which is defined by transmediality, seriality, and digital manipulation of the image. Secondly, it revisits the genre's proclivity for reflections on individuality and difference, specifically on a different kind of family that struggles with fragmentation only to work towards reconciliation, furthering a narrative of identity-defining difference and what Fawaz calls alternative solidarities.[14] Thirdly, the series exemplifies a tension between real and unreal that is specific to the post-cinematic age and is here connected to diegetic concerns about constructedness and artificiality, which in the case of Grace, are linked to notions of gender and its performativity. Lastly, these many factors contribute to an overall sense of self-awareness regarding the genre's narrative and aesthetic workings that results in a representation of (super)power which (re)produces the unsettling affective power of constructedness itself, whether it be the constructedness of stories, media, images, or women.

It is through the tension between real and unreal/simulated/artificial that an anxiety can be identified, which the post-cinematic modes of representation that the superhero genre in the 21st century is imbricated in bring forth with true vigor. If anxiety, which ambivalently implies a desire for something and an unease about the same, is at the center of the affective map drawn by *The Umbrella Academy*, it is because it unsettles the values attributed to realness. Post-cinematic media confront the viewer with the digitally (re)constructed image that encapsulates the uncertainty *of* and potential irrelevance *for* the perceiving subject either of reality and objective truth, or of the notion of essentiality. Whether Grace is a "real" woman and mother and what that means may matter to some and may remain unclear or immaterial to others. The same can be said of Pogo. Simultaneously, the narrative's ironic engagement the teleological workings of the genre through its insistence on the futility of grand schemes reifies the condition of its viewership. This is a viewership that is perpetually asked to invest in a media regime and genre which, by virtue of its seriality and transmediality, demands continued investment in the (not entirely reconcilable) notions of individualist empowerment that the superhero embodies and that of familial/communal cooperation and reunion.

Overall, *The Umbrella Academy* repeats old tropes of the genre but with an uncanny edge that caters to a viewership that desires repetition with a difference. The last episode of the second season, ironically titled "The End of Something," concludes with another repetition: after finally reuniting and averting the apocalypse once more, the siblings of the Umbrella

Academy travel through time, returning to the future. When they arrive in 2019, however, they seem to find themselves in an altered future in which there is a Sparrow Academy, but no Umbrella Academy. The homecoming for which they longed—the root of nostalgia—offers no relief. Luther, surprised to see his father alive, blurts, "I'm just happy that we're home and together again," only to be corrected by a surprisingly alive Hargreeves: "'Home'? This isn't your home." With their past and present erased, a new cycle is set to begin. The difference at work in *The Umbrella Academy* thus seems to be the embrace of self-awareness and an irreverence towards or even denial of certainty, be it in our encounter with media or with the world they reflect. These superheroes, whose very existence both derives from and mocks their inherent nostalgia, cannot stand for absolute values, and their struggle to fulfill their roles as saviors is laden with irony. By no means does this convey insignificance; instead, it suggests a sense of whimsical engagement with the very idea of superheroes and their cultural omnipresence in today's media regime, which is unsettling in and of itself.

## Notes

1. The second season of *The Umbrella Academy* premiered during the editing and publication of this volume. While the essay itself could not be entirely rewritten, some points relating to the second season are addressed in the footnotes.

2. This is obviously a very reductionist condensation of these works' creative origin. Grant Morrison contextualizes their creation and success at length in *Supergods* (2012).

3. Felix Brinker, who also addresses the seriality and political economy of superhero franchises, points out that "big-budget tentpole features, it seems, no longer function as singular apexes of cinematic production whose central task is to outperform other movies, but have instead become nodes in networks of related media texts and fulcra for audiences' ongoing engagement with constantly expanding entertainment franchises" (434). Liam Burke addresses the networks of media convergence in terms of the "universes," as established by Marvel, for instance (32).

4. Transmedial storytelling is a key aspect of the post-cinematic paradigm, which Henry Jenkins outlined in *Convergence Culture*, as story worlds extend across media channels that supplement each other in the construction of a larger narrative.

5. Leaning on Umberto Eco's concept of "catalyzers of collective memory," Felix Brinker explains, "they draw on a wealth of preexisting storylines, character constellations, motifs, and iconographies, and restage these elements in a different context in order to present them as simultaneously new *and* as already familiar" (452).

6. As Linda Hutcheon writes, "The desire to transfer a story from one medium or one genre to another is neither new nor rare in Western culture. It is in fact so common that we might suspect that it is somehow the inclination of the human imagination—and, despite the dismissive tone of some critics, not necessarily a secondary or derivative act" (108). This desire and resulting pleasures of recognition can be linked to what Brinker calls a politics of activation of serial media, which draw an audience into continuous engagement with these media on a narrative level (435).

7. This self-referential gesture is not unique to this series, as other superhero series, films, and comic books have done this as well. For instance, Liam Burke points out that the TV series *Agents of S.H.I.E.L.D.*, which ties into the larger Marvel Comic Universe, included "Avengers action figures and other commercially available merchandise within the diegesis" (37).

8. Fawaz names the Hulk, the Fantastic Four, and the X-Men as prime examples of this "fluxability," brought to the fore by their "unruly and in flux bodies" which illustrate a "state of material and psychic *becoming* characterized by constant transition or change that consequently orients one towards cultivating skills for *negotiating* (rather than exploiting) multiple, contradictory identities and affiliations" (11).

9. This is made clear in the comic book, but not reiterated as such in the Netflix adaptation.

10. The second season will, then, address Pogo's creation.

11. It is the portrait of Madame Jacques-Louis Leblanc (Françoise Poncelle, 1788–1939), painted by Jean Auguste Dominique Ingres in 1823, which is exhibited at the Metropolitan Museum of Art in New York City.

12. In season two, it is revealed that Grace is actually a reconstruction of a woman who worked for Hargreeves and whom he dated in the 1960s. As a seemingly inferior copy, Grace emphasizes the condition of (gendered) hyperreality, not only as a projection of his desire, but also because the original is both lost and irrelevant to those that encounter the copy. As a mother figure, she has been reduced to an index of femininity rather than one of individual identity.

13. Levitt's investigation surrounds the question of life and/in media, as she asks, "how new forms of life and modes of vitality emerge at the spectator-screen intersection as this transforms over time" (3).

14. The second season repeats and arguably intensifies the gesture of generic self-awareness by repeating the story of reunification, engaging more explicitly with nostalgic sentiment, and underlining the relevance of alternative solidarities. The superhero family is once again torn apart by the vagaries of time travel, as its members are scattered across the early years of the 1960s and confronted with a potentially apocalyptic future. The iteration of the entwining story arcs of familial melodrama and superhero morality tale is framed by the political crises of the historical moment—the assassination of JFK, Jim Crow laws, the Vietnam War. While this adds an overtly political dimension to the show, any sense of nostalgic pleasure is imbued with ambiguity as the indulgence of aesthetic pastiche clashes with political realities, past and present. The show addresses the history of racism and segregation in the U.S. as Allison, a woman of color, becomes a civil rights activist and faces racially motivated police violence (a part of the story that has gained poignancy in the context of the protests against institutionalized racism and police violence in the summer of 2020, when the season was released). Meanwhile, Vanya struggles with a sense of disempowerment as she falls in love with a married woman. Her "fluxable" body, dangerous before because of its awesome supernatural powers, is now marked as threatening because of her queer desires. These two story arcs strongly underline the relevance of difference to the individualist argument of post–World War II comic books Fawaz describes, using the historic displacement to highlight its political dimensions.

## Works Cited

Brinker, Felix. "On the Political Economy of the Contemporary (Superhero) Blockbuster Series." *Post-Cinema: Theorizing 21st-Century Film*, edited by Shane Denson and Julia Leyda, Reframe, 2016, pp. 433–473.

Burke, Liam. "'A Bigger Universe': Marvel Studios and Transmedia Storytelling." *Assembling the Marvel Cinematic Universe: Essays on the Social, Cultural and Geopolitical Domains*, edited by Julian C. Chambliss, William L. Svitavsky and Daniel Fandino, McFarland, 2018, pp. 32–51.

Butler, Judith. *Gender Trouble*. Routledge, 2007.

\_\_\_\_\_. "Performative Acts and Gender Constitution: An Essay in Phenomenology and Feminist Theory." *Theatre Journal*, vol. 40, no. 4, Dec. 1988, pp. 519–531.

Fawaz, Ramzi. *The New Mutants: Superheroes and the Radical Imagination of American Comics*. New York University Press, 2016.

Hutcheon, Linda. "On the Art of Adaptation." *Daedalus*, vol. 133, no. 2, Spring 2004, pp. 108–111.

Hutcheon, Linda, and Mario J. Valdés. "Irony, Nostalgia, and the Postmodern: A Dialogue." *Poligrafías* 3, 1998–2000, pp. 18–41.
Jenkins, Henry. *Convergence Culture: Where Old and New Media Collide*. New York University Press, 2006.
Levitt, Deborah. *The Animatic Apparatus: Animation, Vitality, and the Futures of the Image*. Zero Books, 2018.
Mele, Rick. "How the Umbrella Academy Brought Pogo the Monkey Butler to Life." *SYFY Wire*, February 20, 2019, https://www.syfy.com/syfywire/netflix-the-umbrella-academy-pogo-chimp-ape-butler. Accessed January 10, 2020.
Morrison, Grant. *Supergods*. Spiegel & Grau, 2012.
Seymour, Mike. "Umbrella Academy: Dr Pogo at Weta Digital." *Fxguide*, April 1, 2019, https://www.fxguide.com/fxfeatured/umbrella-academy-dr-pogo-at-weta-digital/. Accessed January 10, 2020.
Shaviro, Steven. *Post-Cinematic Affect*. O-Books, 2010.
Sobchack, Vivian. "The Scene of the Screen: Envisioning Photographic, Cinematic, and Electronic 'Presence.'" *Carnal Thoughts: Embodiment and Moving Image Culture*. University of California Press, 2004.
*The Umbrella Academy*. Created by Steve Blackman and Jeremy Slater, Netflix, 2019–2020.
Wagmeister, Elizabeth. "'Umbrella Academy' Series Based on Comic Books Headed to Netflix." *Variety*, July 11, 2017, https://variety.com/2017/tv/news/netflix-umbrella-academy-tv-series-1202492594/. Accessed January 10, 2020.
Way, Gerard, and Gabriel Bá. *The Umbrella Academy: Apocalypse Suite*. Dark Horse Comics, 2008.
Weta Digital. "The Umbrella Academy VFX." *YouTube*, May 28, 2019, https://youtu.be/VU_XrdPOYQg. Accessed January 10, 2020.

# Extraordinary Bodies and the Language of Pain

*Disability in* Apocalypse Suite *and* Dallas

Dana Fore

Reviewing the history of superheroes creates the impression that modern incarnations of the genre have achieved an ironic triumph for ideologies of multiculturalism and tolerance—ironic because from the moment of its creation in the 1930s, the genre served a public hunger for fantasies that were unabashedly patriarchal and Eurocentric. Early critics dug even deeper below the surface to argue that these otherworldly crusaders for justice were not only "super" but also uncanny and potentially dangerous, insofar as their powerfully attractive qualities could just as easily legitimize fascism, homosexuality, and the kind of violence that psychologist and Wonder Woman creator William M. Marston memorably linked to "blood-curdling masculinity" (Ong 34–44; Wertham 46–52; Medhurst 238–243, Robbins 55). Whether working consciously against these detractors or not, subsequent writers and artists at least found common ground in the belief that superheroes had the potential to promote virtuous ideas, and the genre is kept alive by continually redefining what these virtues are and how well these characters meet society's changing standards.

In an unexpected move, this genre—born of fascination with physical power and perfection—has expanded its range of heroic "identities" to include those from the field of disability studies. This analysis of *The Umbrella Academy* takes place in light of this historical moment, arguing that the adventures of the paranormal Hargreeves children display a sensitivity to issues of disability and identity that goes beyond even that which has been explored in the thematically similar franchise of the *X-Men*. Rather than merely refiguring the adventures of Professor Xavier and Company with more millennial angst, *The Umbrella Academy* adds liberal doses of Gothic horror and satire to its superhero narrative to create a story that exposes the double-edged nature of the positive concept of "extraordinary." The use of this term becomes especially fraught whenever it is applied to so-called "freaks," or to people considered disabled. When it is used to define the former group, the term normalizes a stigmatizing gaze directed toward nonstandard bodies—a gaze which (as Rosemarie Garland-Thomson points out) serves to assuage the anxieties of "normal" people regarding their own physical vulnerability, by projecting these fears outward and away from the general public (*Extraordinary* 65–68); when it is applied to people with disabilities, it masks the hidden revulsion of the able-bodied as often as it expresses admiration.

Because *The Umbrella Academy* has been recognized as being closely aligned in spirit to superhero teams like *Watchmen* and the *X-Men*, it is productive to read the Hargreeves saga as what Geoff Klock calls a "revisionary superhero narrative," one which "organizes the contradictory signifying field" surrounding a similar type of story and which then forms it "into a coherent story that is itself a commentary on the history that has come before" (133). Although not dealing specifically with the vexed concept of so-called extraordinary bodies, previous analyses of the *X-Men* franchise have established credible links between superhero narratives and disability, and these issues are in turn refashioned in *The Umbrella Academy*. For example, Romona Ilea argues persuasively that Professor Xavier and his mutants expose the ambivalent relationship between disabled and nondisabled people in particularly vivid ways. She points out that like the X-Men, living as a disabled person means continually negotiating one's place in a society that more often than not views disability through the lens of a "medical model" that sees physical and mental impairment or difference as things to be eliminated through "cures"—and this view leads all too often to resentment or hatred against disabled people who resist the idea that they are "defective," or who simply cannot be "cured" (Ilea 171–175; 178–181). Michael M. Chemers is even more enthusiastic about the idea that the *X-Men* articulate the experiences of disabled people in particularly nuanced ways. He declares that by presenting a mutant community whose diversity seems to mirror our own, and by continually foregrounding similarities between "mutant" and disabled existence, the film *X2: X-Men United* "confound[s]" the "hyper-ableism" of traditional superhero narratives and "solidifies the growing legitimacy of disability-related discourse as part of American aesthetic and historical discourse" (Chemers).

The narrative of *The Umbrella Academy* becomes distinctively darker and more nuanced by addressing the blind spots in these optimistic assessments of disability experience and the superhero genre. Granted, Chemers and Ilea effectively outline the ways in which superhero narratives expose stereotypes and therefore help to articulate the struggles of disabled people, but their views are limited to the degree that they ignore Professor Xavier's less-than-altruistic qualities: he is operating a quasi-military organization, not a commune, so not every mutant can become part of the X-Men team. Some mutants are simply born with physical deformities, and these people are useless for Xavier's needs. More importantly, Chemers and Ilea downplay the destabilizing effect that the villain Magneto and his mutant followers have on positive views of disability. The presence of these characters keeps this self-consciously forward-thinking franchise rooted in the past (albeit unintentionally) by legitimizing the long-standing fear among the able-bodied that disability from whatever cause has a "natural" Jekyll-and-Hyde-type effect that overwhelms any positive aspects of a person's character, until people with disabilities are ultimately transformed (at best) into insufferable narcissists "beyond the reach of therapy" (Siebers 45), or "Demonic Cripples" consumed by thoughts of vengeance and pathological envy and hatred of able-bodied people (Kriegel 32–34; Longmore 67–68). Magneto and his crew, in other words, allow able-bodied audiences to retain the psychological mechanisms that seek to assign people with disabilities to "absolute" categories (Garland-Thomson *Extraordinary* 34), which in turn, allows them to be blamed for their own suffering. In addition, the readings of Chemers and Ilea retain an "us-versus-them" mentality regarding the origins of these stereotypes. In other words, both Ilea and Chemers suggest that prejudice against the disabled and its attendant problems could be eliminated if able-bodied people could let go of the blatantly irrational idea that disabled people are potentially dangerous, defective freaks. The adventures of the Hargreeves children prove that eliminating stereotypes is not always just a matter of re-educating bigots: The effects of even "positive" stereotypes are not always easy to gauge because prejudice does not have to be extreme to remain harmful, and some of the most damaging misconceptions are those that victims themselves cling to. In order to understand why the "extraordinary" body becomes the catalyst for horrors in *The Umbrella Academy*, it is helpful to consider the range of negative attitudes and paradoxes that the concept of *extraordinary* helps to gloss over. A brief overview of attitudes toward disability is useful toward this end.

    Historian Henri-Jacques Stiker suggests that the status of disabled people in society has been precarious since ancient times. In *A History of Disability*, Stiker states that fears of "disease, death, and monstrosity" all coalesce in attitudes toward disability, and therefore, negative reactions toward perceived impairment—which extend in various degrees to people with disabilities—tend to be extreme. Stiker puts it bluntly: the "desire to kill" is never far away when the able-bodied contemplate people with disabilities (8). He elaborates:

> We should not hide from the fact that major disability, especially mental, generates such an urge to make it disappear that it must be called by its name. In embryonic form the desire to kill, to see dead, is extended to all those who are stricken. The practice in antiquity of doing away with deformed children originates in a sense of eugenics, in the will for a pure race, and thus reveals what lies in the human heart. Let's not have any illusions; we carry within ourselves the urges to kill, because death and fear, like aggression, have their roots there. It is obvious that this violence toward the different resolves itself in other ways than the elimination of the disabled, thanks to socialization ... [but we] must constantly remind ourselves of these desires, urges, and fears buried within us, which hide from and elude our clear consciousness but which are always alive and active [8–9].

Stiker's dramatic diction perhaps works to his disadvantage here, given that this passage—with its invocation of "eugenics" and "the will for a pure race"—evokes the specter of the so-called "euthanasia" program in the Third Reich and risks creating a knee-jerk dismissal of his ideas among contemporary readers who resent being implicitly cast as Nazi sympathizers. It is no doubt more comforting for a 21st-century readership to take refuge in Stiker's own admission that "socialization" over the centuries has significantly reduced the urge to simply "eliminate" people with disabilities. Yet subsequent research into the nature of disability and stigma suggests that even more enlightened societies have failed to eliminate the heart of darkness behind disability prejudice that Stiker identifies. Instead, the modern valorization of identity and self-esteem has simply led to the creation of discourse that is more successful at masking the love/hate relationship between nondisabled and disabled people, while proliferating the number of paradoxical attitudes toward nonstandard bodies.

What is most relevant for a discussion of superheroes is the fact that while more ostensibly "enlightened" societies moved away from viewing people with disabilities as objects of quasi-supernatural fear and hatred, they essentially began to create and promote definitions of "heroism" that people with disabilities would be expected to conform to in order to pass as "normal" and to assimilate successfully into the society of the able-bodied. For example, Martha Stoddard Holmes' analysis of Henry Mayhew's *Labour and the London Poor* notes Mayhew's tendency to define the virtues of Victorian-era cripples based on their emotional responses to their impairment, rather than focusing on their physicality (28–29). Holmes argues persuasively that this focus on the disabled as emotional creatures promotes the idea that the nature of people with disabilities can be accurately defined through binary conceptions of good or evil, which in turn allows an able-bodied readership to respond in "uncomplicated" ways through either pity or outrage (30). This focus on the inner spirit of crippled or deformed people also reinforces the view that disability is caused by a character flaw (*ibid.*). These findings suggest, by extension, that the most "heroic" response to one's disability is to ignore it and to cultivate a persona of quiet endurance.

Similar conclusions emerge in G. Thomas Couser's study of modern autobiographies written by authors with disabilities. Couser finds that that the stereotypes of heroism and impairment that Holmes identified in the Victorian period have endured into the present time, primarily because the nature of the publishing business helps to ensure that authors with disabilities are more likely to get published if their personal experiences tend to validate the stereotypes that able-bodied people associate with the disability experience (79). Thus, Couser finds that the most popular novels written by people with disabilities tend to rely on genre clichés of "triumph over adversity," many times while also relying (paradoxically) on conventions of Gothic horror, whereby the deformities and pain of disabled bodies are described in minute detail to provoke a sense of horror and disgust in able-bodied readers (81–83). Couser also notes without surprise that many of these ostensibly "inspirational" novels also end with the death of the author, or they valorize the idea that death is the most fitting or heroic end to a life with impairments (84–85).

The work of Paul K. Longmore confirms that stereotypes of heroic endurance and achievement continue to have a life outside of sociological studies and inspirational biographies. Linking extraordinary bodies to popular "dramas of adjustment" in the media, Longmore describes their effects succinctly. These stories

> stem from the common notion that with the proper attitude one can cope with and conquer any situation or condition, turning it into a positive growth experience. [...] This belief in the power of a positive mental outlook ... not only currently but throughout American history, suggests a primary reason for the popularity of stories about disabled people adjusting and overcoming. It points to one of the social and cultural functions of that image and to one of the primary social roles expected of people with disabilities: In a culture that attributes success or failure primarily to individual character, "successful" handicapped people serve as models of personal adjustment, striving and achievement. In the end, accomplishment or defeat depends only on one's attitude toward oneself and toward life. If someone so tragically "crippled" can overcome the obstacles confronting them, think what you, without a "handicap," can do.
>
> Another obvious social function of the psychologized image of physical and sensory disability is to make it an individual rather than a social problem. [...] In fictional productions, nondisabled persons usually treat disabled people badly, not because of bias, but out of insensitivity and lack of understanding. It becomes the responsibility of the disabled individual to "educate" them, to allay their anxieties and make them feel comfortable [74–75].

The length of the description above hopefully gives some sense of the intensity with which society is invested in blaming disabled individuals for their own weaknesses while it simultaneously praises any "extraordinary" achievements. Thus, failure to "overcome" a disability is never presented as an option—and disabled people are keenly aware of what is expected of them. Being marked as having an "extraordinary" body becomes a double-edged sword: It has the potential to single people out for widespread acclaim, but it can also drive individuals to engage in harmful behaviors as they attempt to overcompensate for their perceived flaws and to "pass" as normal, which in turn can create more psychological trauma or even greater physical damage as they strive to achieve goals that may be impossibly high for people with physical or mental limitations (Siebers "Withered" 27–29).

The previous discussion raises questions that should be answered before proceeding further, namely, how far can a disability reading of *The Umbrella Academy* be sustained? Notwithstanding the superficial similarities between the Hargreeves children and the X-Men—beings who are also born with their powers rather than being changed through science—is it credible to say that any of Reginald Hargreeves' wards share the same level of freakishness as Professor Xavier's associates that would set them apart as "disabled?" After all, research has generally confirmed the findings of sociologist Erving Goffman, who, in his groundbreaking 1963 study of stigma confirmed that ostracized people with severe, visible impairments tend to suffer more than people with hidden flaws (127); if one concedes that this is true, then the only member of the Academy that might have trouble "passing" within a society of so-called "normals" is Luther a.k.a. Spaceboy, with his freakishly overdeveloped simian torso. The rest of the Hargreeves family is conventionally attractive, their powers can be easily hidden from the world at large, and many would probably argue that their special skills are grounds for envy rather than persecution by so-called "normal" people.[1] Yet even if one sees the Hargreeves children as being blessed with youth, good looks and superpowers, they still represent unexplored truths behind the disability experience because even their apparent blessings place them in a class of individuals with a firm kinship to disabled people. The latter can be defined as people with nonstandard bodies from whom society expects not only gratitude (for the tolerance of "normal" people) but also silence regarding their day-to-day struggles, owing to the belief—among the able-bodied—that any problems associated with their disabilities have been rendered irrelevant (or at least tolerable) through some kind of physical or mental "compensation." This notion of quasi-supernatural compensation is promoted in everyday life, for example, through stories of blind people who develop extraordinary hearing, or feel-good narratives about people with mental disabilities who display an "amazing" capacity for being able to enjoy life without materialist distractions, while they love others deeply, without prejudice. As uplifting as such stories might be, they are still implicated in the cultural scripts described by Longmore and others that are used by able-bodied people to allay their anxieties about people with disabilities.

*The Umbrella Academy* also accommodates readings as a text about disability because its story recognizes—in the same way that disability researchers do—that *disability* represents more than the personal challenge of having to function with an injury or deformity. It means having to come to terms with the ways in which the larger society stigmatizes and places limitations on people who are *considered to have* significant mental or physical differences from the norm. Characters like Klaus and Vanya and Number Five help to represent the struggles of people with invisible disabilities like PTSD, addiction, or Body Dysmorphic Disorder. Through the adventures of the Hargreeves children, one sees not only the traumas caused by having one's self-worth continually linked to physical achievements by society at large, but also the harm caused by internalizing these destructive ideals. Finally, *The Umbrella Academy* is a disability text because it recognizes darker truths behind supposedly enlightened attitudes toward non-standard bodies, to a degree that the *X-Men* does not. First and foremost, it recognizes that the concept of *extraordinary* is doubly euphemistic: It can refer to a sense of unexpected amazement, as when people think, in Longmore's words, "If someone so tragically 'crippled' can overcome the obstacles confronting them, think what you, without a 'handicap,' can do" (74). But *extraordinary* can also hide the fact that for many, to be disabled is the ultimate terror, the *ne plus ultra* of degradation (Stiker 7–9; Sherry 31–38). In these cases, the word is a polite mask for the flash of horror felt when a disabled person's achievement reminds people of their own vulnerability. At times like this, open praise of a disabled individual's accomplishments comes with a shudder, and the silent admission, "I would rather be dead than be that way."

To develop this paradoxical idea that the extraordinary body is both an impossible ideal of perfection and a symbol of ultimate monstrosity, *The Umbrella Academy* forges intimate links between the conventions of a modern superhero genre holding out the ideal of bodily perfection in a utopian future, and tropes of the Victorian triumph-over-adversity novel that cling to binary representations of the disabled body as a symbol of either ultimate evil or absolute saintliness. This approach infuses the disabled body with the power of what philosopher Edmund Burke calls "the sublime"— the paradoxical ability of terrifying things to create passionate feelings of "astonishment" and "horror" as well as "admiration" and "reverence" (180).

After having established these connections, the text employs extreme, "torture-porn" levels of violence to expose and satirize them. Satire, in turn, becomes the conduit through which the text acknowledges the disabled body as what Peter Stallybrass and Allon White define as a "grotesque" and "classificatory" form—a symbol of physical and psychological excess which a dominant culture uses to reinforce its own concepts of "high" and "low" social class as well as concepts of normal behavior and appearance (20–22). *Volume One: Apocalypse Suite* sets the stage for the bloody business to follow by introducing the stunning achievements of its first extraordinary body, Sir Reginald Hargreeves. Sir Reginald is "a world-renowned scientist and wealthy entrepreneur. Inventor of the Televator, the Levitator, the Mobile Umbrella Communicator, and Clever Crisp Cereal. Olympic Gold Medalist and recipient of the Nobel Prize for his work in the cerebral advancement of the chimpanzee" (Way, *Apocalypse*). Because he is recognized as the person who adopts the otherworldly members of the Umbrella Academy, Sir Reginald qualifies as an extraordinary body, even though he is not considered to be freakish or deformed by the general public. This classification is apt because in modern media portrayals of disability, the charitable nature of so-called normal parents who are willing to adopt children with disabilities is frequently regarded with the same level of amazement as the disabled children they care for.

Yet there is a significant disjunction between the laudatory tone of the text, and the images they are linked to. For example, the narration praising Hargreeves as a "world renowned" scientist and entrepreneur is placed in a panel showing a medium shot of Hargreeves' face, a cigarette dangling laconically from his lips, his grim features washed in shadow. In the background, over Hargreeves' shoulder, we see his loyal servant Abhijat, standing at attention. And upon closer inspection, we see that at the servant's feet are the sprawled, bloody forms of vanquished enemies, fallen amidst the hilts of what might be swords or daggers. In broad strokes, this arrangement of text and visuals works to create the same kind of creeping unease—leading slowly to horror—that one finds at the beginning of Jonathan Swift's infamous satire "A Modest Proposal," where the narrator's polished upper-class persona crumbles as he moves from platitudes about trying to help poor children become "sound and useful members of the commonwealth" to cold-blooded prescriptions for genocide through cannibalism (305–307). Similarly, Sir Reginald's uncertain—and possibly predatory—relationship to other people is suggested gradually. He is portrayed in anomalous terms: Even though he exists in a stereotypical science-fiction world where exotic-sounding "Televators" and celebrity "space squid[s] from Rigel X-9" are apparently commonplace (Way, *Apocalypse*), his gaunt, balding face is distinguished by its handlebar mustache and monocle. These antiquarian characteristics combined with the presence of a specifically Indian valet mark Hargreeves as a creature with strong affinities to the 19th century, especially the *Raj*, the era of British colonial rule in India, when England was at the height of its imperial powers and well-known for its willingness to use mass violence against colonized subjects to maintain order. In this context, the barely-visible limbs of his vanquished opponents are doubly disturbing: placed as they are at the furthest points of Hargreeves' introductory portrait, they become the very prototype of the "discreet" war photo described by Susan Sontag—a carefully constructed bit of *mise-en-scène* that downplays the true costs of war by using partially visible corpses, in a way that confirms the "scale of war's murderousness" while simultaneously "destroy[ing] what identifies people as individuals, even as human beings" (367). This paradox, in turn, also creates an undercurrent of unease in the viewer by rendering violence banal and suppressing any clue as to the guilt or innocence of the dead victims, or of the people (Hargreeves? Abhijat?) who killed them.

The presentation of Sir Reginald as a bundle of paradoxes and anachronisms is also doubly significant because these characteristics make him an "allegorical" figure in the sense defined by film scholar Adam Lowenstein, and this allegorical quality in turn shapes the treatment of disability issues in *Apocalypse Suite* and *Dallas*. To briefly explain: In his discussion of horror films dealing with national traumas, Lowenstein uses the term "allegorical moment" to describe instances when all the reality-distorting elements of film combine to create images that are both intensely horrific yet, at the same time, so compelling that the viewers' attention is riveted, and they begin to reflect deeply on the things they see and feel. In Lowenstein's words, the allegorical moment is "a shocking collision of film, spectator and history, where registers of bodily space and historical time are disrupted, confronted, and intertwined"; the effect of this shock "produce[s] forms of knowing not easily described by conventional delineations of bodily space and historical time" (2).

If one transfers Lowenstein's transgressive notion of "allegorical" from moving film to the images in *Apocalypse Suite* and *Dallas*, it seems clear that the depiction of Sir Reginald's appearance and actions are meant at the most basic level to "confront" and "disrupt" assumptions about the readability of people's personalities through their physical appearance—a problem that people with disabilities have to face on a daily basis. On a more fundamental level, Sir Reginald's uncanny combination of 19th-century trappings and cold-blooded demeanor serve as notice that the story over which it presides as catalyst and guiding spirit is nothing less than a dark parody of stereotypical 19th-century "triumph over adversity" stories. Like the worlds of Oliver Twist, David Copperfield, and Jane Eyre, the world of the Umbrella Academy is a realm where twists of fate cast children out into a harsh world—as orphans, or as virtual orphans, set adrift by abusive or absent families. Through his cold and unpredictable nature, Sir Reginald steps into the role of menacing foster parent, like Edward Murdstone to David Copperfield, Aunt Sarah Reed to Jane Eyre, and Fagin to Oliver Twist.

Ominous hints about Hargreeves' true nature lead up to the dramatic discovery of his foster children. Upon hearing the news of the otherworldly births, Hargreeves rushes off to collect as many of the children as he can find, in a ship which, according to rumor "is powered by the remains of King Amen-Kharej IV" (Way, *Apocalypse*). This odd detail suggests that Hargreeves is not troubled by any scruples regarding the supposedly sacred nature of human bodies, and that he is willing to save them, or exploit them, according to his needs. His behavior at the children's public debut seems to confirm that his attitudes are not unambiguously paternal. After 43 "extraordinary" births, the narration tells us that "He only found seven of them" (Way, *Apocalypse*).

Significantly, the panel introducing the children is arranged like a series of snapshots, and we see that each of the children wears a form-fitting black half-mask—the traditional badge of the superhero—which renders their eyes into uncanny white blanks. Since the children are infants at this point, we can assume that Hargreeves is the one who has supplied these masks and arranged the children in this orderly row for inspection. This style of presentation confirms Hargreeves' callous and exploitative nature since it replicates the strategies of freak show and beauty pageant promoters, as outlined by disability scholar Rosemarie Garland-Thomson. In "The Beauty and the Freak," Garland-Thomson explains, for example, that traditional freak shows often included people who were not obviously disabled, but who were "cultural freaks," and these individuals were presented to the public in ways that facilitated unimpeded staring by the "ordinary and normal" masses—for instance by presenting their bodies in "assembly line" rows, or by "exotic[izing] them through costumes and props" (187; 188; 192). This process of cultural enfreakment is completed once a reporter asks Hargreeves why he has adopted the children, and he responds grandiosely, "To save the *world*, of course" (Way, *Apocalypse*). Once again, Hargreeves' superficially benevolent words create troubling associations since saving the world through extraordinary babies evokes the propaganda of 19th-century eugenicists or 20th-century Nazis.

Early in *Apocalypse Suite*, there is confirmation that Hargreeves is at least emotionally abusive to his children: he tells the children not to call him "Dad," and he refers to them by numbers, rather than by names. The task of naming the children falls to the robot mother that he has created to care for them. But his deep-seated lack of empathy for them reveals itself even in the construction of this surrogate: The face of the "mother" looks human and speaks articulately, but the body is a haphazard (and uncanny) construction: the torso is an anatomical study dummy with exposed heart and lungs; the lower half is the plastic frame of a dressmaker's mannequin. This creature is so unsettling that even as an adult, Diego "The Kraken" cannot stand the sight of it. He disrupts Hargreeves' funeral by impulsively stripping the trench coat from his "mother," screaming that she is just another "lie," and "a piece of plastic" (Way, *Apocalypse*).

This reference to a "plastic" mother and the visual of her lower torso as nothing more than a wire frame creates a startling allusion that reveals another level of Hargreeves' inhumanity: it draws connections between Hargreeves' personality and the work of psychologist Harry Harlow, who studied the emotional needs of children in the 1950s. In his most famous experiment, Harlow isolated groups of monkeys with inanimate mother surrogates in order to determine whether food or emotional bonding was more important for an infant's psychological development. The substitutes were made out of cloth with rudimentary faces, or they were simply wire frames. He found that having a maternal bond was crucial for the healthy development of infants: the monkeys isolated with only wire surrogates and food were left with profound psychological problems (Suomi 319–342). To silence any remaining doubts about Hargreeves' nature after this point, his cruelty is finally unmasked in a short story from *Volume One: Apocalypse Suite*. In "But the Past Ain't Through with You," the Academy crew are mystified by the discovery of a double of The Rumor. The body is human, but dead. Before they can unravel the mystery, they are called upon to defeat a psychopathic magician and his equally insane assistant who have created a gigantic "Murderbot." Hargreeves arrives at the scene after their victory, and he is surprised to see The Rumor alive. A library card found on the body of the dead Rumor allows Spaceboy to solve the mystery: The Rumor lied about going to the library when she was in fact meeting a lover. But because Rumor's lies are transformed into reality, a duplicate manifested itself at the library, and this double was murdered by the mad magician and his assistant before their final battle. Upon learning the truth, Hargreeves remarks, "To think I led the murder magician to a copy. Fascinating!" Enraged, The Kraken screams, "What? You told that psycho where to find her? Why would you do that?!" "To teach her a lesson," Hargreeves replies, "Class dismissed" (Way, *Apocalypse*).

The children's subsequent adventures suggest that Hargreeves' cold indifference to bodily fragility and human suffering are not simply the flaws of an individual. Instead, Hargreeves represents the spirit of his age—an era where "extraordinary" bodies are targets for exploitation, or they are transformed into something ridiculous, malevolent, or both. Above all, it is an era where heroic quests more often than not take on the trappings of a "torture porn" movie. The work of Aaron Michael Kerner suggests that the ethos of torture porn films is well suited for critiquing societies that treat bodies like disposable commodities, especially if these values stem from toxic concepts of masculinity. In *Torture Porn in the Wake of 911: Horror, Exploitation and the Cinema of Sensation,* Kerner argues that central to the structure of torture porn is the idea that "not only does our culture perpetuate acts of violence but this violence is institutionalized" (19). He goes on to note that these films do not share the obsession over the punishment of feminine sexual transgressions that marked the "slasher" films of the 1980s; rather, they expose the flaws of sadistic father figures. "It is abject fathers," Kerner outlines,

> not mothers, that spawn dread in torture porn. Dexter, in the Showtime series, lives by the Code of Harry as dictated by his father Harry Morgan; similarly [...] Jigsaw [from the *Saw* franchise] and the Elite Hunting Syndicate (headed by the paternalistic Sasha) in *Hostel* subscribe to libertinage. In all these cases, we witness the perversion of "proper" Law by paternal figures. With these twisted paternal figures, we find the outlines of a Frankenstein motif in torture porn. Madeline Smith, along these lines, observes that the *Saw* franchise is populated with the monstrous-masculine (set in contrast to [Barbara] Creed's monstrous-feminine). The monstrous masculine gives birth to abject agents. [...] The torture chamber, like Frankenstein's laboratory, might be viewed as an artificial womb from which monsters are conceived [27–28].

Following Kerner's paradigm, *Apocalypse Suite* validates the notion of institutionalized violence through gruesome satire: The first "monster" that the children face is an Eiffel Tower suddenly rendered sentient and homicidal through the genius of equally monstrous (and extraordinary) creator Zombie Gustav Eiffel. A similar encounter with the murderous/extraordinary recurs when the Academy crew must defeat a living version of the Lincoln Memorial which has gone berserk. The murderous nature of everyday life is also alluded to through the story of the mad magician mentioned above. This supervillain does not unleash his leviathan Murderbot on an unsuspecting populous from the safety of a hidden lair. Rather, the monster and his creator make a very public debut in front of an appreciative audience of the Lucifer Clark talk show (Way, *Apocalypse*).

The mad magician is not alone in his creative zeal. The world of the Umbrella Academy is rife with would-be Frankensteins and their monstrous progeny: disease-wracked villain Dr. Terminal creates the Terminauts, flying robots with death rays who resemble sentient frappuccino containers; Hargreeves transforms his son Luther into the half-human, half-simian Spaceboy; the timeline guardians of the Temps Aeternalis

Agency preside over an army of robots and physically enhanced assassins; and the psychopathic Conductor of the Orchestra Verdammten has a lab where he converts Vanya Hargreeves' and her musical talent into the apocalyptic power of the White Violin.

Amidst any discussion of the machineries of death and destruction in the world of the Umbrella Academy, the Temps Aeternalis deserves a special note, since the agency creates another unsettling level of parody in the narrative. By introducing an organization that is homicidally dedicated to maintaining the "status quo" by eliminating "anomalies" throughout time and space (Way, *Dallas*) the story recognizes (although probably unintentionally) intimate links between the very foundations of "normality" and destructive real-world attitudes toward disability, as outlined in the work of disability scholar Lennard J. Davis. In "Constructing Normalcy: The Bell Curve, the Novel, and the Invention of the Disabled Body in the Nineteenth Century," Davis asserts that so-called "normality" is a construct with connections to a specific historical context. He implies that earlier societies recognized that ideal body types were impossible to attain (10–11), and he blames industrialization and a set of practices related to nationality, criminality, and sexuality for creating the modern conception of "normal" with its concomitant view of disability as an "abnormality" and a "problem" (9–10). He notes, for example, that the word "normal" in its commonly understood sense only entered the language around 1840—before that, the term meant only "perpendicular" (10). Davis explains that the concept of "normality" emerged from an interest in statistics—specifically, the impulse to discover the characteristics of an "average" social class. This interest in group characteristics led, in turn, to the desire to define the characteristics of the "average" man (Davis 11). Unfortunately, a darker worldview developed from these relatively innocuous early studies because all the famous statisticians who engaged in this work were also devoted eugenicists, who would go on to use their statistical data to add scientific legitimacy to stereotypes of "deviance" and abnormality once the idea of a universal "norm" had gained general acceptance (Davis 14–19). These theories, of course, were the basis for the genocides of Nazi Germany and other nations. In light of this information, the text of *Dallas* creates a fitting (and backhanded) tribute to the spiritual forefathers of the Temps Aeternalis when leaders in the agency describe their program of murder as simply the "removal" of "anomalous" elements, and their two most successful assassins are shown gleefully gamboling off to their next assignment clad in SS uniforms.

The Academy itself provides another example of violence connected to extraordinary bodies. In addition to the examples of parental neglect mentioned previously, the experiences of the "normal" sibling Vanya are noteworthy in this regard. In a flashback from *Apocalypse Suite*, we see Vanya as a child, running down a corridor of the mansion screaming, "I hate you! I hate you!" She runs into her room and slams the door, screaming, "I don't belong here!" When the young Pogo arrives to comfort her, she sobs, "I'm useless. I'm so w-w-worthless. There's nothing special about me. I–I'm not like the others. I can't *do anything*." Pogo responds, "You're right. You're not like the others. You don't need to *destroy things* to prove yourself" (Way, *Apocalypse*; original emphasis). To understand the significance behind this brief interlude—or more specifically, the significance of *the language* in this interlude—it is helpful to consider Elaine Scarry's ideas about the inexpressibility of pain. In *The Body in Pain*, she suggests that pain tests the descriptive power of language to its very limits, because "its resistance to language is not simply one of its incidental or accidental attributes but is essential to what it is" (5). With this central idea in mind, she moves on to discuss torture as a process with its own distinct language, one designed to "[convert] absolute pain into the fiction of absolute power," or in other words, to create an unshakable sense of justification and certainty in the mind of the torturer, while destroying the victim's sense of reality and identity (Scarry 27–28).

A key moment in the torture process is what Scarry calls "the betrayal." This is the moment when the victim provides some kind of verbal response to the torturer's interrogation. Scarry explains that it is wrong to equate "confession" with "betrayal," which suggests that simply acknowledging the torturer's questions is enough, probably because even the torturer realizes that answers given under duress may be false (35). The true sense of "betrayal" in this context comes not only from providing secret information that could endanger others; instead, it comes also from feeding into the torturer's sense of justification and power by providing any response other than silence, thereby making the torturer's sense of the world "larger," while destroying the victim's sense of reality (37). Scarry notes that the words surrounding the moment of "betrayal" have a distinctive psychological power. Presumably, once they are laid down into transcripts or transformed into propaganda, by publicizing the "idiom of betrayal," the torturer can "[discredit] the prisoner, making him rather than his torturer, his voice rather than his pain, the cause of his loss of self and world" (Scarry 35). These statements create an "absolution of responsibility" for the torturer while shifting responsibility onto the victim. They "turn the moral reality of torture upside down." Scarry declares that "as soon as the focus of attention shifts to the *verbal* aspect of torture, [lines of moral responsibility] have begun to waiver and change their shape in the direction of accommodating and crediting the torturers" (35; original emphasis).

What we see in the interlude between Vanya and Pogo is proof that the world of the Umbrella Academy is steeped not only in the language of pain, but also of torture. On the surface, Vanya's intense sense of torment prevents her from clearly articulating its causes. She can only scratch the surface with euphemisms like "belong" and "special" and "do anything." Pogo's more explicit response about "destroying" things reveals that these words are intimately connected to violence. To "belong" and to be "special" in the world of the Academy is to be familiar with violence—how to inflict it, how to defend against it, and undoubtedly how to endure it when it is inflicted on oneself. On a deeper level, Vanya is using the "idiom of betrayal" favored by Scarry's torturers: by calling herself "useless" and "worthless," she is shifting responsibility for her pain onto herself and shifting the "moral reality" and responsibility for her suffering away from Sir Reginald and his system of education. Vanya herself seems to recognize the paradox of this language as an adult: she writes a tell-all autobiography called *Extra Ordinary*, which the Conductor of the Orchestra Verdammten reminds her is full of "nasty things" about her family. But ironically—or perhaps predictably—this attempt to tell the truth fails to achieve any sense of closure or catharsis. Vanya is treated like a traitor to her family and ostracized by the other members (Way, *Apocalypse*). Unfortunately, we see that the morality-blurring vocabulary of pain and torture within the Academy is the lingua franca of the world beyond its walls: When Vanya is a child, Sir Reginald tells her point-blank that there is "nothing special" about her; the time police from the Temps Aeternalis refer to their system of assassinations and disaster creation as "manipulations and removals," and the Conductor from the Orchestra Verdammten refers to his monstrous transformation of Vanya as making her a "star" (Way, *Apocalypse*; *Dallas*).

At one point in *Apocalypse Suite*, Number Five sums up his childhood by saying, "My brothers and sisters have spent their lives being dissected by the people Hargreeves raised us to protect" (Way). By evoking images of bodies kept at arm's length, while being subjected to violence and close scrutiny, the metaphor of "dissection" comes close to issues at the heart of the narrative. Through its treatment of people with nonstandard bodies and the euphemistic language used to describe them, *The Umbrella Academy* acknowledges what disability scholars have long recognized: disabled bodies create a sense of the uncanny, and they generate paradoxes by seeming to exist "between" worlds. They are "*on the border* of other groups that are fairly well recognized" [italics in text] (Stiker 69); even when they are integrated into society as a whole, charitable attitudes by able-bodied people are also frequently linked to a sense of entitlement or "burden of gratitude" (Keith 19); and even if they are accepted, a stigma remains, a lingering sense that they are "not quite human" (Goffman 5) and they "impose their presence on the 'normals'" (Kriegel "The Cripple" 33).

In the final analysis, *The Umbrella Academy* proves that the superhero genre is still extremely effective at creating role models with lasting psychological resonance and allegories with extraordinary emotional impact. Its treatment of disability is linked in spirit with the franchise of the *X-Men*, but these similarities are destabilized—to the point of parody—through the presence of characters like Sir Reginald Hargreeves and the murderous Temps Aeternalis agency. Any critique of disability stereotypes in the *X-Men* is blunted by the presence of Professor Xavier, who seems to serve the same purpose as the quasi-omniscient narrator that J. Hillis Miller identifies in *The Form of Victorian Fiction*. Xavier, to use Miller's words, seems to have "perfect knowledge of a world [he] has not made" (65), so therefore he is entitled to speak as "the general mind of the community" (88). Granted, Xavier's actions show that he is keenly aware of hatred and distrust between so-called "normal" humans and mutants. But his calm in the face of disorder is the equilibrium of the sage and mystic, and his continual calls for peace and acceptance between normal humans and mutants take on the weight of prophecy, leaving little doubt that even if violent conflict between humans and mutants occurs in the present, everyone will be able to achieve harmony at some point, once they recognize their shared interests and band together for the common good. Thus, the *X-Men* franchise takes on the optimistic worldview of the triumph-over-adversity drama and *Bildungsroman*, narratives in which problems like disability will become irrelevant upon the dawning of a more enlightened era.

In contrast, *The Umbrella Academy* recognizes the trappings of 19th-century optimism in franchises like the X-Men and sneers at it through parody and horror movie aesthetics: Sir Reginald Hargreeves gives us Dickensian villainy with a science-fiction twist and the genetically enhanced mass murderer Number Five destroys the saintliness of every preternaturally wise child from Oliver Twist to Tiny Tim with every murder he commits. *The Umbrella Academy* does not believe that there will ever come a time when disability will not matter and presents the reader with a parade of exploding, vivisected, incinerated, stabbed and bullet-riddled bodies to underscore its point. The Hargreeves children live in a universe where zombies and vampires and robots and aliens are commonplace, beyond Xavier's land of tribal struggle between humans and mutants; yet, even in a universe such as this, neither society nor the members of the Academy themselves have come to terms with their ambivalence toward freakish or disabled bodies. That this ambivalence is never far away from violence is suggested on a cosmic level by the presence of the Temps Aternalis Agency, which controls the universe by destroying any "anomalies" that crop up in time or space (Way *Dallas*). At the local level, the intimate link between disability and violence is suggested through the sociopathic coldness of Sir

Reginald toward his children, and his sadistic methods of educating them. The Hargreeves children are liminal creatures, existing "between" states of normality and abnormality, acceptance and ostracism. As such, they exist in a web of paradoxes, as what disability scholar Henri-Jacques Stiker has called "the cared-for, integrated marginalized" (69). The horrors they face are not bred from the naked hatred of bigots; instead, they stem from the evils of half-hearted acceptance.

Within the graphic novels and the Netflix series, the language of pain becomes a conduit through which the adventures of the Hargreeves children become double- and triple-voiced. It is language that validates the experience of ableist gaslighting that disabled people endure; it aligns reality with a universe of Swiftian satire and Grand Guignol horror, and yet it holds out hope—albeit a slim and distant one—that the possibility of progress and improvement still exists. In *Volume Two: Dallas*, this language takes on its darkest incarnations, providing concrete proof that it can, in Elaine Scarry's words, make the world of torturers "larger" while destabilizing the reality that victims experience (37). In the graphic novel, Number Five attempts to fight the Temps Aeternalis by thwarting the assassination of JFK; the agency negates this humanitarian impulse through blackmail: They threaten to kill Allison unless Five completes his original mission. As part of the new assassination plot, The Rumor is also corrupted. Kennedy, Five decides, "is something special." He embodies a sense of hope, "*an idea*" that cannot be destroyed with mere bullets. This hope, Five concludes, is something that "you have to take down with *words*" (Way, *Dallas*; original emphasis). Thus, after all the other gunmen are destroyed, it is Allison (disguised as Jackie Onassis) and her gift of reality-altering speech that ensures Kennedy's death. Hence, the world is saved, to the extent that the Temps Aeternalis timeline is restored to the post–Kennedy reality that modern readers know, where the evils we face are at least familiar in their banality.

In Season 2 of the Netflix series, this language of pain still holds sway. The episodes are shot through with tropes of faulty or abusive speech. Our heroes tumble through a time warp into the early years of the 1960s. Black civil rights leaders are beginning to articulate their struggle, yet not effectively enough to end the racism around them; The Rumor is recovering from an injury and cannot use her powers for a year; an accident plunges Vanya into an amnesiac state, and she is sheltered in the home of Sissy, a woman struggling to raise a non-verbal autistic son; Klaus becomes a cult leader and then abandons his followers; Diego lands in a psychiatric hospital, where he struggles to convince people that Kennedy is about to be assassinated, and Number Five is faced with the task of convincing the whole family to come together again as a team in order to prevent another apocalypse. The only character who enjoys boundless freedom and an unfettered power of speech is the venomous Handler, who bends an army of lackeys to her will with lies and half-truths in her quest to seize control of The Commission that controls the timelines of the universe. It is fitting that the Handler wields such power in the plot because her character resonates powerfully in the American cultural consciousness. Her successes validate a modern sense that people's lives are being controlled by a capricious and sadistic hand, in a land where "American exceptionalism" has joined the ranks of "inspirational" and "extraordinary" as an outdated and destructive cliché. Her downfall keeps alive the hope that the idealism of the 1960s was not just a pleasant "idea," and that we will once again be able to separate truth from lies while moving step-by-step and word-by-word toward better days.

## Note

1. To recap the Hargreeves' playbook: Number Five (The Boy) is a genetically enhanced super assassin who can shift back and forth through time; Allison (The Rumor) makes lies (or "rumors") into reality by simply declaring them true; Luther (Spaceboy) is a human/simian hybrid with super strength; Diego (The Kraken) can control the path of moving objects, making him unstoppably lethal with throwing knives; Klaus (The Séance) can communicate with the dead; the (now-deceased) brother Ben moves objects with energy tendrils that sprout from his body, and Vanya (the White Violin) can convert emotions into apocalyptic levels of telekinetic power.

## Works Cited

Burke, Edmund. *The Writings and Speeches of Edmund Burke in Twelve Volumes. Volume One.* Little, Brown and Company, 1901. Babel.hathitrust.org. https://babel.hathitrust.org/cgi/pt?id=hvd.32044010665776&view=1up&seq=11. Accessed November 1, 2020.

Chemers, Michael M. "Mutatis Mutandis: An Emergent Disability Aesthetic in *X2: X-Men United*." *Disability Studies Quarterly*, vol. 24, no.1, 2004, dsq- sds.org/article/view/862/1037. Accessed November 1, 2020.

Couser, G. Thomas. "Conflicting Paradigms: The Rhetorics of Disability Memoir." *Embodied Rhetorics: Disability in Language and Culture*, edited by James C. Wilson and Cynthia Lewiecki-Wilson, Southern Illinois University Press, 2001, pp. 78–88.

Davis, Lennard J. "Constructing Normalcy: The Bell Curve, the Novel, and the Invention of the Disabled Body in the Nineteenth Century." *The Disability Studies Reader*, edited by Lennard J. Davis, Routledge, 1997, pp. 9–28.

Garland-Thomson, Rosemarie. "The Beauty and the Freak." *Points of Contact: Disability, Art and Culture*, edited by Susan Crutchfield and Marcy Epstein, University of Michigan Press, 2003, pp. 181–196.

\_\_\_\_\_. *Extraordinary Bodies: Figuring Physical Disability in American Culture and Literature.* Columbia University Press, 1997.

Goffman, Erving. *Stigma: Notes on the Management of Spoiled Identity*. Simon & Schuster, 1963.

Holmes, Martha Stoddard. "Working (with) the Rhetoric of Affliction: Autobiographical Narratives of Victorians with Physical Disabilities." *Embodied Rhetorics: Disability in*

*Language and Culture*, edited by James C. Wilson and Cynthia Lewiecki-Wilson, Southern Illinois University Press, 2001, pp. 27–44.

Ilea, Ramona. "The Mutant Cure or Social Change: Debating Disability." *X-Men and Philosophy*, edited by Rebecca Housel and J. Jeremy Wisnewski, John Wiley and Sons, 2009, pp. 170–182.

Keith, Lois. *Take Up Thy Bed and Walk: Death, Disability and Cure in Classic Fiction for Girls*. Women's Press, 2001.

Kerner, Aaron Michael. *Torture Porn in the Wake of 9/11: Horror, Exploitation and the Cinema of Sensation*. Rutgers University Press, 2015.

Klock, Geoff. "The Revisionary Superhero Narrative." *The Superhero Reader*, edited by Charles Hatfield, et al., University Press of Mississippi, 2013, pp. 116–135.

Kriegel, Leonard. "The Cripple in Literature." *Images of the Disabled, Disabling Images*, edited by Alan Gartner and Tom Joe, Prager, 1987, pp. 31–46.

Longmore, Paul K. "Screening Stereotypes: Images of Disabled People in Television and Motion Pictures." *Images of the Disabled, Disabling Images*, edited by Alan Gartner and Tom Joe, Prager, 1987, pp. 65–78.

Lowenstein, Adam. *Shocking Representation: Historical Trauma, National Cinema, and the Horror Film*. Columbia University Press, 2005.

Medhurst, Andy. "Batman, Deviance, and Camp." *The Superhero Reader*, edited by Charles Hatfield, et al., University Press of Mississippi, 2013, pp. 237–251.

Miller, J. Hillis. "The Narrator as General Consciousness." *The Form of Victorian Fiction*, edited by J. Hillis Miller, University of Notre Dame Press, 1968, pp. 53–90.

Ong, Walter. "The Comics and the Super State." *The Superhero Reader*, edited by Charles Hatfield, et al., University Press of Mississippi, 2013, pp. 34–45.

Robbins, Trina. "The Great Women Superheroes." *The Superhero Reader*, edited by Charles Hatfield, et al., University Press of Mississippi, 2013, pp. 53–60.

Scarry, Elaine. *The Body in Pain*. Oxford University Press, 1985.

Sherry, Mark. "Does Anyone Really Hate Disabled People?" *Disability Hate Crimes: Does Anyone Really Hate Disabled People?*, edited by Mark Sherry, Ashgate, 2010, pp. 29–54.

Siebers, Tobin. "My Withered Limb." *Points of Contact: Disability, Art and Culture*, edited by Susan Crutchfield and Marcy Epstein, University of Michigan Press, 2003, pp. 21–30.

\_\_\_\_\_. "Tender Organs, Narcissism, and Identity Politics." *Disability Studies: Enabling the Humanities*, edited by Sharon L. Snyder, et al., MLA, 2002, pp. 40–55.

Sontag, Susan. "Regarding the Pain of Others." *Fields of Reading, Motives for Writing. Tenth Edition*, edited by Nancy R. Comley, et al., Bedford St. Martin's, 2013, pp. 366–372.

Stallybrass, Peter, and Allon White. *The Politics and Poetics of Transgression*. Methuen, 1986.

Stiker, Henri-Jacques. *A History of Disability*. Trans. William Sayers, University of Michigan Press, 2002.

Suomi, S.J., and H.A. Leroy. "In Memoriam: Harry F. Harlow." *American Journal of Primatology*, vol. 2, 1982, pp. 319–342.

Swift, Jonathan. "A Modest Proposal." *Fields of Reading, Motives for Writing. Tenth Edition*, edited by Nancy R. Comley, et al., Bedford St. Martin's, 2013, pp. 305–311.

Way, Gerard, and Gabriel Bá. *The Umbrella Academy Volume One: Apocalypse Suite*, Dark Horse Comics, 2008.

\_\_\_\_\_, and \_\_\_\_\_. *The Umbrella Academy Volume Two: Dallas*, Dark Horse Comics, 2009.

Wertham, Fredric. "The Superman Conceit." *The Superhero Reader*, edited by Charles Hatfield, et al., University Press of Mississippi, 2013, pp. 46–52.

# Part 3
# Forces of Violence

# Domestic Abuse

## *Normative Violence and Child-Superheroes*

### Alokparna Sen

To be a superhero is to use violence. It is all about the enhanced strength, the telekinesis, the martial arts skills and so on. Even the likes of Professor X (Charles Xavier, a telepath from the *X-Men* series), with their strictly "mental" capabilities, are performing a more insidious kind of violence, going into their enemies' heads and rearranging things to their own benefit. The superhero genre relies on violence as a foundational element. Once the superhero is brought from the purely visual to the audio-visual medium, this reliance on violence only becomes more noticeable because the screen requires action and action usually translates to violence.

It is perhaps, on some level, difficult for the audience to accept that the hero has actually made an impact of some kind unless that impact is represented as the result of fighting. Encapsulating the struggle between good and evil in a series of battles makes it easier to grasp. Violence produces a tangible result and a genre that is rooted in escapist wish-fulfillment is justified in its liberal use of it. The bad guys will not just be defeated, they will be incapacitated or killed, and if that does not happen, they will at least limp away from their final altercation with the hero sufficiently injured. The violence against the villain who occupies a significant position in the narrative, whose malicious acts the viewer has witnessed in detail, who has caused harm on a personal basis to the hero the viewer identifies with, allows the viewer to feel a sense of cathartic satisfaction. With reference to Seymour Feshbach, Marjorie Heins mentions that violence in the form of dramatic fantasy is historically established and vicarious participation in such fantasies on the part of the audience does seem to satisfy some human needs (4). Casual violence against minor criminals is simply a shorthand used to establish the superhero as a superhero, as we see in the pilot episode ("Into the Ring") of Marvel's *Daredevil* (2015), a television series adapted from the *Daredevil* comics. Generally speaking, the superhero is a superhero because he or she has the ability to use violence against those who are deserving of it.

The heroes themselves will also be subjected to violence from their enemies and even their friends. The hero's enemies usually fight back. Heroes are injured and killed regularly by their enemies. Because of the nature of the medium of comic books, neither injuries nor death last very long unless the plot demands it. But it is expected that the hero will suffer physically and otherwise, and that different kinds of violence will be enacted against them. They simply have to persevere and be capable of striking back. Heroes often inflict violence on each other, given the popularity of narratives that pit heroes against each other. Events like *Civil War* and *Civil War II* by Marvel comics, in which heroes who are friends turn against each other, point to the degree to which violence is embedded within identity formation among superheroes. Violence is always a go-to option regardless of context. Violence can be used with impunity against friends and allies in the event of disagreement, because it is the most effective weapon in the arsenal of a superhero. A hero suffering violence at the hands of another hero will usually view it in terms of the inextricability of the use of force from the hero lifestyle and accept it as something natural and expected. If heroes fight each other, they will do it with their fists, weapons, or powers, rather than just their words. That is to say, violence is fundamental to how superheroes relate to the world and to each other.

Hannah Arendt wrote that violence is instrumental and that like all means, violence, too, has to be guided and justified through its intended end (51). Violence, then, is the ultimate instrument employed by superheroes, their preferred means to achieve any end. In some ways, superheroes themselves might be considered to be instruments of violence, which occurs explicitly in certain contexts, like Steve Rogers undergoing a scientific procedure that gives him enhanced strength, agility, and durability, and being given the title of Captain America afterwards so that he can be used in the war against the Axis powers in *Captain America: The First Avenger* (2011). Superheroes not only use violence as a means to pursue an end but are themselves made into the means to an end. Given the power dynamics involved, one might consider young sidekicks of adult superheroes, and children and teenagers who are trained or permitted to work as superheroes by adults in terms of this idea of superheroes as tools of violence, wielded by and for others.

As sidekicks or as superheroes in their own right, children and teenagers are a staple of the superhero genre. With reference to Arendt, Guido Parietti states that "violence is not intrinsically wrong or evil, though it is always to some extent destructive […]" (9). Where the impact of the destructive nature of violence on children is concerned, it has been found that school-aged children and teenagers exposed to community violence and family violence display symptoms of anxiety and depression, and behave in aggressive, violent ways themselves (Osofsky 37–38). Support from parental figures and the community can mitigate the effects of exposure to violence on children (Osofsky 39). This is what many child superheroes essentially lack, because even when they ostensibly have parental figures as well as their community aiding them and encouraging them, what they are being aided and encouraged to do is putting themselves in danger. Being trained to use violence as part of learning martial arts or self-defense can have a positive effect on children, particularly girls. It can lead to improved self-confidence, self-discipline, physical performance, academic performance and knowledge of ways to ensure one's safety (Gray Matter Research 6, 9–10). But for children who act as superheroes, being trained to use violence even in self-defense is complicated by the fact that on a fundamental level, they are meant to prioritize the safety of civilians over their own. Their use of violence in self-defense is ultimately always meant to facilitate their use of violence in defense of others.

Where the reliance of the superhero genre on violence becomes problematic is when children enter the equation. For the viewer, the concept of the child superhero requires a certain amount of willingness for suspension of disbelief. Of course, the superhero genre as a whole requires plenty of suspension of disbelief as well. This suspension merely operates on different levels. Mutations that result in superpowers are a complete impossibility in the real world. A child possessing the requisite maturity and skill to regularly fight criminals is highly unlikely, if not logically untenable, depending upon the context. Heroes like Batman and Green Arrow, whom the reader accepts as flawed, but well-intentioned, allowing children to endanger themselves in the pursuit of justice with token justifications while still retaining some degree of moral authority, also necessitate suspension of disbelief. Because the kid hero is considered to be a more effective audience surrogate, the narrative will defend their existence except on select occasions, like Superman castigating the wizard Shazam over Billy Batson's involvement in the trials and tribulations of superhero life. However, in general, the child superhero is someone who is good at their job, and any adult who tries to stop them is rightfully conflicted about it, as is the case in *Young Avengers* (2005). A child or teenager who is in possession of a superpower (Peter Parker/Spider-Man), notable physical training (Dick Grayson/Robin I), above-average intelligence (Riri Williams/Ironheart), or any combination of the above, along with a suitable motivation, ranging from a traumatic bereavement (both Parker and Grayson) to the desire to help an adult hero (Tim Drake/Robin III), will take up a life of constant exposure to violence, as both perpetrator and victim, and this is endemic in the superhero genre.

The genre is not blind to the inherent vulnerability of a child hero. The second Robin, Jason Todd's infamously brutal death at the hands of the Joker comes to mind (he got better, of course, but he stayed dead for a remarkably long time by comic book standards, to say nothing of his subsequent character development as a violent, murderous villain/anti-hero) and so does the disbanding of the first version of the Young Avengers team, which involved the deaths of two members (one of them at the hands of a third) and a fourth member's descent into a prolonged depressive spiral. Yet, the fundamental aspect of superhero comics is perhaps that nothing is permanent. Any message that is delivered by one writer can be undone by another. Kid superheroes understand the precariousness of their position in one run and in the next, circumstances conspire to put them right back where they were before, within a defining framework of violence.

Professor X trains teenagers and children because they have powers and exposes them to dangerous situations. Their powers are the primary factor here that necessitates the rest. If one has powers, then they must use them against criminals and supervillains, making themselves the target of retaliatory violence. The process of learning to use one's powers is itself not free of violence. Powers are not necessary for a hero to be able to perform violence, but they certainly enhance the extent to which they are able to perform violence. The adults who train children in the use of violence and tacitly or actively permit their participation in dangerous situations that involve violence enacted by and against children are technically guilty of child abuse and child endangerment. For the members of the Umbrella Academy too, it is their powers that bring about their entry into the framework of violence, both within and without the familial structure.

In live-action media, the presence of child heroes has become more common recently, depending on the requirements of the narrative. Roy Harper and Wally West, a young teenager or child during their original tenures as Speedy and Kid Flash in the comics, are aged up for their appearances on CW's *Arrow* (2012) and *The Flash* (2014) as they are not the primary focus characters on those shows and their younger age would create needless complications. On the other hand, Peter Parker in the Marvel Cinematic Universe is 15 in his first appearance, and shows like *Cloak and Dagger* (2018) and *Runaways* (2017) also represent teenaged heroes, and their age is an important component of their narratives. Significantly, these teenage characters are not recruited into becoming superheroes by adult characters. Even Peter Parker in the MCU is already active as a small-time hero before Tony Stark recruits him, though the latter then both encourages and enables him to put himself in danger.

In *The Umbrella Academy,* we see children being raised with the explicit intention of making them superheroes. Reginald Hargreeves,[1] more than any adult mentor-figure, imposes superheroism upon the children in his care, rather than those children being in a position to demand training for themselves. The focus is on the siblings as adults (and an adult in a child's body, in Five's case) but their experiences as children are significant. That is to say, the fact that Luther,[2] Diego,[3] Allison,[4] Klaus,[5] Five,[6] and Ben[7] were young teenagers when their careers as superheroes began is a defining element of their personalities. Except for Luther, who went on missions until his injury, Diego, who continues to be a vigilante up until the present day (and perhaps Ben, depending on how the series will frame his death), the majority of their tenures as "proper" superheroes were spent as teenagers.

In its deconstruction of the conventions of the superhero genre, *The Umbrella Academy* emphasizes the debilitating effects that prolonged exposure to the violence of a life as a superhero has on children with regard to their development into adults. Violence becomes inextricably linked to how the Hargreeves siblings interact with each other and with other people. Additionally, the fact that they do not possess secret identities and operate with the approval of the authorities and the community when they are young means that there is no aspect of their lives that is not tied to their work as superheroes and no reason other than their own, personal discontent to think of their situation in negative terms. An illicit element that is present in many child superhero activities is absent for the Hargreeveses. Their treatment at the hands of Reginald is legitimized by other people within the narrative.

The public in the universe of *The Umbrella Academy* thus functions as an analogue to the general reading/viewing public of superhero media. The age of the Hargreeves siblings is given secondary consideration in comparison to their abilities and skills. Despite the narrative making it clear that such an upbringing did not benefit the siblings themselves, the domestic violence they undergo, in terms of the child endangerment their caretaker is openly guilty of, is not acknowledged by those who are saved by them and those who look up to them as celebrity figures. They are not given the same entitlement to safety that "normal" children have. Their powers set them apart, make them something Other, and thus the domestic violence they face is rationalized. A similar rationalization is carried out by the audience of superhero media where child superheroes in a non-deconstructionist framework are concerned. Vanya's[8] book on her and her siblings' abusive childhood is sensationalized and Reginald Hargreeves' behavior remains uncriticized by her readers from what we see, before interest in the book drops off, as is usually the case with celebrity memoirs. Even Vanya, because of the specific nature of the abuse she herself suffers as a child within the family structure, cannot recognize her siblings' experience as abusive because of the glorification of the superhero lifestyle. Instead, she craves the opportunity to be one of them, symbolized by the scene where she draws the symbol of the Academy on her wrist with a marker to mimic the tattoos that are being forced upon her siblings without their consent, feeling justifiably excluded but overlooking the actual physical pain involved ("We Only See Each Other at Weddings and Funerals").

Reginald Hargreeves' exposure of his children to the hyperviolence that drives their lives takes place within a larger context of prolonged emotional abuse in which he rates the children's worth and importance in terms of their usefulness at handling hyperviolent situations. The domestic violence the Hargreeves siblings undergo incorporates both emotional and physical abuse within the home as well as the perilous situations their father sends them into. Being superheroes is an experience of abuse for Luther, Diego, Allison, Klaus, Five and Ben. The audience sympathizes with most of their negative feelings towards Reginald Hargreeves because he is explicitly shown to be a man who did not care for his children and was usually cruel and harsh in his dealings with them. But it is Reginald's behavior in their day-to-day lives that his children find problematic. The very act of grooming his children to be superheroes, rather than the specifics of how he went about doing it, is not questioned on the same level in the show. Allison, for example, tells her daughter bedtime stories about the missions the Academy went on. The violence her father subjected her to has become normalized in her mind because it has been normalized by the adults she grew up with, the governmental authorities, the masses, and the media. Allison in turn normalizes it for her daughter. Within the hyperviolent context of a society where superheroes and superpowers exist, children participating in sanctioned violence is destigmatized, depending on who the children are. The ordinary definitions of child abuse and child endangerment are put on hold.

So, to what extent can the treatment of child superheroes by mentor-figures be considered domestic violence within this hyperviolent framework? The answer would be that knowingly allowing children to participate in the hero lifestyle always constitutes abuse and endangerment by real-life standards. However, in a fictional context we are well-used to the concept of child-heroes in general. Their existence in superhero media is only more egregious depending on the specifics of the narrative. But superhero media also desensitizes us to the violence inherent within it. In many works involving child protagonists, there is an implicit or explicit understanding that the adults cannot do what the children can, for various reasons. In superhero media, this need for children to step up is not there. Children and adults deal with the same situations and threats. That is to say, because most superhero media provides a wide array of protagonists of different ages across various titles, all of them equally significant in terms of the narrative they inhabit, the structure of texts like the *Harry Potter* series by J.K. Rowling, the *Percy Jackson and the Olympians* series by Rick Riordan, or *The Hunger Games* by Suzanne Collins, where for various reasons, the narrative focus comes to rest on a few young protagonists only, is not replicated in superhero media. There are adults in the DC and Marvel universes who can take over the duties performed by their younger counterparts, but do not, perpetuating a doublethink situation wherein civilian children are to be protected, but sidekicks and young heroes, some of whom are their own offspring, are allowed on the battlefield. In *The Umbrella Academy*, there are no adult superheroes, invoking the necessity for children to fill the role. Interestingly enough, in the Netflix series, during the Academy's "glory days," there do not appear to be any threats that require intervention beyond that which the police or the military are capable of providing. By contrast, in the very first issue of *Uncanny X-Men* (1963), Magneto uses his powers to attack humans, and the X-Men arrive to fight him in a way ordinary people cannot. The intervention of sixteen-year-old Bobby Drake is needed in this situation (though it can be argued that his older teammates could have dealt with the matter without him). Yet, the Umbrella Academy only seems to fight non-powered robbers and thieves when the siblings are young. Sending children to resolve situations that do not urgently require intervention they alone could provide is child endangerment without nominal justification.

The siblings, particularly Ben, are also shown using excessive force, because they are capable of it and have been taught to do so, even when they can defeat the people they are fighting without doing so. They are encouraged to perform the hyperviolence which their powers only create the possibility for. This unnecessary hyperviolence against people who are not capable of fighting back on their level does lasting damage to their psyche where the normalization of the use of violence against others and themselves is concerned. In his discussion of *The Boys*, Aaron Bady asks, "After all, in the absence of supervillains, what 'crime fighting' could a superhero do that couldn't be done just as easily (and with less destruction) by normal-powered police officers?" This can, of course, also be applied to the television adaptation of *The Umbrella Academy*. The apocalypse Reginald claims to be focused on is years away when he sends his children out to incapacitate and kill criminals. Besides, training at home (which is also abusive because of Reginald's particular methods) seems a better way of preparing the Academy to deal with an eventual apocalyptic scenario than making them superheroes, which (presumably) killed Ben and could have potentially killed the others, too, leaving no one to face the threat Reginald was worried about. All in all, there is no justification within the narrative for the child endangerment that Reginald practices.

Taking that into account, I would argue that *The Umbrella Academy*'s specific case of child superheroes practicing and facing violence counts as domestic violence against them within the narrative as well as from a meta-textual perspective. While the hyperviolent framework the siblings operate within as adults includes the presence of the Commission, the one they operate within as teenage superheroes is constituted by the behaviors their father has inculcated in them alone. The world of *The Umbrella Academy*'s past is hyperviolent because Reginald makes it so. Unlike most child superheroes, the Academy does not meet hyperviolence from others but only doles it out because their father has conditioned them to do so by raising them in a violent environment. It might be said that while constructing his children's superhero identities, Reginald constructs the hyperviolent space he expects superheroes to exist within. Superhero media normalizes extreme violence to the point that children being involved in it can become a matter of course, a commentary on how no one is exempt from the violence that pervades these texts. While this ever-present air of violence can make it difficult to draw definite conclusions about what constitutes abuse and complicates the question further by bringing in the issue of needing to use excessive violence as a defensive measure against others wielding it as well, these qualifiers are absent where the Academy, as teenage heroes, is concerned.

Reginald Hargreeves chooses to adopt the children and put them through rigorous training and introduce them to a dangerous lifestyle because of their powers and justifies his behavior in terms of his children's innate exceptional nature. The impact of his treatment of them is severe enough that in the second season, even while dealing with a version of him from the past, who has not yet adopted them or abused them, the adult Diego is driven to tears and a resurgence of his childhood stutter by his insults. Prior to this incident, Luther mentions that their father, who is not yet their father, will certainly play "mind games" with them and turn them against each other, and the siblings do fail to adequately support each other when faced with the young Reginald's disapproval, illustrating the trauma from their upbringing ("A Light Supper"). When raising the children, besides enforcing a militaristic emphasis on physical conditioning, Reginald performs other, more specific acts of abuse. He denies his children free time beyond a bare minimum, as well as any opportunity to exert their individuality, by forcing a rigidly structured lifestyle upon them that includes standard uniforms as daily wear. Most egregiously, he does not name the children in his care, and does not call them by the names which they come to possess. He locks Klaus in a mausoleum (with the justification that it will strengthen his ability to communicate with the dead), and Vanya in a soundproofed cell (because her power involves manipulating sound waves to produce destructive force) for extended periods of time, and he makes Allison use her power of manipulating minds to make Vanya forget about hers when they are four years old, because he fears the intensity of Vanya's ability. The siblings literally live in a space pervaded by violence as children, as symbolized by the drawings illustrating unarmed combat techniques lining a wall. This is a way of life that is chosen for the siblings and it comes to define the relationships within the family.

Teaching children martial arts and other such practices or having them participate in physical exercise is by no means abusive in itself. It is the specific context within *The Umbrella Academy*, of children being taken in with the sole intent of raising them as soldiers, with no other choices being made available to them but to take part in the training, which brings in the abusive connotations. When questioned on his parenting methods by Klaus, Reginald claims that he wanted them to live up to their potential. Thus, Reginald Hargreeves draws a clear connection between the siblings' powered status and his abusive behavior. However, for all his justifications, Reginald, like any abuser, is primarily concerned with maintaining control over the children, which becomes clear when he decides to suppress Vanya's power because she cannot control it, and thus he cannot control it through her. He isolates the children from their peers and other adults, from what we see, and raises them in a household where the other "adults," Grace (an android built by Reginald) and Pogo (a chimpanzee who became sapient due to a procedure performed by Reginald), are subservient to his wishes, both being his creations and subject to his abuse as well (Grace not being allowed to leave the grounds, for example). He continuously denies them agency. He withholds information from them, making them dependent on him, and while he talks about the importance of their collective strength, he nevertheless encourages them to compete with each other in training, keeping them from forming effective alliances against him. He conditions them to accept their situation and take pride in their work as superheroes, though this ceases to work as the siblings grow older and begin to develop wishes and ideas of their own despite Reginald's best efforts. But Reginald keeping his children from realizing that their living conditions are less than desirable by making himself the only source of trustworthy knowledge regarding how things are meant to be in their lives for as long as he could is also a recognized technique used by abusers.

One of the reasons abusive parents isolate their children is to prevent "exposure to people with other worldviews" which could "encourage them to think differently and eventually rebel against the worldview that the family rules are based on," according to *Emotional Abuse Answers*. Reginald gaslights his children where Vanya and her powers are concerned. Psychological maltreatment has been defined by Garbarino, Guttman and Seeley as "a concerted attack by an adult on a child's development of self and social competence, a pattern of psychically destructive behaviour" (8). This is classified into five behavioral forms, *viz.*

    1. rejecting: behaviours which communicate or constitute abandonment of the child, such as a refusal to show affection;
    2. isolating: preventing the child from participating in normal opportunities forsocial interaction;
    3. terrorising: threatening the child with severe or sinister punishment, ordeliberately developing a climate of fear or threat;
    4. ignoring: where the caregiver is psychologically unavailable to the child andfails to respond to the child's behaviour;
    5. corrupting: caregiver behaviour which encourages the child to develop falsesocial values that reinforce antisocial or deviant behavioural patterns, such asaggression, criminal acts or substance abuse [Tomison and Tucci].

Out of these, Reginald Hargreeves definitely carries out the behaviors associated with rejecting, isolating, ignoring and corrupting. Other than making them superheroes and sending them to fight criminals, he mostly abuses his children in recognizable ways. Their existence within a superhero narrative and his focus on their powers provide a foundation for the abuse, but the specifics of the abuse can be easily correlated with to real-world behaviors. Reginald places the onus for his treatment of the siblings on the siblings themselves, but he is not bringing them into a pre-existing framework of children being trained to fight crime, and thus nothing can distract from the fact that his methods are clearly abusive. Not a superhero or a person in possession of powers himself (though non-human), he exists outside the hyperviolent structure he creates and makes his children a part of. His own violence against them is mundane and familiar and differs mainly in terms of the resources available to him that are not present or difficult to obtain in reality, like Allison's power and the soundproof cell that he subjects Vanya to. It becomes a matter of scale, rather than motivation or action.

    Reginald's domestic violence against his children is separate from the domestic violence his children themselves perpetrate because of it. Mostly, in superhero media, the mentor directly responsible for training child heroes and allowing their participation in superheroic activities is active within the framework of hyperviolence or at least capable of being active within it. Batman, Green Arrow, and the Flash are all superheroes who use extreme violence. Professor X, while not an active crimefighter on account of his disability, can and does use his telepathy to enact violence, and is not essentially different from his students. He is one of the persecuted mutants, just like them. As far as general perceptions are concerned, Reginald does not share in his children's Otherness. While he is canonically an alien who arrived on Earth in the 19th century ("The White Violin") and stands out in the late 20th century because of how he retains the fashion of the early 20th century in his personal wardrobe, he hides his own Otherness from society at large by utilizing the general expectation of a rich man to have eccentric habits and mannerisms.

His status as an alien, besides carrying a problematic implication that his cruelty and lack of empathy stem from his non-human nature, relieving him of taking responsibility for his behavior, does not noticeably set him apart from society to the same degree as his children in their youth. His violence against them does not fall into the same paradigms as violence between superheroes/people with powers. Despite his lack of superpowers, as an adult, rich, apparently white man who satisfies society's expectations, he holds all the actual power in the household and this imbalance is what is truly significant in *The Umbrella Academy*. In deconstructing the tropes associated with superhero media, the narrative strips the siblings of the power that other child heroes usually possess. The physical violence the siblings are willing to perpetrate against each other as adults is not based on power imbalance but invokes the normalization of violence between people who are capable of it and have been conditioned to use it. The emotional and verbal abuse they engage in is simultaneously a corollary of this physical abuse between superheroes/powered people and rooted in the cycle of realistic abusive behavior Reginald introduces into the familial structure. But the siblings still appear to abuse each other primarily as people for whom violence of all kinds is natural, which is differentiated from Reginald's nominally motivation-driven, actually control-seeking abuse. However, the fact that it is Reginald's parenting that normalizes violence for the siblings in this specific case has to be kept in mind.

The siblings perform domestic violence against each other in *The Umbrella Academy*. As children, Luther, Diego, Allison, Klaus, Five and Ben are separated from Vanya in terms of how they are raised, creating an inability to empathize with each other between the six of them and her. The exclusion of Vanya from the activities of the other siblings when they are younger is something that Reginald is directly responsible for because of the way in which he teaches them to think of themselves in terms of their powers and relative usefulness being their most important aspect. As Allison points out, the continued ostracization of Vanya into adulthood is the responsibility of her siblings. At the root of it is Vanya's apparent lack of superpowers. Many of the acts of verbal and emotional abuse perpetrated by Diego against Vanya are based on her fundamental difference from her siblings. It should be noted that Vanya's lack of superpowers does not create a power imbalance between her and her siblings in the sense that they can wield authority over her. Interestingly, once the existence of Vanya's powers is revealed, Luther performs physical violence against her by asphyxiating her. While Allison argues for a peaceful, diplomatic approach, the brothers are resolved to use physical violence against the White Violin, as Vanya is now on their level, so to speak, and can be dealt with as superpowered people are meant to deal with each other. Allison's refusal to engage in this can be traced back to her realization that she has used violence against her daughter by mind-controlling her, which happened because she has been conditioned to view family members as unexempt from violence and violence as something expected of her. Thus, her repentance leads her to prioritize the familial connection with her sister over Vanya's powered status. Even knowing that it is wrong, Allison tries to use her power against Vanya to subdue her in the cabin because abusive behavior is ingrained in her; however, she shows her growth by taking accountability for her actions afterwards. Diego, who is the only one of the siblings who has remained a superhero, or rather, a vigilante, lacking the public support the Academy once had, is quick to verbally berate Luther as well as Vanya, and he expresses a desire to physically attack Five after Patch's death and punches Klaus to keep him from going back on his own decision to undergo detox. Five knocks Diego unconscious during the latter's fight with Hazel. Both Five and Diego lead more violent lives than the rest of their siblings and their actions reflect it, but they are also emulating Reginald's lack of consideration for family members. The siblings are quick to strike at each other's vulnerable spots, from Luther threatening to throw Delores out of the window, to Diego saying their father made Luther a monster.

Both the casual violence and the verbal/emotional attacks are a result of being raised in a hostile environment, as combatants first and foremost. Yet, even from a metatextual viewpoint, the perpetration of assault both with and without weapons and superpowers amongst the protagonists of a work of superhero fiction is what is expected by the audience, especially since *The Umbrella Academy* also uses the proliferation of violence as a source of black comedy. However, while combat between protagonists of superhero media is often driven by particular circumstances like mind control (*The Avengers* [2012]; *Avengers: Age of Ultron* [2015]), misunderstandings (*Batman vs. Superman: Dawn of Justice* [2016]), ideological disagreements (*Civil War* [2006]; *Civil War II* [2016]), and so on, in *The Umbrella Academy*, protagonists do not always require such circumstances. In both cases, violence is inevitable and a matter of course, but where *The Umbrella Academy* is concerned, there is an additional level of normalization of violence at work on account of the familial context of abuse. Additionally, the significance of inter-sibling violence is often minimized despite it being the most common form of interfamilial aggression (Hernandez 7). The fight between Luther and Diego at Reginald's funeral evokes a cultural idea of adult brothers being quick to engage in physical altercations. Basically, their sibling rivalries and willingness to be violent do mirror real-world relationships, but they fundamentally operate within a structure determined by their possession of superpowers. Overall, the violence between the siblings and otherwise enacted by the siblings is tied to their status as main characters within an action-driven medium, and from an internal perspective, their behavior is also logically derived from Reginald's abusive upbringing of them.

The series also seems to indicate an inherent link between powers and aggression that precedes the effects of conditioning and normalization. It is seen in Vanya's actions most explicitly, as she does not actually undergo much of the training that her siblings do and, as a result, lacks their externally imposed tendency towards violence. As a child of four or less, Vanya uses her powers to seriously injure and likely kill a series of caretakers. As an adult, the process of her recovering the use of her ability is rooted in violence, against the men Leonard hires to attack them. Subsequently, she accidentally injures Allison and intentionally kills Leonard. There is an implication that Vanya's power was always uncontrollable and thus any serious use of it invariably led to destruction and violence. I would argue that Vanya's use of her ability is overwhelmingly violent, once again, as a result of her upbringing. Before being made to forget about her power at the age of four, Vanya was also trained, with the same purpose as her siblings, and afterwards, she grew up in an environment where Reginald repeatedly asserted the association between powers and violence through his treatment of her siblings. Though she was not conditioned to use violence as a child superhero, Vanya was nevertheless conditioned to think of superpowers as being meant for a violent use, something Leonard is aware of when he correctly decides that without the presence of people to defend against, Vanya will not be able to access her power. The hyperviolence is not a spontaneous outcome of superpowers but ultimately a creation of Reginald Hargreeves' worldview and methods in this case as well. Vanya, too, is part of the family structure that has normalized lashing out against loved ones. Vanya, like Allison, gets caught up in a cycle of abuse outside the immediate Hargreeves family, but as victim rather than perpetrator. While Allison cannot quite conceptualize her treatment of her daughter as abusive at first because of her own abusive childhood, and her husband, with an outsider's perspective, seeing her as a mother rather than a superhero, recognizes it for what it is, Vanya is unable to see through Leonard's lies and manipulation because as AnnaLivia Chen points out, he preys on her trauma by validating her resentment of her family's abuse for his own purposes. Leonard, as a victim of childhood domestic violence himself, is able to find common ground with Vanya and uses that against her. Leonard's abuse of Vanya is based on his desire to introduce her into the hyperviolent structure of interactions between superpowered people. He differs from Reginald only in his use of more subtle, insidious methods rather than openly forceful ones. Otherwise, he literally follows Reginald's notes, and like him, seeks to make an instrument out of a superpowered person. Leonard arrives at this idea because he has grown up in a society which has normalized superpowered violence as conceptualized by Reginald and because of his own experiences, which suggest to him the endemic nature of interfamilial aggression.

Despite the similarity in the fact that the domestic violence perpetrated by Reginald and that perpetrated by his children both evoke abusive techniques in the real world while being essentially rooted in the existence of superpowers within the narrative, there is a differentiation as well. Reginald's rhetoric of the children never being "just kids" ("The Day That Was") but instruments for saving the world is an external reason for abuse. He confers upon himself a position of righteous pragmatism and refuses to acknowledge that his behavior was questionable. As against Reginald's utilitarian stance which is further legitimized by the public support for the Academy, as stated earlier, the siblings' abuse of each other is perpetuation of long-standing as well as learned behaviors, and something that they are so used to, that rather than denial, they possess an inability to recognize their actions as abusive. Only Allison truly makes progress on this front, recognizing her and her siblings' culpability in the continuing cycles of abuse in their lives, and even noting that her father made her an "accomplice" ("I Heard a Rumor") in his abuse of Vanya when they were four. Vanya, not yet able to see the structure of violence they have all been raised within, interprets Allison's confession as an autonomous, individual act. The domestic violence the siblings engage in is internalized behavior, with no overarching ultimate purpose, which Reginald claims it to have. People of whom violence is constantly expected engage in violence in interpersonal relationships as well, as reports on abuse in families where members are part of the military or the police show. A study conducted by Andrew H. Ryan, Jr., across seven law-enforcement agencies in the Southeast and Midwest areas of the United States found that over half of the respondents indicated they were aware that another officer in the department was an abuser. Stacy Bannerman speaks about domestic violence perpetrated by veterans of the Iraqi war in an article called "PTSD and Domestic Abuse: Husbands Who Bring the War Home." She writes that, "the majority of studies of treatment-seeking veterans with post-traumatic stress disorder (PTSD) or combat-related mental health issues report that at least 50 percent of those veterans commit wife-battering and family violence." The siblings' abusive actions are a by-product of their lifestyle and upbringing, audience expectations of violence aside. There is no nominal goal to strive towards via abusive behavior where they are concerned. By explicitly framing Reginald's abuse in terms of a goal, the series de-emphasizes the real-world associations of his actions. The siblings' relationships, on the other hand, become a more organic depiction of abuse, despite being rooted in the nature of the genre.

In the last episode of season one, the series simultaneously subverts and upholds conventions. On the one hand, it stresses the negative effects of the violence the superhero lifestyle is intrinsically linked to via the validation of Allison's viewpoint of how Vanya should be dealt with. On the other hand, it portrays Vanya's breakdown as a loss of self in the face of her power reaching its peak and a desire to bring about death and destruction. In satisfying the generic expectations of an inherent link between powers and aggression, *The Umbrella Academy* backs away from exploring the implications of prolonged abuse, as Chen states. The association between powers, the superhero lifestyle, and violence is a construct, and its ramifications take the form of the dysfunctional familial relationships we see. Acknowledging the constructed nature of this association is something the series fails to do in a satisfactory manner, in the same way that it fails to acknowledge the impact of Reginald's parenting being visible in the violence that exists in the siblings' interpersonal relationships as adults.

*The Umbrella Academy* is a deconstruction of the tropes associated with the genre of superhero fiction. Among others, it deconstructs the concept of the child superhero by representing the detrimental effects of such a lifestyle on said children. While child superheroes are common in superhero media, *The Umbrella Academy* differentiates itself by portraying the superheroism as something imposed upon the Hargreeves siblings through abusive methods by their father. Allowing or helping children participate in perilous situations is child endangerment, which is considered to be a component of child abuse. Many adult protagonists in works of superhero fiction commit it. This child endangerment is generally based on audience expectations of sidekick figures and other child fighters that the genre has created. From a metatextual viewpoint, the existence of child superheroes is inherently based on child abuse as well as audience satisfaction. That is to say, the factor of child abuse is mainly recognized from an external perspective, and the audience expectations that necessitate it are also external to the narrative.

There is an internal explanation for the child endangerment in *The Umbrella Academy* in the form of Reginald's awareness that the children born on October 1, 1989, can be trained to prevent the coming apocalypse. But making them superheroes and sending them into danger at an early age is counter-intuitive, as Ben, for example, dies before the apocalypse arrives. While the series explains Reginald's actions in terms of the existence of the siblings' powers and how they can be implemented for the greater good, it has to be acknowledged that Reginald's behavior is abusive in ways that can be recognized via their real-world resonances. The significance of this abuse is somewhat lessened by placing it within a context of normalization of violence in superhero media, but since it is Reginald himself who introduces that context in the society that exists within this text, the justifications of his behavior are weakened. The siblings internalize Reginald's constant emphasis on the need to use their powers and engage in fights and perform abusive behaviors themselves as adults. The casual violence they are willing to perpetrate against each other is played off as comedic, but there are also serious implications where the results of the pervasive presence of violence in one's life from an early age onwards are concerned. Rather than an inbuilt connection between powers and violence, *The Umbrella Academy* depicts that it is a matter of learned behavior, conditioning and societal constructs. Domestic violence perpetrated by Reginald creates all of this in this narrative. His children abuse each other as an organic result of their upbringing, not because they wish to use each other. The normalization of abusive behaviors in interpersonal relationships in superhero media is challenged primarily by Allison, who is forced to acknowledge her own abusive behavior as a parent, unlike Reginald, who refuses to do so, and her stance is validated by the narrative. Yet, the series ultimately suggests that violent impulses are inevitable for someone with powers who has not undergone Reginald's abusive regime of training to the fullest extent. The series itself, however, shows that Vanya's actions can be traced back to Reginald's parenting as well.

This essay does not cover the implications of the existence of child superheroes with audience support, but doing so would provide interesting insight into the intersection of children reading comics needing audience surrogates and adult consumers of superhero media both expecting those child heroes to continue inhabiting the narrative and a more realistic look at the consequences of children fighting crime. A propensity for superhero media itself becoming "darker and grittier" after a certain point following the advent of the Bronze Age of Comic Books around 1970 contributes to this more realistic approach. While child superheroes will continue existing, it depends on the nature of the narrative as to whether the harm to them caused by their lifestyle will be acknowledged or not.

## Notes

1. Hargreeves is the adoptive father of Luther, Diego, Allison, Klaus, Five, Ben, and Vanya. He collects them as infants because of the unusual circumstances of their birth, and trains them, with the exception of Vanya, to be superheroes. A cold, eccentric, and powerful man, he is later revealed to be an alien. His death prompts the reunion of most of the siblings at the start of the Netflix series.

2. Originally known as Number One. His ability involves enhanced strength and durability. As an adult, in the present-day timeline of the series, he has the body of an ape because of a procedure performed to save his life. The most loyal to Reginald and his wishes out of his siblings. Eventually forced to confront his father's abusive behavior for what it was.

3. Originally known as Number Two. He has the ability to hold his breath indefinitely and throw knives with pinpoint accuracy. He carries on working as a vigilante independently, unlike his siblings, in adulthood.

4. Originally known as Number Three. She has the power of controlling someone's behavior/beliefs by speaking the phrase "I heard a rumor…" followed by the desired result. Estranged from her husband, partly because of her use of this power on their daughter.

5. Originally known as Number Four. He can see and communicate with ghosts and is eventually able to make a ghost corporeal. It is implied that he has the ability to come back to life after being killed as well.

6. Known only as Number Five. He has the ability to teleport and travel through time. As a teenager, he traveled to a post-apocalyptic future where the human race had been decimated and unable, to return, grew up there. He worked as an assassin for a period of time. In the present-day timeline of the series, he is chronologically 58 but biologically 13.

7. Originally known as Number Six. He has extradimensional beings trapped under his skin. He dies prior to the start of the series and appears as a ghost that only Klaus can see and interact with at first.

8. Originally known as Number Seven. At first, she, her family, and the audience believe that she has no powers. She is the only one of her siblings not trained as a superhero, which alienated her from them. It is later revealed that she has a power, manipulating sound waves to generate force, which she was made to forget about because Reginald deemed it uncontrollable. Her power was suppressed via medication she was manipulated into taking. Ultimately, Vanya brings on the apocalypse with her power, spurred on by her anger at her family, and the antagonist of the first season, Leonard Peabody/Harold Jenkins, for their lies and betrayals.

## Works Cited

Arendt, Hannah. *On Violence*. Harvest Books, 1970.

*Arrow*, season 3, created by Greg Berlanti, Marc Guggenheim, and Andrew Kreisberg. CW, 2014.

*The Avengers*. Directed by Joss Whedon, performances by Robert Downey, Jr., Chris Evans, Chris Hemsworth, et al., Marvel Studios, 2012.

*Avengers: Age of Ultron*. Directed by Joss Whedon, performances by Robert Downey, Jr., Chris Evans, et al., Marvel Studios, 2015.

Bady, Aaron. "Superheroes, They're Just Like Us." *The Week*, 31 Jul. 2019. theweek.com/articles-amp/855506/superheroes-%20theyre-just-like. Accessed 3 Dec. 2019.

Bannerman, Stacy. "PTSD and Domestic Abuse: Husbands Who Bring the War Home." *Daily Beast*, 25 Sep. 2010. https://www.thedailybeast.com/ptsd-and-domestic-abuse-husbands-who-bring-the-war-home. Accessed 6 Dec. 2019.

*Batman Vs. Superman: Dawn of Justice*. Directed by Zack Snyder, performances by Ben Affleck, Henry Cavill, Gal Gadot, and Jesse Eisenberg, DC Entertainment, 2016.

Bendis, Brian Michael. *Civil War II*. Marvel Comics, 2016.

*Captain America: The First Avenger*. Directed by Joe Johnston, performances by Chris Evans, Hayley Atwell, Hugo Weaving, and Sebastian Stan, Marvel Studios, 2011.

Chen, AnnaLivia. "Abuse Causes the Apocalypse: Cycles of Harm, Transformative Justice, and *The Umbrella Academy*." *Voices*, 9 Apr. 2019. swarthmorevoices.com/content-1/2019/4/9/xb9crfr3thzhgly7efnmpwfgbbw3vj. Accessed 3 Dec. 2019.
Collins, Suzanne. *The Hunger Games*. Scholastic, 2008–2010.
"The Day That Was." *The Umbrella Academy*, written by Ben Nedivi and Matt Wolpert, directed by Stephen Surjik. Netflix, 15 2019.
Ewing, Eve. *Ironheart*. Marvel Comics, 2019.
Feshbach, Seymour, Ruth Leeds Love, and Robert D. Singer. "Television and Aggression: An Experimental Field Study." *Contemporary Sociology*, vol. 1, no. 4, 1972. pp. 365–367.
Finger, Bill. "Batman and 'Robin the Boy Wonder.'" *Detective Comics*, vol. 1, issue 38, DC Comics, 1940.
*The Flash*, season 2, created by Greg Berlanti, Geoff Johns, and Andrew Kreisberg. CW, 2015.
Garbarino, James, Edna Guttman, and Janis Wilson Seeley. *The Psychologically Battered Child*. Jossey-Bass Publishers, 1986.
Goddard, Drew. *Marvel's Daredevil*. Marvel Television and ABC Studios, 2015.
Gray Matter Research. *Literature Review of Research Into the Effectiveness of Self Defence Programmes for Girls as a Sexual Violence and Family Violence Prevention Strategy*. Ministry of Social Development, Government of New Zealand, 2016.
Heinberg, Allan. *Avengers: The Children's Crusade*. Issue 8–9, Marvel Comics, 2012.
\_\_\_\_\_. "Sidekicks." *Young Avengers*, vol. 1, issue 6, Marvel Comics, 2005.
Heins, Marjorie. "Violence and the Media: An Exploration of Cause, Effect and the First Amendment." Freedom Forum Institute, 2001.
Hernandez, Kaylyn. *Exploring Sibling Aggression*. 2015. Humboldt State University, MA thesis.
"I Heard a Rumor." *The Umbrella Academy*, written by Lauren Schmidt and Sneha Koorse, directed by Jeremy Webb. Netflix, 2019.
"Into the Ring." *Daredevil*, written by Drew Goddard, directed by Phil Abraham. Netflix, 2015.
"Isolation." *Emotional Abuse Answers*. emotionalabuseanswers.org/emoabu/emotional-abuse-behaviors/isolation/. Accessed 4 Dec. 2019.
Kripke, Eric. *The Boys*. Sony Pictures Television and Amazon Studios, 2019.
Lee, Stan. *Daredevil*. Marvel Comics Group, 1964.
\_\_\_\_\_. "Spider-Man!" *The Amazing Spider-Man*, issue 15, Marvel Comics, 1962.
\_\_\_\_\_. *Uncanny X-Men*, Marvel Comics Group, 1963.
\_\_\_\_\_. "X-Men." *Uncanny X-Men*, vol. 1, issue 1, Marvel Comics Group, 1963.
"A Light Supper." *The Umbrella Academy*, written by Aeryn Michelle Williams, directed by Ellen Kuras, Netflix, 2020.
Millar, Mark. *Civil War*. Marvel Comics, 2006.
Moench, Doug, Chuck Dixon, and Alan Grant. *Batman: Knightfall*, vol. 1, DC Comics, 1993.
Osofsky, Joy D. "The Impact of Violence on Children." *The Future of Children*, vol. 9, no. 3, 1999, pp. 33–49.
Parietti, Guido. "Arendt on Power and Violence." *The Anthem Companion to Hannah Arendt*, edited by Peter Baehr and Philip Walsh. Anthem Press, 2017, pp. 197–220.
Pokaski, Joe. *Marvel's Cloak and Dagger*. Wandering Rocks Productions, ABC Signature Studios, and Marvel Television, 2018.
Riordan, Rick. *Percy Jackson and the Olympians*. Penguin Books, 2005–2009.
Rowling, Joanne K. *Harry Potter*. Bloomsbury Publishing, 1997–2007.
Ryan, Andrew H. "The Prevalence of Domestic Violence in Police Families." *Domestic Violence by Police Officers*, edited by Donald C. Sheehan. U.S. Department of Justice, Federal Bureau of Investigation, Behavioral Science Unit, 2000, pp. 297–307.
Schwartz, Josh, and Stephanie Savage, creators. *Runaways*. ABC Signature Studios, Marvel Television, and Fake Empire Productions, 2017.
*Spider-Man: Homecoming*. Directed by Jon Watts, performances by Tom Holland, Michael Keaton et al., Columbia Pictures and Marvel Studios, 2017.
Starlin, Jim. "A Death in the Family." *Batman*, vol. 1, issues 426–429, DC Comics, 1988.
Tomison, Adam M., and Joe Tucci. "Emotional Abuse: The Hidden Form of Maltreatment." *NCPC*, no. 8, Sep. 1997.

*The Umbrella Academy*. Created by Steve Blackman and Jeremy Slater, Netflix, 2019–2020.
Waid, Mark. "Inherit the Wind!" *Flash*, vol. 2, issue 63, DC Comics, 1992.
"We Only See Each Other at Weddings and Funerals." *The Umbrella Academy*, written by Jeremy Slater, directed by Peter Hoar. Netflix, 2019.
"The White Violin." *The Umbrella Academy*, written by Steve Blackman, directed by Peter Hoar. Netflix, 2019.
Winick, Judd. "Bring It On!" *Green Arrow*, vol. 3, issue 47, DC Comics, 2005.
\_\_\_\_\_. *Superman/Shazam: First Thunder*, issue 4, DC Comics, 2005.
\_\_\_\_\_. "Under the Hood." *Batman*, vol. 1, issues 635–641, 645–650, DC Comics, 2004.
Wolfman, Marv. "A Lonely Place of Dying." *Batman*, vol. 1, issue 440–442. *The New Titans*, issues 60–61, DC Comics, 1990.

# Crystal Moments
## Sites of Music and Violence

### Lisann Anders

Extra-diegetic music sets the tone of a film and creates a certain atmosphere, be it the mood within a scene or themes for certain characters as an attempt to grasp their character and intentions. While extra-diegetic film music is usually meant to be subtle enough to not be noticed consciously, sometimes, songs can also be foregrounded—not in the form of musical numbers but as what Phil Powrie calls "crystal songs" that not only dominate a scene but are pivotal for the story. I would like to go a step further and argue that these songs also create a heterotopic space. Heterotopias, according to Michel Foucault's definition of space in 1967, can be described as non-spaces or anti-spaces meaning that they offer a space that is set in reality and yet, subverts the very same by presenting their own set of hegemonic rules. However, heterotopias do not necessarily have to be geographical places as such; they can be imagined spaces, heterotopic in their exclusive nature. Thus, songs and in particular extra-diegetic crystal songs, can be regarded as mirror images of the real that serve as a mode of self-reflexivity.

In the first two seasons of the Netflix series *The Umbrella Academy* (2019 and 2020),[1] the interaction between sound and space serves primarily two functions. On the one hand, on an intra-diegetic level, it helps to create and emphasize relationships between characters. The songs unite the protagonists, in particular the siblings.[2] This is further stressed by the choice of songs used for individual scenes, in which the lyrics add an extra-diegetic layer to the characters and the action that not only enriches the perception of the scene but also deepens the understanding of the respective character. On the other hand, the suspension of disbelief is broken, and the songs draw attention to the fictionality of the audio-visual medium. This function is usually used in scenes in which hyperviolence is depicted. Therefore, songs serve as heterotopic crystal moments. Moreover, music and sound are also spatialized by means of Vanya—especially in season one. Not only does she perform in the heterotopic space of the concert hall, she also learns to control her powers in the remoteness of the woods—a trope usually used in fairytales to show a character's coming of age. In addition, Vanya's body is portrayed as a space of music when she transforms into a white ghost-like figure who is dominated by music and turns the latter into a destructive force. This physical spatialization of music becomes even more evident in the first volume of the comic book series of *The Umbrella Academy*, *Apocalypse Suite*. Not only does the title highlight the importance of music within the story, but Vanya's body is literally transformed into an animated white violin.

This essay will take a closer look at the crystal scenes and songs and explain how music is used as inter-medial heterotopia of theatricality in the Netflix show *Umbrella Academy*. Furthermore, I would like to analyze the physical manifestation of heterotopias in the body of Vanya in the comic book series and in the Netflix adaptation, respectively. Before discussing the comics and show of *The Umbrella Academy* in a close analysis of the songs, the terminology of the usage of music in film needs to be specified. There are three categories of music that are to be outlined as they are fundamental to the perception of music in the series. First, the distinction between intra- and extra-diegetic music needs to be understood. The discussion of the advantages as well as limits of this theory will give the songs a clearer position in the narrative and the space of the diegesis. Second, the notion of the musical moment as developed by Amy Herzog will serve as a basis to grasp the importance of songs in audio-visual media. This exploration will then lead to the third section, namely Phil Powrie's concept of the crystal-song in order to explain the function of songs in films and other media.

Film music usually describes accompanying music that supports a movie in its narration, character exploration, atmosphere, and the audience's emotional reaction. The same holds true, of course, for music in TV productions. Film music is generally divided into extra-diegetic and intra-diegetic music. The latter is part of the diegesis as the music is played as part of the narrative or as background music on the radio. Intra-diegetic music thus seems to be natural and more mimetic, "We may accept the presence of music in the narrative space of the film, then, partly as a sign of the fictional state of the world created on screen. It is an indicator that the universe in which the events we are watching takes place is not real; and having accepted that, music's presence seems entirely natural [...]" (Winters 229). Extra-diegetic music, on the other hand, is superimposed in the editing process. The characters of the diegesis are usually not aware of the soundtrack and even the audience might only notice it if it is pronounced through songs with lyrics or if the tone of the music is juxtaposed to the content of the scene. Winters explains,

> [...] extra-diegetic might be understood as music or sound whose logic is not dictated by events within the narrative space, and therefore does not seem to be part of the film's *fabula*. This is music that accompanies certain montage sequences, or seems to be deliberately distanced from the here-and-now of the narrative space's everyday world: it may have a self-consciously narrative function or may even be perceived as an expression of the filmind's own emotional reaction [...] [237].

If we follow this logic, intra-diegetic music might create a lesser emotional reaction in the audience and is also less theatrical in its narrative function than extra-diegetic music.

The definitions are thus rather limiting here since intra-diegetic music and especially songs can be as performative as their extra-diegetic counterpart; this can be seen, for example, by means of the song "I Think We're Alone Now" in the first episode of the first season of *The Umbrella Academy*, which will be discussed in detail later in this essay. Likewise, extra-diegetic songs do not necessarily have to have a narrating function only. The dichotomy between extra- and intra-diegetic music thus has to be deconstructed in order to open up the music's position within the audio-visual medium. Winters points out that in order to do so, we need to distinguish between the "narrative space" and the "narrative voice" (225); the film music needs to be understood in spatial terms within the narrative rather than from a purely narrating angle. If music and narrative spaces are combined, music becomes part of the characters' world; hence, "[...] accepting music's location in the same realm as the characters as an instance of film-thinking potentially allows it far greater agency to influence the other aspects of the diegesis; the filmind can suddenly allow the music to be heard by the characters, or imagine it influencing their actions, without requiring it to cross what Robynn Stilwell called the 'fantastical gap' between the non-diegetic and diegetic" (Winters 235). Breaking down the binary oppositions thus means that music can have the same agency as space. In the audio-visual medium, space is visualized through the mise-en-scène. It does not have to be an actual place that influences the character, but it can also be a character's vision.

A scene in *The Umbrella Academy*, which exemplifies this notion of a musical space that is placeless is the dance seen between Luther, or Number One (Tom Hopper), and Allison (Emmy Raver-Lampman), also known as Number Three (Episode 6, "The Day That Wasn't"). The scene depicts the two adopted superhero siblings in a dream-like space of fairy lights and warm colors. That this space is a mere fantasy and expresses the characters' desire to be together is emphasized by their sudden change of clothes and Luther's normal physique. While the story portrays him as ape-shaped due to a failed mission, the dance shows Luther in his human body shape. The visuals thus suggest a mere glimpse into the characters' minds and emotions, which are expressed through the use of music. Therefore, this scene highlights the interdependence on the visual space and the force of music as both define and develop the characters. The music in this scene would be extra-diegetic but the characters still react to it, thus confirming Winters' claim to break up the extra- and intra-diegetic opposition.

Focusing on the individual song rather than music in general, it is also the above-mentioned dance scene, which highlights what Amy Herzog calls a "musical moment." The latter "occurs when music, typically a popular song, inverts the image-sound hierarchy to occupy a dominant position in a filmic work" (Herzog 7). In this scene, the song "Dancing in the Moonlight" by Toploader is used to create a romantic connection between Luther and Allison, which is then underlined by the fantastical setting. The song "disrupt[s] the flow of the narrative" (Herzog 6) as it distracts from the primary narrative, namely the stopping of the approaching apocalypse. The dance routine to the song dominates the scene as it is used for emotional expression and bonding between Luther and Allison, which makes this scene a musical moment. Herzog compares these kinds of moments that are composed of pop songs to classical Hollywood musical productions:

> [...] there is a unique type of musical moment, one that relies on popular music yet is distinct from the compilation score, that is best exemplified by the production numbers in classical Hollywood musicals. The images during these musical interludes are constructed entirely according to the demands of the song. The rhythm of the music prescribes the cinematography and the pacing and timing of edits. The temporal logic of the film shifts, lingering in a suspended present rather than advancing the action directly. Movements within the frame are not oriented toward action but toward visualizing the trajectory of the song; walking becomes dancing, and objects and people become one in a complex compositional choreography. Space, too, is completely reconfigured into a fantastical realm that abandons linear rationality [6–7].

This transportation to the realm of an aestheticized fantasy that follows its own temporal and spatial structure is thus facilitated by the music or rather the song, as can be seen in Luther's and Allison's dance scene.

However, *The Umbrella Academy* is not a musical and thus does not strictly fall into Herzog's category of analysis as she identifies the musical moment not only as music that enables a dance routine but as a song that is sung, often by the characters themselves. Of course, the dance scene is accompanied by a song that contains lyrics, but the characters are not the singers. The scene can still be regarded as a musical moment, but it has to be acknowledged that this moment is not part of a musical. Phil Powrie addresses exactly this issue in his work on contemporary French cinema. He identifies musical moments in movies that are no musicals. Since the term musical moment can mislead to the assumption that a song that meets the criteria of Herzog's definition is automatically part of a musical, Powrie coined the term "crystal-song," describing a "momentous musical moment" in film (Powrie 2). His general definition of crystal-songs is similar to Herzog's musical moment; he explains that a crystal-song "is the moment in a film when the coming together of sound and image transports us, if only momentarily, to a different place, a place of difference, when the music takes flight, and we fly with it, whether that flight is soaring emotion or searing insight, or, more properly for what I call the 'crystal-song,' a combination of the two" (3). However, he clearly sets his concept of the crystal-song apart by outlining that the latter is a mere fragment of a film and not necessarily expected as in a musical:

> It is my contention that the musical moment I wish to define as a crystal-song occurs in films other than the film musicals or the broader category of musical films that Herzog considers. The crystal-song can occur in any film, whether a popular comedy or a "high-brow" art cinema film. Indeed, its difference may well be more apparent if it does not form part of a sequence of musical numbers in a film that could be defined as a film musical, precisely because it functions as a critical fragment rather than as a part of a series closely tied to the narrative [Powrie 11].

While Herzog talks about film musicals and Powrie broadens the theory to adapt it to films, both concepts can also be found in TV shows. Not only do many TV series include musical episodes, making way for Herzog's musical moments, but they can also include crystal-songs that are shaping the narrative of an episode or even the entire series.³

In the case of *The Umbrella Academy*, it is individual episodes that make use of popular songs in order to enhance the importance of a scene and to evoke an emotional reaction in the audience.⁴ By doing so, the song not only transports us "to a different place, a place of difference" (Powrie 3) but it also marks the space of the musical scene as different. In *Umbrella Academy*'s season 2, episode 8, "The Seven Stages," this is emphasized by the song "Pepper" by the American rock band Butthole Surfers. The song stresses the hallucination scene, in which Vanya is drugged by the FBI and finds herself in a fantasy version of her childhood home. Here, space and time are blurred by the notion of imagined memory. The song lyrics substantiate this through verses which play with the notion of self-perception and image. Herzog explains, "Film and recorded music are media marked by their manipulations of time and space, their emotional affect arising from the space between the reproducibility of the material form and the seeming etherealness of the aesthetic experience" (2). The spaces that are occupied by the crystal-songs are thus highly aestheticized ones and they become places of transformation and revelation and thus, they are turned into heterotopias. By means of adding the spatial component, the crystal-songs become part of, what I would like to call, a "crystal moment." The latter combines Herzog's musical moment and Powrie's crystal-song, but it encompasses the entire mise-en-scène. This means that the combination of the visual presentation, the audio component, as well as the diegetic space that draws attention to itself through the music elevates a scene to an artistic, theatrical expression in its self-reflexive performativity.

This self-reflexivity of the crystal moments can be best described by Foucault's heterotopia as heterotopic spaces are in themselves theatrical in the sense that they subvert norms. Foucault outlines that

> There are also, probably in every culture, in every civilization, real places—places that do exist and that are formed in the very founding of society—which are something like counter-sites, a kind of effectively enacted utopia in which the real sites, all the other real sites that can be found within the culture, are simultaneously represented, contested, and inverted. Places of this kind are outside of all places, even though it may be possible to indicate their location in reality. Because these places are absolutely different from all the sites that they reflect and speak about, I shall call them, by way of contrast to utopias, heterotopias [24].

However, heterotopias do not necessarily have to be geographical spaces or rather places as such, which is congruent to Foucault's claim that heterotopic spaces are not publicly accessible but are exclusive. Heterotopias can also be seen on a more abstract level. Thus, mirrors would be an example of a heterotopic space. In a mirror we see ourselves; yet, what we see is just a reflection and not our real self. It is a picture of us captured in the frame of the mirror. The mirror image cannot be grasped because it only represents the real without ever being the real space. In a similar way, crystal-songs are also mirror images of the real. In season 1, episode 6, Allison's and Luther's dance scene thus depicts their real feelings for each other while simultaneously portraying an imagined heterotopic space in which reality is defied. Hence, crystal-songs reflect on the characters, the presented situation, and the space of a scene, thus making the song an integral part of the narrative space, as Winters suggests (230). In that way, the crystal moment is the musical embodiment of Foucault's heterotopia.

In *The Umbrella Academy*, the merging of space, characters, and songs is even taken a step further as here, the music not only defines the characters but their body. Again, the romantic dance routine Luther and Allison perform serves as an example of the body's importance as well as performativity since Luther's huge ape-like body is reduced to a normal physical shape. The focus thus lies on the transformation of the body in this heterotopic space of Luther's and Allison's shared imagination. Another example of a crystal moment, in which bonding is demonstrated through the physical activity of dancing is presented in season 1, episode 1, "We Only See Each Other at Weddings and Funerals." Here, the siblings are shown a couple of scenes after a discussion about the circumstances of their adoptive father Reginald Hargreeves' death, in which Luther implicitly accuses his siblings that one of them has murdered their father. Everyone is shown reminiscing in different parts of the house, highlighting the characters' loneliness through piano music. They are separated in the space that should unite them, namely their childhood home. In order to unify them in their separation, Luther harnesses pop music to create a heterotopic space of emotional connectivity. Through the change from extra-diegetic to intra-diegetic music and through the act of dancing to the pop song by Tiffany, "I Think We're Alone Now," the siblings use the space of the house as a stage to perform to the song. The utilization of the heterotopic space in this song is striking as the siblings are spatially separated but united through the act of dancing. Luther and Allison are in their adjacent bedrooms, Klaus a.k.a. Number Four (Robert Sheehan) is in the basement kitchen, Diego a.k.a. Number Two (David Castañeda) in the living room, which he intentionally closes off, and Vanya a.k.a. Number Seven (Elliot Page) is situated in the hallway. The latter space is particularly interesting in so far as it portrays a transitional space—it is not a room but also not outside. This positioning shows Vanya's role in her family—she is both part of it and is yet excluded. The scene zooms out from Vanya into a cross section of the house, enabling every character to be seen for the viewer. Vanya is in the center of this shot, foreshadowing that she is the center of the plot, the person the apocalypse revolves around. In this scene, all the siblings are shown as equal, making Vanya part of the family and showing the non-heroic human side of the Academy. While the song suggests that the siblings "are alone now," it ironically makes them less alone and allows them to share a moment of togetherness. The music does not only bring the siblings closer together emotionally but also physically as the song is cut abruptly upon the dramatic arrival of Five (Aidan Gallagher), who appears not only from a space in the sky but also from another time, uniting all the (living) siblings in the space of their childhood home and in the present.[5]

That music is a force of unison is, then, also carried on to the second season. In episode 5, "Valhalla," Klaus, Allison, and Vanya kill time in the beauty parlor Allison works in. Since the second season plays mostly in the 1960s, the three are already out of place here by their mere existence since they do not belong in this time but are from 2019. Vanya can neither remember herself nor her family, which makes this scene all the more important in terms of acknowledging that a broken family can be mended. While Klaus points out the dysfunctionality of the family, Vanya embraces the family—quite literally—in a group hug with Klaus and Allison. The song "Twisting the Night Away" performed by Sam Cooke is played as intra-diegetic music on the radio and the three siblings dance together. This scene can be regarded as a development to the "I Think We're Alone Now" scene from season 1 as here, three of the siblings are not spatially separated anymore but actively bond through dancing.

The uniting space music creates is already touched upon at the very beginning of the series when the siblings are introduced. Even though they are not yet physically united, the music establishes a link between the siblings as the intradiegetic music also serves as an extradiegetic accompaniment, which is shown in the addition of instruments throughout the song. Vanya is performing a violin medley of Andrew Lloyd Webber's *The Phantom of the Opera* interpreted by Lindsey Stirling in front of empty theater rows. The only audience is the extradiegetic viewer, who gets to know the characters of the show through the musical presentation. The musical parts are not only linked to the characters but also their spaces. We are first introduced to Luther through Lindsey Stirling's eerie and slow interpretation of the song "The Phantom of the Opera." This eeriness is reflected by the heterotopic space Luther finds himself in, namely the moon. Not only is the moon remote from society and any form of civilization but it is also unreal in its unsuitability for human life. Luther is shown as a figure that longs for living—he tenderly cares for a small plant in his trailer—but who does not have any experience of life; he literally and metaphorically lives on the moon. The song cuts to a fast rock version of "Phantom of the Opera," showing Diego in a family home. Yet, this space, which should be a place of peace and safety is depicted as a space of violence, which is substantiated by the music style. Luther and Diego are thus framed by the same song but in different styles. While Luther is the phantom on the moon, watching out for phantom threats, Diego is the phantom in the family home. He is shown as a vigilante, who saves a family that is taken hostage in their own home. We see Diego appearing out of nowhere, wearing a mask and fighting the intruders. He presents himself as a phantom, a mysterious hero.

Likewise, Allison is also framed by this song on the red carpet where she is the center of attention of photographers and journalists. She is the phantom in that she is a movie star that seems out of reach and that is only known through the public persona created around her. The red carpet can also be regarded as a heterotopic space as it is temporary, transitory, and not openly accessible to everyone. The latter also holds true for the moon, of course. The cameras focusing on Allison connect the scene to

Vanya. While everyone is looking at Allison presenting herself on the stage of the red carpet, Vanya is not noticed despite her extraordinary performance since there is no audience. Yet, through the song, Vanya is indirectly in control of what the extradiegetic audience sees. She is the actual phantom behind it all.

When the song moves on to the next part, the camera jumps to Klaus. The music settles down and becomes calm again shifting to Lloyd Webber's "Angel of Music." This choice seems fitting as Klaus' ability is to conjure the dead. He is shown in a rehab center—a heterotopia of deviation, an institution sheltering people outside the norm. The music hints at the proximity to death of the institution's inhabitants and Klaus' aspiration to be constantly high to be calm. The song itself, even though presented without lyrics here, talks about the dream and hope of an angel who would come and comfort the singer as a father figure. It is exactly this what Klaus wishes for, but his angel of music is materialized in drugs, which numb him and his fears. The connection to the missing father is then taken further as the scene cuts back to Luther who is watching the sunrise and who learns about his father's death. Even though we do not know what has happened, yet, we see Luther reading and reacting to the message. "Angel of Music" therefore portrays loss—the loss of hope for a caring father and the death of the actual father, Reginald Hargreeves. The music changes to "Think of Me" and the camera jumps back to Diego, who sees his father's death on TV in the home of strangers. Allison receives the news on the red carpet and is framed by the same song. Through its connection to Hargreeves' death, this song serves as a reminder to remember the father and to reconnect with the latter. Klaus is, however, not ready to do this, yet, which is why he is shown buying drugs in the fragment of the song.

The music shifts to a rock-style again and "Music of the Night" and, more precisely, to "abandon your defenses" (even though the lyrics are never sung). Klaus' abandoning of defenses is shown in his drug consumption and his proximity to death. This part shows Klaus in an ambulance where he is reanimated and brought from the eternal night of death back to life. It is also in this location, again a transitory space, in which he learns about his father's death. The medley ends with "Music of the Night" and Vanya playing the violin on stage; however, the last note is missing. Vanya is shown on stage framed by a spotlight on the theater stage she is standing on. The song is calmed down by reducing the instruments to the sound of the violin. This very glimpse of Vanya foreshadows that she is supposed to be the center of attention and that she is framing the narrative. However, she is not granted attention just yet, which is accentuated by the abrupt end of the song. The latter remains incomplete—just as she is incomplete without her powers—and the switching off of the spotlight highlights her role in the family. Nevertheless, the song starts and ends with her—she frames not only this introductory scene by her musical performance but also the entire show revolves around her music. Not only does she discover her repressed powers through music, but at the end of the first season, Vanya is also shown on stage again, performing the "Apocalypse Suite." However, instead of being in the spotlight here, she is the spotlight as she turns into the white violin, radiating light from her body. This destructive energy, which streams out of her body and is aestheticized by her performance at the concert emphasizes the performative violence of the entire show.

The performativity of violence is primarily shown through the use of rather upbeat songs and hyper-violent encounters. The violence depicted is thus not only aestheticized in an entertaining way but through its theatricality it gains a self-reflexive quality that draws attention to the fictionality of the respective scene of violence. Interestingly enough, the songs chosen for these representations of hyperviolence often revolve around movement and space. When taking the origin of the word "violence" into account as being an active and moving force, the merging of violence with movement and space makes sense:

> Etymologically the word "violence" has many connotations aside from our usual associations of force and destruction. It stems from the Latin *vis*, meaning force and strength, as well as vigor, vitality [...]. It is also connected to *vim*, meaning energy. [...] The Latin *violentia* connotes vehemence and impetuosity, as well as the more familiar sense of violation, a physical force inflicting injury upon or damage to persons or property [Schenk 129].

In the first episode of the show, the members of the Umbrella Academy are shown as vigorous and energetic children in the act of stopping a bank robbery. The song that accompanies this scene is called "The Walker" by Fitz and The Tantrums. Hence, the confined space of the bank is juxtaposed with movement here through the song. Simultaneously, the siblings are shown moving in and stopping the movement of the bank robbers. Especially Five and Ben stand out here as Five jumps between spaces and Ben's movement is just vaguely shown in a side room, in which he unleashes his power, culminating in the bloody deaths of the criminals. The justification of such violence used by children is thus not questioned but celebrated, which the subsequent scene in front of the press highlights. Violence is thus trivialized in the diegesis, which the use of the indie pop song highlights.

This trivialization comes full circle in episode 10, "The White Violin," the last episode of season 1. After Vanya has destroyed the childhood home because of its spatial embodiment of the Umbrella Academy she was never part of—which is depicted in the first episode and the bank robbery scene when she asks her father why she cannot partake in the mission and Reginald Hargreeves points out that she is not special—the siblings reconvene at the bowling alley to discuss how to stop Vanya from causing the apocalypse. Their meeting is disturbed by a group of masked assassins, who were sent by Five's former employer, the Commission, in order to enable the apocalypse. The encounter starts with a mere beat but during the fight a disco lightshow and disco music are accidentally turned on. This intra-diegetic music is then used again to juxtapose the hyperviolence with the pop song "Saturday Night" by the Bay City Rollers. This place of innocent Saturday night entertainment where kids celebrate birthdays is transformed into a space of hyperviolence. This is not to say though that this violence is not entertaining in a perverse way. The music and the lighting effects are in sync with the shooting and add an unreal and performative quality to the scene, consequently turning the bowling alley into a heterotopia. Moreover, the lyrics of the song display the entertainment of dancing and thus, just like in the bank robbery scene, movement. The addition of the song and its emphasis on moving one's body for entertainment therefore exposes violence in the show as a physical performative expression. This performance, then, can be seen as a space of its own and thus seen as a heterotopic space of illusion, a theatrical heterotopic space. The necessity to move and more precisely to move forward is finally made clear by the siblings running for their lives and toward Vanya.

Movement is also shown through the movement of time and thus change, which is emphasized further in the shooting at the diner and doughnut shop, Griddy's Doughnuts, in episode 1 of season 1. In this scene, adult Five (who is trapped in the body of his thirteen-year-old self) reminisces about the change of the diner over time and how he and his siblings used to enjoy themselves in this place. His nostalgia is interrupted by the aforementioned hitmen his former employer sent to terminate him. Through the violent invasion of the doughnut shop, the space is made uncanny in the sense that something familiar is made unfamiliar. While the presentation of the diner of the past can be classified as a utopian memory, the invasion completes its decline into a dystopian space. The indie song "Istanbul (not Constantinople)"—the 1990s We Might Be Giants cover of the original Four Lads version—not only stresses the hyperviolence of this scene by juxtaposing it with its light musical style, but it also highlights the significance of change. The lyrics reflect on the name change of Constantinople to Istanbul without having an explanation for it. This can be read as quasi-allegorical to the change of the diner and as a metaphor of time. Of course, the emphasis on time comes as no surprise in this scene since Five dominates the latter and his superpower is not only to teleport between and through spaces but also time. In fact, the assassins are part of the time police who try to keep timelines stable and thus unchanged. However, as the song and the death of the gunmen at Five's hand substantiate, time and change go hand in hand. This is again picked up in season 2, episode 9, "743," where Five tries to kill his younger self in an older body. The absurdness of time and space is highlighted in their jumps across the lawn and parking lot and the song "Dancing with Myself" by Generation X. First of all, the song fits perfectly as it describes the fight between both Five versions as a dance, marking the scene as a crystal moment. Second, the continuity of time is highlighted by the band's name, namely Generation X—the generation of people born between 1965 and 1980. Five was born in 1989 but due to his time travelling ability, he is older. The episode plays in 1963, however, and thus the time that was dominated by the baby boomers. All generations are thus present in the scene, which shows how relative time is. Therefore, the interdependency of time and change is portrayed by incorporating a song from 1981 in the scene, turning it into a crystal moment.

Again, the underlying meaning of change through time is taken up toward the end of season 1. In episode 8, "I Heard a Rumor," Cha-Cha who, together with Hazel, is sent by the temps, i.e., the time control unit, to ensure the apocalypse, burns down Griddy's Doughnuts. Her motive for doing so is Hazel's decision to quit his job and start a new life with doughnut baker and waitress Agnes. Cha-Cha's reluctance to this change is musicalized in the song "Stay with Me" by Mary J. Blige. She does not want to let go of her working partnership with Hazel and reacts with jealousy and acts of vengeance. Until the very end of the first season, she tries to correct the timeline and turn back time in the sense that she longs for the partnership with Hazel to go back to where it was. While Five is about active movement and the constant attempt to change time, which is substantiated in his powers and the "Istanbul" song in episode 1, Cha-Cha is presented as the paradox of an active and yet stagnating character, who is not able to adapt to change or to change herself.

Cha-Cha's stagnation is a gradual process, though over the course of the episode and is only completed in her fight against Hazel, in which the song "Sunshine, Lollipops and Rainbows" by Lesley Gore juxtaposes the violence she uses, on the one hand, and manifests her emotional connection to Hazel, on the other hand. The scene takes place in a motel room, which is, according to Foucault's space types, a crisis heterotopia, in which activities of personal development take place but remain hidden from the public eye. Cha-Cha's as well as Hazel's development from rational killers without any personal attachments to emotional human beings (even though still killers) with wants, needs, and hopes thus finds its climax in this transformative heterotopic space of the motel room. The title of the episode, "Changes," further underlines Hazel's and Cha-Cha's development. The emotional development is, then, substantiated in the crystal moment, in which their feelings are expressed. Both characters long for love and happiness. However, while Cha-Cha finds this in Hazel and her job, Hazel has found it with Agnes and the hope for a simpler life in the here and now. Since their dreams are not compatible, the space of the motel also turns into a crisis heterotopia by portraying this actual crisis, the confrontation with each other and their changed personalities. It comes as no surprise that their confrontation is played out in a violent physical fight, which takes on the form of a performance as Agnes watches them, tied up and at the risk of falling into the jacuzzi behind her and to her death at any moment. The theatrical quality of the scene itself is thus dominated by physical movement, but it takes on a self-reflexive feature when the scene is suddenly disrupted by being turned into a heterotopia of time, i.e., a heterochrony, a break in time, a space that is inside and outside of time. The scene literally freezes except for Hazel and Cha-Cha, who are amazed by Agnes being frozen in mid-air while she is falling into the pool. Time is put on halt by their boss, the Handler, who ends their fight in order to make them focus on their mission again to ensure the apocalypse. This play with movement is picked up in season 2 in the song "Everybody" by the Backstreet Boys (episode 7, "Öga for Öga"). Here, the lyrics in the chorus are linked to violence in the depiction of Allison fighting the Swedes, who have come to eliminate her. The fight takes place in her new home, where she lives with her husband Raymond Chestnut. The violent invasion of the home space is highlighted through the use of music, turning the scene into a crystal moment of violence.

The pattern of movement and pause yet strikingly dominates the characters of Hazel and Cha-Cha throughout season 1. On the one hand, they are trying to put a stop to the continuation of time by pushing the apocalypse; on the other hand, they are described as moving from one job to the next. Their movement is further expressed in their use of physical violence, which is often displayed in elaborately choreographed fight scenes with distinct songs emphasizing their actions. Two scenes stand out as crystal moments here, showing violence in heterotopic spaces and aestheticizing the latter into performances through the use of song. The first crystal moment can be seen in episode 2, "Run Boy Run," in which Hazel and Cha-Cha chase down Five at a department store, where the latter is meeting his girlfriend, the inanimate mannequin Dolores. The Queen song "Don't Stop Me Now" accompanies this scene and transforms it into a moment of performative hyperviolence. Not only does the song suggest movement but it suggests action. This action is visualized in a shootout in the confined space of the department store, in which escape is nearly impossible and Five is trapped. While he can jump through space and time, in this scene he is stopped and not able to transport himself out of the store. Hazel and Cha-Cha are finally interrupted in their mission of assassinating Five by the arrival of the police, even though they can get away before being arrested. While neither Hazel and Cha-Cha nor Five want to be stopped in this moment as the song suggests, ironically, they all are held back. Here, the binary oppositions between freedom of movement and confinement are mirrored in violence and fun (as represented in the song).

This narrative device of crystal moments that create a space of conflict is taken up repeatedly, be it in season 2, episode 4, "The Majestic 12," where Five, Diego and Lila, the daughter of the Handler, fight the Swedes, three brothers, who were ordered to kill Diego, to the Kiss song "I Was Made for Lovin' You," adding an ironic tone to the scene, or the scene in which Hazel and Cha-Cha are on drugs and burn the laboratory down, in which Five tried to find clues about the apocalypse (season 1, episode 4, "Man on the Moon"). The same holds true for Cha-Cha's and Hazel's invasion of the Umbrella Academy home in season 1, episode 3, "Extra Ordinary." This scene is interesting in so far as two songs define the crystal moment here. First, Klaus listens to the song "We're Through" by the Hollies. This intra-diegetic music is then turned into the extra-diegetic soundtrack of the home invasion. The song emphasizes that the speaker was torn apart by another person and is now better off without the person. This song adds various layers to the scene. Since Klaus is listening to the song, it might be argued that Klaus is through with his siblings and better off without them, even though it turns out later, after he is abducted by Hazel, that he very much needs help. However, since Hazel and Cha-Cha are the focus of the scene as they are looking for Five, it is more plausible to read the song in connection to them. Therefore, the song can be seen as a foreshadowing of the future relation between the two assassins as it suggests that the two will be torn apart by this mission and they thus would be better off without it. The music shifts then to Nina Simone's jazz song "Sinnerman" when Vanya is attacked and the fight between the killer duo against Luther, Diego, and Allison starts. The song comments again on movement and stasis as the lyrics describe the sinnerman running to a rock to hide. The "sinnerman" then implicitly mirrors the violent action in the scene making all the participants in the fight sinners as all of them engage in physical violence. The choreographed melee fighting then adds a performative aspect to the scene as the violence is aestheticized on a meta-level. It is reminiscent to the dance scenes in the show as this fight also creates a certain intimacy between the siblings; they have to work together, and they discover Luther's true body shape as the chandelier crashes on him. The bond between them is undermined, however, when the music turns out to be intra-diegetic and is only heard by Klaus, who does not partake in the fight nor notice the latter. The scene thus plays with the notion of crystal moments as relationships are foreshadowed, formed, and broken. This is then shown by Luther running away from Diego, Allison, and Vanya, the temporary separation of Hazel and Cha-Cha, and the abduction of Klaus without his siblings noticing.

What was only hinted at indirectly so far is that since the show (and the comic book series) is about seven siblings who used to be child superheroes, physicality is shown, on the one hand, through the extraordinary powers that are linked to the characters' bodies and, on the other hand, through the use of physical violence. Indeed, the characters are often shown in a crystal moment when they discover parts of themselves that are either linked to their physical abilities or their desire to be without these abilities. The line that is then established between physicality and music is often (even though not always) leaning toward violent encounters between the inner self of a character and the physical superpowered self, reminiscent of the scenes in which Hazel and Cha-Cha are depicted using hyperviolence. It is therefore not only the identification of crystal moments in *The Umbrella Academy* which is of interest here but also their connection to and presentation of physical violence in the show and the comics. Music is, then, turned into crystal moments of self-destruction and/or self-discovery. This is especially apparent in the characters of Number Four, i.e., Klaus, and Number Five.

The song by Woodkid "Run Boy Run" in the eponymous episode (season 1, episode 2) plays with the notion of forward movement to the future and the danger of stopping. In the scene that is defined by the song, Five tries to prove his father wrong and instead of merely jumping between spaces, he attempts to jump forward in time. Indeed, he succeeds but is unable to return due to the limitation of his powers. He finds himself in the apocalypse amidst the ruins of his home and his siblings' dead bodies. While the scene is not violent in the actions portrayed, the aftermath of hyperviolence is still visualized in the end of all movement. For Five, the song and the movement of the scene presents a crystal moment as it leads to self-discovery. Even though there is no choreographed action, it is still performative in that Five wants to showcase his abilities and in that he becomes the sole witness to and audience of the apocalypse. He realizes that he should have listened to his father and that he was not ready for time travel, yet. This combination of a heterotopic space—the apocalypse is after all a nowhere space since all places are destroyed—and performance on an intra-diegetic story level and on the extra-diegetic musical level that dictates the character's narrative, thus determines a crystal moment for Five. Moreover, it is striking that it is his ability that creates a heterochrony and heterotopia at the same time. Since Five defies time and space through his superpowers, his body, from which his powers originate, shown in the use of his fists to create portals, becomes a heterotopia, too. Through the physicality of his powers and the song, which even tells him to "run," Five transforms his body into a crystal space, a heterotopic space that is accompanied and defined through the narrative of music.

Similarly, Klaus experiences self-discovery through the use of extra-diegetic music and crystal moments. In season 1, episode 6, "The Day That Wasn't," he, too, travels through time but not due to his abilities but by means of a time machine briefcase. He finds himself among US soldiers in the Vietnam War, surrounded by bombs and despair. Yet, his self-discovery, while violent in its spatial setting, has a more positive note to it than Five's. Klaus experiences true romantic love for the first time in his life when he dances with Dave in a bar. Similar to Allison's and Luther's dance scene, the bar is shot in a warm-colored lighting and addresses the emotional bond Klaus and Dave form here while the song "Soul Kitchen" by The Doors is playing. The title of the song is, of course, ambiguous as souls are lost in the fire of the war surrounding them but the bar presents a space where the soul can indulge in physical and emotional pleasures. Yet, the song foreshadows that Klaus cannot stay here as it is time to go, move on, and forget. Klaus finds himself in a static time capsule that is ironically surrounded by physical action and movement; however, he cannot remain in this paused space that is outside his reality and time forever. When Dave is killed in action, Klaus returns only to find himself unable to move on and let go of Dave. His crystal moment of the soul kitchen, in which he discovered his emotional side, is then turned into self-destruction as he starts taking drugs again. Interestingly enough, it is not the discovery of his hidden powers that is accompanied by a crystal song but only his emotional journey, making him discover love in a world that is dominated by violence.

The search for love can also be seen in Leonard Peabody's story line, a.k.a. Harold Jenkins, which is established in episode 7, "The Day That Was." Harold's childhood is, similarly to the Umbrella Academy, defined by violence. However, instead of using violence to do good and save people, Harold experiences domestic violence. His childhood is filled with dreams of superpowers that are then shattered by another father figure, Reginald Hargreeves. Since Harold constantly experiences rejection and abuse, he turns to exactly those means to free himself when he kills his father. The montage is accompanied by Three Dog Night's song "One." While this is not a crystal moment on the diegetic level, the song turns the sequence into a crystal moment for the audience as the montage creates a meta-diegetic space that connects the sequence. It is thus a heterotopia of time due to the summary thereof and of space due to the merging of different spaces and places into one sequence. Again, this heterotopic space is, then, linked to the violent content of child abuse and patricide. This poses an interesting parallel to the Umbrella Academy as Luther accuses his siblings of the murder of their father, which turns out to be a suicide. Hence, while the siblings also suffer from their father's treatment and are confined to their superpowered bodies and abilities without escaping the violence that comes with them, Harold Jenkins is spatially imprisoned (by literally being sent to prison) due to the use of violence against his father. Even though he does not possess powers, he still uses his body for destruction.

His character is mirrored by Vanya's as she, too, seems to be merely ordinary. Of course, this powerlessness is nothing but an illusion; her uncontrollable powers were stopped by her father by means of sedative medication as he feared her violent behavior.[6] While she appears to be a harmless, innocent, and powerless character just like Harold Jenkins, she turns out to be a destructive force, though. While she does not have a crystal moment in terms of a popular song that accompanies her development or her violence—except for a very brief glimpse of the song "Barracuda" by Heart after Vanya has discovered her full potential and destroyed the home of the academy (episode 10, "The White Violin")—it is classical violin music which determines her character throughout the series. Not only does she discover her powers through music and sound waves, she also learns to control them. Like Harold Jenkins, she uses violence to take revenge on the Umbrella Academy as well as Harold, whom she knows as Leonard. Leonard's and her siblings' betrayal as well as the latter's lack of empathy and trust causes her emotional breakdown as it appears to her like the end of the world. Therefore, she takes this metaphorical emotion to literal action by ending the world. While the other characters are narrated through heterotopic spaces, Vanya defines space by destroying it and by creating a new form of heterotopia through her body. On the stage of the Palladium Theater where she started at the beginning of the show, she not only dominates the performance of the concert since she is first chair now, but she ends up on stage alone playing the "Apocalypse Suite" (composed by Jeff Russo) and thus causing the notion of space and time to collapse altogether by unleashing the destruction of everything. Her violin performance slowly transforms her body into the white violin showing the intricate relationship between music and physicality in the series. Her crystal moment is thus the performance of the destruction of the world, combining once again space and theatricality with violence. However, this time, all of it is personified in Vanya's body, which is turned into a site of music and violence.

This spatial embodiment of music and destruction is visualized in more detail in the first volume of the comic book series. Here, music dominates through a silent representation of it. While the Netflix show can, of course, make use of the auditory aspects of the medium, the comic is restricted to visuality and words.[7] Nevertheless, it is not surprising that the comics make music the focal point since, on the one hand, "Comics have had a long-standing relationship with music. Popular song lyrics have routinely cited superheroes" (Summers 122) and, on the other hand, because writer Gerard Way is a musician himself. While the Netflix show pays homage to the writer of the comics and thus emphasizing the meta-theatrical aspect of the music in the show by including the song "So Happy Together" in episode 5 ("Number Five"),[8] which he performs with Ray Toro, the comic book uses visual means to present crystal moments. The musical notations that appear in the first volume *The Umbrella Academy: Apocalypse Suite* add a layer of filmic quality to the images, as Brown points out by referring to the inclusion of a visualization of music in comics in general:

> The addition of musical elements in each of the examples represents a significant intervention into comics' traditional dichotomy of word and image. While each borrows from the language of music, breaking notation down into elements that combine more readily with word and image on the page, the examples each maintain the otherness of music, via the use of separative strategies such as the occupation of the margin and the use of depth. This separation has a marked effect on the sequencing of the comics via both the rhythm and timings inherent to notation and the continuity between the music and the panels and between the musical sections themselves over multiple pages. The result in each is an encompassing and pervasive depiction of music, loosely comparable to a film's soundtrack [1].

Not only do the musical notations in the comic reveal hidden messages in words such as "bye" or "hit," hinging Vanya'a violin play on violence (chapter 6), but the musical visuals are closely linked to the bodily representation of Vanya as her body is literally transformed into a white violin by the conductor of the Orchestra Verdammten (chapter 4).

The play with the words "violin" and "violence" becomes thus even more striking in the comics. While both words have a different origin, they share not only visual similarities but also auditory ones. While the connection is not often made due to the different word stems, Schenk hints at a link by referring to Greek philosopher Heraclitus:

> Heraclitus wrote, "The name of the bow (*biós*) is life (*bíos*), but its work is death" (Wheelwright 2964, 91), indicating the intertwining aspects of life and death. The paradox is addressed in a different way in another of Heraclitus' statements, "People do not understand how that which is at variance with itself agrees with itself. There is a harmony in the bending back, as in the case of the bow and the lyre" [...]. "Bending back" brings music and hitting the mark, life and death, together in harmony. At its etymological roots, violence is associated with the intermingling of life and death [129].

This connection between music and violence is thus materialized in the instrument of the lyre and its bow or, in this case, the bow and the violin, connecting life and death in an aesthetic way. This aestheticization is then taken a step further by turning Vanya's body into a violin, making it the ultimate heterotopic space of life and death. The white color of the violin, then, epitomizes her force as it is shown to be able to create a void in time and space and its full potential is unknown. Her body becomes a non-space or rather a space beyond time and space, as Leonard puts it in the show describing Vanya's discovery of her power as an "out-of-body experience" (episode 5, "Number Five").

In both the first volume of the comic book series and the Netflix series, bodies thus dominate as a spatial force of violence and music. They are portrayed in a performative way, adding a meta-theatrical and thus self-reflexive quality to the show and the comics. The use of crystal songs adds to the performativity of the show by highlighting and aestheticizing violence, on the one hand, and by showcasing the characters' identity formation through the creation of relationships in crystal moments, on the other hand. Hence, while the comics become theatrical in their use of intermediality between music, images, and text, making the comics heterotopic on a meta-diegetic level, Netflix's *The Umbrella Academy* uses crystal moments to show intermedial heterotopias of theatricality. These heterotopias are then presented in the characters' bodies, which are ultimately turned into sites of music and violence.

## Notes

1. Season 2 is only marginally considered here. The main focus of the analysis is on season 1.
2. The siblings have designated numbers from 1 to 7 since their adoptive father Reginald Hargreeves attributed numbers to them instead of names. They received their names by their robot nanny Grace, whom the siblings acknowledge as their mother. Alongside their numbers and names, the comic book series also introduces a third category, namely their superhero names.
3. An example for a crystal-song that dominates an entire series even though it does not occur in every single episode would be the song "Toss a Coin to Your Witcher" from the Netflix show *The Witcher* (2019).
4. Powrie elaborates on the emotional reaction by distinguishing between minor and major crystal-songs: "The minor crystal-song corresponds to a greater intensity of perception than reaction, and conversely the major crystal-song corresponds to a greater intensity of reaction than perception; but both modes are present in any experience of a crystal-song. We perceive and react to any musical piece in a film, but some may leave us cold, while others may lead to an extreme physiological reaction" (12).
5. It is interesting that they all meet in the yard since this is also the location of Ben's, a.k.a. Number Six's (Justin H. Min), memorial statue. Thus, all the siblings are in fact united once more in this outside space of their childhood home. Since the dead can be part of the present and since time travel is possible, time and space constantly overlap and collapse in the show.
6. Her use of violence becomes apparent from an early age on as she kills and hurts one nanny after the other since she does not want to eat her porridge. This montage scene is accompanied by the light French music of the song "Lundi Matin-Comptine" by La Superstar des Comptines Rondes et Berceuses, lending the scene a humorous and yet uncanny quality.
7. Summers explains that the inclusion of "song problematizes notions of diegetic space

and its relationship with narrating music by capitalizing upon one of the differences between film and comics: the lack of audio. The ambiguity, however, is not restrictive, but rather liberatory, as meanings and interpretations are opened for the reader's own imaginative play" (138).

8. In the scene this song is used to show a moment of joy, which is immediately juxtaposed with violence. While the male siblings unite against Hazel and Cha-Cha by handing them a fake time briefcase, they get the escape from Hazel's and Cha-Cha's violence in under the wire. Moreover, Vanya is shown hooking up with Leonard while the camera then slowly moves to the latter's attic to reveal the corpse of Helen, the first chair in Vanya's orchestra and her professional rival. Again, the song presents a heterotopia by creating a surreal space of happiness, which is undermined by the violence shown to the audience, making the song an ironic meta-statement.

## Works Cited

Brown, Kieron. "Musical Sequences in Comics." *The Comics Grid: Journal of Comics Scholarship*, vol. 3, no. 1, 2013, pp. 1–6.

Foucault, Michel, and Jay Miskowiec. "Of Other Spaces." *Diacritics*, vol. 16, no. 1, 1986, pp. 22–27.

Herzog, Amy. *Dreams of Difference, Songs of the Same: The Musical Moment in Film*. University of Minnesota Press, 2010.

Powrie, Phil. *Music in Contemporary French Cinema. The Crystal-Song*. Cham, Pelgrave Macmillan, 2017.

Schenk, Roland. *The Appearance of Death in Everyday Life*. State University Press of New York, 2001.

Summers, Tim. "'Sparks of Meaning': Comics, Music, and Alan Moore." *Journal of the Royal Music Association*, vol. 140, no. 1, 2015, pp. 121–162.

*The Umbrella Academy*, created by Steve Blackman and Jeremy Slater, Netflix, 2019–2020.

Way, Gerard, and Gabriel Bá. *The Umbrella Academy: Apocalypse Suite*. Dark Horse Comics, 2008.

Winters, Ben. "The Non-Diegetic Fallacy: Film, Music, and Narrative Space." *Music and Letters*, vol. 91, no. 2, 2010, pp. 224–244.

# Dissonance
## Striking a Chord Through the Silencing of Women's Voices

### J.E. Hornsby

Netflix released Gerard Way's and Gabriel Bà's *The Umbrella Academy* in spring of 2019 after ordering the series in 2017. The show is based on the comic books, first published in 2008. Starting with the terrifying and violently non-consensual births of superchildren, the show explores the dysfunctional relationship of seven supernatural brothers and sisters. The siblings do not necessarily exhibit superpowers that are new to viewers and fans of the superhero genre—time travel, strength, mystical arts, to name a few. However, each of the siblings' bodies are further altered visually in direct correlation to or in contrast with their superpowers. Because of the visualization of characteristics, it seems obvious that each superhero is marginalized from outside and within their group due to their distinctions. Questions concerning age, sexuality, race, gender, cyborgs, and animal-hybridity play out on screen making the viewer wonder what defines humanity with consequences for how to unite around difference.

The first scene of the first episode written by Jeremy Slater, "We Only See Each Other at Weddings and Funerals," begins at a Russian swimming pool where a young woman flirts with a young man. The innocent and youthful romance plays out in a flirtatious pantomime; he gets up and then sits next to her on a bench by the pool; the young man tries to kiss the young woman and she rebuffs him; after a few moments pass, she quickly kisses his cheek and jumps in the pool. The opening sequence to the show starts without much distinction. Young love is a trope that audiences are all too familiar with. However, innocence turns to violence when the camera shows blood emerge in the pool, at the location of the young submerged woman, only for her to surface in the bloody pool, nine months pregnant, and in pain of labor—a physical state she had not been in before jumping into the pool. The women at the pool help her out of the water, surround her, and help to deliver the baby. The violent opening scene begins with a non-consensual pregnancy and labor forced on a young woman who is aided and helped by the other women nearby. The birth destroys all innocence in a visually violent and non-consensual action leaving the viewer to wonder how this could happen, who did this to her, and what is going on. Although the scene is surprising because it defies the natural order, the audience learns that this is not the only birth to take place, that other women from around the world also found themselves instantly pregnant and spontaneously in labor. This scene is fantastical in the sense that it could never happen but quite realistic in another. The visual image of the female body suffering the consequences of a non-consensual act, and then multiple women coming to her aid is a metaphor for the emotional and physical labor[1] women do.

The shocking opening scene of *The Umbrella Academy* is a world-establishing scene that lets the spectator know the superheroes are born from the strange, the weird, and the non-consensual violent act of forced pregnancy. This essay focuses on the two sisters in the Netflix show and how their superpowers are constructed through questions of vocalization or dissonance—or a disagreement over the truth—which echo visually, in a timely manner, the #MeToo movement that went viral on social media in 2017. One sister, Number 3/Rumor/Allison[2] (Emmy Raver-Lampman), who is a Black woman in the show, can control people by saying "I heard a rumor...," which causes people to believe what she said. The other sister, Number 7/Vanya/The White Violin[3] (Elliot Page), who is a white woman, can control sounds and vibrations around and within her and project them into the world with great force and violence.

Both Allison's and Vanya's powers rely on sound, specifically dissonance, in order to control the world. This essay is about the optics of dissonance; specifically, but not exclusively, this essay addresses the visual motif of dissonance in the Netflix series *The Umbrella Academy* drawing on cultural practices embedded in gendered and racial relationships among women. Through an examination and analysis of the visual violence, neglect, and suppression that both sisters encounter and commit, this essay will discuss how "voices" represent that which is feared most by a patriarchal society: power. A close reading of the gendered oppression through systemic silencing of their voices will show how the series examines, challenges, and potentially echoes visual stereotypes of women as untrustworthy gossips or women to be silenced out of fear. While the show uses the dysfunctional family trope to explain each of the superheroes' inability to solve their life problems or to work together to save the world, the two sisters in the story act as a visual metaphor for the contemporary #MeToo movement—that of not believing women and/or of silencing women's voices. I argue that the opening scene and other scenes provide an allegory for assault and harassment the #MeToo movement tries to address in society (externally) as well as the powers and relationship that the sisters (internally) have with each other.

I would like to first contextualize the #MeToo movement in the United States and provide some key moments to the evolution of the movement that I will later link to *The Umbrella Academy*. On October 15, 2017, at 1:21 p.m., Alyssa Milano tweeted, "If you've been sexually harassed or assaulted write 'me too' as a reply to this tweet." Alyssa Milano (1972– ), a white American actress and feminist activist, has a prominence on social media, including Twitter, and uses those platforms in order to discuss politics and social justice. In her tweet, Milano screen-capped an image of text quoted to explain that if women tweeted "Me Too" then people would understand the "magnitude of the problem" concerning sexual harassment and assault. Milano provided no citation for the image, nor did she explain where the idea came from. The "magnitude" refers to the statistics concerning women's lived experiences of sexual harassment and assault. With numbers varying from 1 in 4 to 1 in 5 depending on the research and the question posed in the research.[4]

Milano's tweet went "viral," or spread quickly across social media platforms. Approximately one year later, in the article "How Social Media Users Have Discussed Sexual Harassment Since #MeToo Went Viral" (October 11, 2018), the Pew Research Center analyzed the usage of the term #MeToo on the internet. They reported that the hashtag had been used over 19 million times on Twitter alone, thus creating a viral trend in a popular social medium. The Pew Research Center also noted in the article from their survey that a majority of social media users reported seeing content about sexual harassment and sexual assault in their social media. To add to coverage of the #MeToo movement, The *New York Times* added a "gender editor," Jessica Bennett, to their staff and counts 18 distinct articles[5] covering the #MeToo movement in the United States.

The cultural importance of the #MeToo movement emphasizes similar, lived experiences for women. The hashtag movement has given women the opportunity to express, without force of sharing details, that they have a lived experience with sexual harassment and/or assault. Expression without sharing becomes a vital aspect to the #MeToo movement since women often do not report the crime. Also, nearly one year later, Christine Blasey Ford, a white woman professor, appeared before Congress on September 27, 2018, to testify against Supreme Court Justice Nominee Brett Kavanaugh. Blasey Ford shared her story, accusing Kavanaugh of having groped her, attempting to assault her, and threateningly covering her mouth when she attempted to scream. The incident occurred when they were teenagers. Blasey Ford's testimony made headlines and was discussed heavily in social media as part of the #MeToo movement. However, the days and weeks that followed Blasey Ford's testimony created a backlash of threats, headlines, and discussions to discredit her with people trying to silence Blasey Ford's lived experience. These cultural moments in American history are brought up here for two reasons, which both highlight cultural phenomena of women's lived experiences when recounting their experiences of sexual harassment and assault. The hashtag #MeToo became quickly synonymous with lived experiences of sexual harassment and assault. The movement itself also highlighted prominent men and their behaviors while the public demanded the men be held accountable for their actions. However, the consequential backlash women received surrounding both related moments express a culturally embedded response to accusations of sexual harassment and assault. In the case of Blasey Ford, discrediting the accuser and silencing her voice became part of the cultural discourse. In an article for *Glamour*, Abby Gardner writes, "Immediately following Blasey Ford's decision to go public, however reluctant, doubts were raised about the veracity of the story and the motives behind it" (September 21, 2018). Gardner details how in the days following Blasey Ford's public statement, Blasey Ford was threatened and essentially forced into hiding.

Yet, Milano and Blasey Ford, both white women as previously stated, were not the first to create a movement or to publicly testify before Congress about a Supreme Court Nominee. The viral nature of the movement since Milano's tweet often hides or silences the origin's movement in America. The "me too" movement was founded by Tarana Burke, a Black woman, in 2006. On the website's history page for the organization, it states "The 'me too.' movement was founded in 2006 to help survivors of sexual violence, particularly Black women and girls, and other young women of color from low wealth communities, find pathways to healing." Burke has worked with and developed programs and curricula to help survivors of color in their communities to address assault and harassment. Burke describes a moment she had with a woman who shared her personal experience of assault with Burke and how Burke listened briefly and suggested that the woman see someone else to better help her. Burke states, "I watched her walk away from me as she tried to recapture her secrets and tuck them back into their hiding place. I watched her put her mask back on and go back into the world like she was all alone and I couldn't even bring myself to whisper … me too." From this single moment, Burke was inspired to create the movement to help survivors. Moreover, Anita Hill (1956– ), a Black woman lawyer, accused the then Supreme Court Justice nominee Clarence Thomas of sexual harassment in 1991. Hill also testified before Congress detailing her experiences of sexual harassment by Thomas while working for him. Hill was the first woman to accuse a Supreme Court Nominee of sexual harassment which led to a secondary hearing. Hill faced public scrutiny for her testimony. Both the Hill/Blasey Ford and Burke/Milano moments represent racial relationships between women using their voices to share lived experiences of sexual harassment and assault and amplify the voices of others' experiences. However, in both cases, the white women eclipse and/or erase the original Black women's voices. As we will see, *The Umbrella Academy* visually echoes a cultural pattern of white women's voices overpowering and/or silencing Black women's voices.[6]

It is important to note that *The Umbrella Academy* does not feature, apart from the opening sequence, sexual harassment or assault as a motif or plot point. I am not arguing that the relationship between Allison and Vanya gives voice to the #MeToo movement or represents women's lived experiences with sexual harassment and/or assault. The sisters, Vanya and Allison, offer a familiar visual representation that resonates and replicates the lived experiences of women concerning their voices. Or, to put it more succinctly, Allison and Vanya replicate the lived experiences of women when they tell their stories. The Netflix series cast a woman of color to play Allison, a choice that is not reflected in the original comics series. However, it is argued here that Allison's character visually represents the intersection of race and gender in her lived experiences in systems of oppression with her sister's character Vanya. Allison's power hinges on the spread of gossip or making a statement framed as an untruth—"I heard a rumor…"—which then becomes reality. Allison's power allows her to manipulate people into doing or being what she purports them to do or to be. Allison's power, subsequently, casts doubt on her sincerity, her motives, as well as reality since she creates it from lies. Allison's codename, "Rumor," which directly references her superpower, reinforces and destabilizes her credibility. How can the characters in the diegesis trust Allison when whatever she says may be based on a created lie or story from Allison's rumors?

Tarana Burke succinctly addresses the marginalization of Black women in an interview for the *New York Times*. While discussing the movement she created, Burke discusses marginalized communities and how women of color seem absent from the viral media movement. Burke states, "This is just a theory: I think the media doesn't really care about the stories of black women and the stories of women of color" ("She Founded Me Too" 2018). Allison, the celebrity Black actress, is undermined by her own superpower because her story is a "rumor." In the first episode, the spectator learns that adult Allison has become a famous actress. The first image the viewer sees of adult Allison is on the red carpet, photographed by the paparazzi and reporters, and silent. The career choice Allison makes is ironic. Acting is a career based on presenting a lie for an audience to believe, while tabloids and gossip columns create lies and spread rumors about her public and personal life. Allison's career and life are a representation of her superpower—rumors. However, casting a Black woman to play the part visually reinforces the marginalization of Black women as untrustworthy and not credible.

As the season progresses, Allison's superpowers and story intersect. In the fifth episode, "Number Five," written by Bob DeLaurentis, Allison worries about Vanya's potential love interest and warns her to be careful: "Leonard seems perfectly charming, perfectly thoughtful, perfect. But I've been around long enough to know that when something seems too perfect it's usually anything but" (15:26). Allison's concern is not remarkable. Either Allison's worry is misplaced and merely an overbearing concern for her sister, or she is expressing a ubiquitous concern about a possibly dangerous man based on prior experiences. Margaret Renkle expresses the ubiquitous reality of women being suspicious of men in her article, "The Raw Power of #MeToo." Renkle recounts how she did not raise her teenage sons with stories of growing up and experiencing sexual harassment from men. She explains how her experiences with men have changed her behaviors with regard to safety measures. After citing her own personal examples as well as those of friends, Renkle states, "There is nothing unusual about these stories. They are the ho-hum, everyday experiences of virtually every woman I know, and such stories rarely get told." Allison's words of warning to her sister Vanya express a common and everyday concern for many women. This is the second time in the show that Allison expresses to Vanya her suspicions about the man.[7] Allison expresses clearly why she worries and the problematic behaviors of Vanya's suitor.

However, in the same scene, Vanya responds to Allison's sisterly concern by also calling into question Allison's superpowers. Vanya responds, "Like a woman who's based her whole life on rumors? Some people actually mean what they say" (15:36). Vanya's retort not only questions Allison's sincerity, but it also casts doubt on her story and whether Vanya believes Allison because of her superpower. This moment in the show is a larger metaphor for the optics of dissonance. Allison uses her voice to express concern and worry based on previous experience only to be dismissed as a lie. This scene is all too similar to the backlash both Anita Hill and Christine Blasey Ford experienced during their testimony. Both Hill and Blasey Ford had their credibility questioned, not only by the men they accused, but by the very people to whom they told their story. Abby Gardner analyzed tweets and Twitter commentary for Glamour magazine about Blasey Ford in the days around Blasey Ford's testimony. In Gardner's article, explicitly titled, "Death Threats and Discrediting: The Treatment of Christine Blasey

Ford Is a Reminder of What's at Stake for Sexual Assault Survivors," Gardner argues that the commentary concerning Blasey Ford was more negative than it was for Kavanaugh. Gardner argues, "A quick look at Twitter reveals that many civilians are having a difficult time recognizing the credibility of her claim—yet somehow buy into Kavanaugh's version of the story with ease. Essentially, the situation is a boiled-down version of what it means to be a woman: The burden lies on you to prove your worth and your truth." Similarly, Vanya forces Allison to prove her truth. However, Vanya does so by eliminating any possibility of success through Allison's superpower. As long as Allison can alter reality, or base her life on rumors, Allison cannot be heard as credible.

This moment reinforces visually the dissonance of Black women's voices and their credibility. The intersection of race and gender plays out on screen as Allison's, i.e., a Black woman's credibility is questioned by Vanya, a white woman. Allison who continues to ask the questions, does the work of protecting her family and voices her concerns for the betterment of society, which is consequently refuted and rebuffed by the white woman who she seeks to align herself with as sisters. Visually, this circles back to the Anita Hill testimony against Clarence Thomas. In the interview for the *New York Times*, Burke talks about the intersection of race and why Black women do not share their stories: "I've been told so many bad stories, whispers from Black women in Hollywood or in entertainment, that they just don't feel comfortable coming forward—because they haven't seen themselves in this narrative [...]. We can't wait for white folks to decide that our trauma is worth centering on when we know that it's happening" (Harris: 2018). Hill certainly faced public scrutiny and attacks on her credibility and character. She also suffered career setbacks for sharing her story (Katz: 2018; de Leon 2016; Oliver:2018). Yet, many of the articles concerning Hill's testimony discuss Thomas as a Black man,[8] but do not analyze how Hill's story was scrutinized since she is a Black woman. Or, as Jack E. White analyzed for *Time* magazine in 1991 during the testimony, "Black women's complaints about sexist behavior are taken even less seriously than white women's. Held down by racism and the sexism of both black and white males [...] their attempts to call attention to their plight routinely provoke storms of energy denial of the legitimacy of their complaints." Allison's race and superpower intersect visually in the show to replicate the experience of Black women in America, who are denied credibility.

Vanya's aggressive statement directed towards Allison recognizes that Allison's superpower controls people into believing something that is inherently not true: a rumor. Examples of the nature of Allison's power and her credibility as a character appear throughout the show. In episode 8, "I Heard a Rumor" written by Lauren Schmidt Hisserich and Sneha Koorse, we see Allison with her daughter at night recounting stories about being a superhero. Her daughter asks Allison questions about "Aunt Vanya" and why she did not participate in the stories. Allison responds, "She's a little different than the rest of us" (1:55).[9] However, when it is time for her daughter to go to sleep, Allison's daughter exclaims she is not tired, yet and wants more stories. The sequence shows a parenthood trope of the nighttime routine with a resistant child. The viewer watches Allison use her voice and power to convince her daughter to go to sleep, which her husband witnesses. The viewer then understands the context as to why Allison lost custody and why the marriage ended. Allison's use of her superpower to parent immediately calls into question her credibility as a mother, as well as whether her power is used in sincerity. This scene reestablishes a norm that good mothers would never use such a tactic to raise their children or to deny her child's free-will. The episode reinforces Vanya's retort from earlier. Since Allison uses her power on her child to parent,[10] the viewer cannot trust whether she is credible or just lies to suit her needs and motives. Later in the same episode, "I Heard a Rumor," a shot of Allison driving a car to find Vanya shows Allison lost in thought and thinking about all the times she used her power. The viewer hears her say "I heard a rumor" to her daughter repeatedly in different parenting contexts, as well as career moves, but then the viewer hears, "I heard a rumor that you love me" (3:02). The last statement explains to the viewer that Allison used her power on her partner at some point in the past. The moment in the car again reiterates that Allison and her version of events cannot be trusted. Especially, as is implied by the statement, Allison used her superpowers to potentially convince her ex-husband that he loved her, which was not true. Her version of events, because of her superpower, are always called into question or doubted since they are based on insincerity or falsehoods. The implications for Allison's credibility serve as a metaphor for survivors of harassment and assault as their version, their story, is doubtful and always doubted—and more so for women of color.

Vanya's power which she discovers over the course of the series, is the ability to amplify sounds and use them as a force. Whereas the visual representation of Vanya remains silent or is forced into silence, it is often juxtaposed with how Allison's voice is untrustworthy. Yet, as will be discussed in detail below, it is Allison, the woman of color, who seeks out Vanya, the white woman, hoping to engage with her sister. Allison wants to talk, help, and work with her sister and wants her sister to reciprocate. Allison seeks a coalition[11] again and again with Vanya. However, Vanya continually rejects Allison or ignores what her sister says. The first example given to the viewer of Allison reaching out to Vanya occurs in the first episode, "We Only See Each Other at Weddings and Funerals." The spectator learns that

Vanya wrote a "tell all" autobiography about her experiences with the dysfunctional family—an action that has caused her father figure and siblings to reject her. Vanya's autobiography emphasizes Vanya seeking to use her voice and express her lived experience. The backlash, however, of rejection is felt on a microcosmic level through her family. Images of different family members reading Vanya's story, or the father-figure shelving it unopened, and becoming outraged at her speaking, re-inscribe the importance and necessity of Vanya's silence. Vanya's speaking out causes problems.

A striking visual scene happens during the funeral in the first episode. At their father's funeral, the chimpanzee, Pogo, who acts as a family butler and confidant, asks if anyone wishes to speak (38:03). The film shot frames Pogo in the foreground and in medium close-up with Vanya in the background but in deep focus. As Pogo asks if anyone would like to speak on behalf of their father, Vanya remains in deep focus and silent, forcing the spectator to see her silent in the background. The mise-en-scène and cinematography of the shot reinforce Vanya's position in the family as well as in her life outside the family. Vanya is quiet, isolated, and marginalized to the background. Although it is clear she has the opportunity to speak, Vanya remains silent under the oppressive rejection of her brothers due to her infraction of having written a tell-all autobiography. Vanya's voice is not welcome, whether it speaks the truth or not. The take foreshadows the importance of Vanya's silence as her superpower of dissonance could not only disrupt the status quo but could destroy the world. Vanya's voice is background noise that, when amplified, becomes powerful and dangerous. Again, the show visually juxtaposes and significantly highlights Allison as a Black woman against Vanya's whiteness and the relationship dynamic between them. At their father's funeral, Allison approaches Vanya and extends a proverbial olive branch by welcoming her. Allison seeks Vanya and encourages her to be a part of the family. Allison seeks to build a coalition, as sisters. Throughout the first season episodes, Allison continuously seeks out Vanya to build a relationship and forge a bond between the women. However, Vanya does not seek Allison during the show and does not reach out to her sister to build a relationship. The varying scenes of Allison talking to her sister, asking her questions, and chasing after her reiterate Allison working at a relationship with Vanya. By contrast, Vanya continually refutes, rebuffs, and runs from her sister.

When Vanya slowly discovers and realizes she has superpowers, she does not seek out her sister to help her or discuss her abilities. Vanya instead only reveals her powers to Allison after Allison seeks out Vanya to help her and protect her from the man who is a threat to Vanya and the family. Allison seeks out Vanya to tell her the truth. While Vanya explains that she, too, has powers, and rebuffs Allison's story about Vanya's love interest, Allison remembers that their father-figure used her own powers to convince Vanya that she was ordinary. In the episode, "I Heard a Rumor," Allison recalls and realizes that "[their father] made me an accomplice" (44:07–45:44). The flashback tells the viewer that at the age of four, when Allison's and Vanya's father-figure isolated Vanya out of fear she would use her own superpower to resist his authority, he ordered the Rumor to use her power and say to Vanya, "I heard a rumor you think you're just ordinary." Allison recognizes her complicity in silencing her sister's voice. The scene becomes a metaphor of women in a patriarchal society upholding the systems of oppression by silencing other women's voices. In this case, after being asked to silence Vanya by their father, Allison silences Vanya into believing that she is normal and without powers. However, this flashback scene takes place when both Allison and Vanya are four, which only reinforces their upbringing and initiation into a culture of silencing women's voices. But Allison's age also highlights her inability to understand the consequences of her actions and how she should not be held accountable for them.

As previously mentioned, the twist of Allison's powers being used to suppress Vanya's creates a paradox that calls into question the very nature of Allison's powers. As the show continues, the viewer discovers that Vanya maintained her power in spite of the Rumor's suggestion. The paradox of the sisters' powers is the dissonance created by their powers—both sisters use sound to create dissonance by silencing others. Allison's power is used to silence Vanya, and ultimately, Vanya becomes strong enough to resist or realize the "lie" in her sister's superpower to overcome her and silence Allison in return. Both sisters are complicit in upholding the silence of the other. In episode 8, "I Heard a Rumor," the viewer sees a flashback of Vanya being trained by their father figure. But rather than participating in the training, Vanya resists him and uses her superpower to hurt their father. Later in the episode, a flashback shows Vanya being led to a silent and locked chamber to contain her because of her threat to their patriarchal father. Vanya's power could hurt the father figure which acts again as a metaphor for female voices challenging male authority. Allison recognizes her complicity as an adult. However, it is the patriarch that forces her to comply and to help him by manipulating a child. Yet, in this instance, although Allison is indeed guilty of complicity, she is not responsible for it.

To show the extent of the father figure's intent to dominate and force the children to submit to his authority, Episode 9, "Changes," opens with a scene about Vanya. A young Vanya sits at a table, looking indifferent. She is silent during the scene. The scene centers on various nannies attempting to get her to eat her oatmeal. However, while they sing to her and attempt to spoon feed her oatmeal, the tea kettle whistles on the stove, triggering

Vanya's powers and thus enabling her to resist; she uses her powers to throw the nannies across the room, down the stairs, out a window, etc. Vanya clearly does not like oatmeal and does not want to eat it. However, Vanya does not state nor use her voice to explain what she wants or does not want. Rather, she uses her power to control sound waves to express her resistance to the coercion of doing what she does not want to do. Vanya's dissonance is, each time, always met with a new nanny attempting and repeating the scene. Ultimately, Hargreeves creates Grace, an android and future mother figure, who is introduced as impossible to hurt or maim. At the realization that she cannot resist the mother figure, Vanya ultimately submits and eats the oatmeal. The scene reinforces the father figure's domination in the home and his use of women to enforce his rules and policies. When male domination does not suffice, the father figure employs women to do what he cannot. Thus, the father figure creates a mother figure that Vanya cannot resist in order to silence her.

Allison shows Vanya that she feels guilty for her participation in silencing Vanya. The eighth episode culminates in the two sisters talking and arguing about Vanya's and Allison's powers. In a shot that shows Allison kneeling in front of a sitting Vanya, Allison makes her intentions clear when she says, "I love you. And I just want to be here for you as your sister" ("I Heard a Rumor" 43:17). Allison seeks Vanya's forgiveness for participating in hurting Vanya. However, Vanya responds by again questioning Allison's version and her credibility in the following dialogue:

> VANYA: You did this to me.
> ALLISON: I didn't realize.
> VANYA: You knew this whole time? That I had powers. ["I Heard a Rumor" 46:06–46:18]

Both Vanya and Allison want to be heard and believed. Both women want their voice to count. However, their patriarchal father created a system that forced the two women to work against each other, which presents again a metaphor for women's stories in patriarchal society. Vanya argues and questions Allison by first accusing her and then questioning Allison knowing the truth but creating a lie. As with the autobiography, Vanya's story and voice had been dissonant and resistant, but the one person that should have been her ally was complicit in silencing her. The argument leads to a key moment in the series that vocally and visually represents the cultural framing of the #MeToo movement. After Allison admits how she complicity silenced Vanya, in "I Heard a Rumor," and that, as a child, she did not understand what she was doing or why, Vanya screams, "You destroyed my life!" (46:38). Vanya's phrasing that she was denied access to her powers—because she was silenced by her sister at the request of the father figure—shows her recognition of its effect on her life experiences. The silencing of Vanya, because she resisted her father figure's authority, forced her into the family's background. Vanya's brothers and sister marginalized her because her voice, and superpower, were taken away. Similarly, the #MeToo movement argues that women are not permitted to tell their stories, that they are forced into silence in order to protect the accused men. Women's forced silence, often because of the complicity of other women, has a negative impact on their careers and relationships due to the trauma. As the example of Vanya shows, women become marginalized either for their experiences or for trying to resist the control and manipulation of a perpetrator.

Vanya's outcry about being silenced evokes a strong reaction from Allison. Allison responds, "Oh Please! Vanya, everything is out in the open. We can move on!" ("I Heard a Rumor" 46:42). Allison's response to Vanya metaphorically represents the idea that sharing the truth, exposing it, allows those traumatized to move forward and past the trauma. This is not dissimilar to Tarana Burke's work on harassment and assault survivors, nor Anita Hill's testimony against Clarence Thomas, nor Christine Blasey Ford's testimony against Brett Kavanaugh. All three women opt to openly speak the truth and seek to move forward and move society forward. For Allison, the truth being "out in the open" allows the sisters to work together and work past the trauma. As the metaphor for the #MeToo movement plays out visually between the sisters, Vanya responds to Allison's hopeful idea that they can move on with the truth in the open. Allison wants to work together and form a relationship as sisters. However, Vanya does not accept Allison's proposal and responds, "I'm moving on, but not with you!" ("I Heard a Rumor": 46:43). This particular scene captures the gendered racial tensions of American culture and the #MeToo movement. More precisely, this sequence between the two sisters captures the centering of the white woman's story over the Black woman's story. The visual moment between the Black Allison being told by the white Vanya that she will move on without her offers the viewer a cultural representation of white women taking the work and claiming the movement as their own while erasing/silencing the work of the Black women before them. The violent culmination comes when Allison starts to use her power/voice out of fear of Vanya's emotional and violent reaction. The moment shows Vanya violently using her violin bow to slice Allison's throat and thus physically silencing her. In a violent moment, Vanya moves on from her sister's voice by silencing her.

The realization of her brutal and permanent silencing of her sister leads Vanya to say, "I didn't mean to" ("I Heard a Rumor": 48:13). Vanya's apology is not an apology as much as it speaks to her intent. Vanya did not intend to hurt nor permanently silence her sister; however, in spite of her intentions, that is exactly what she did. Similarly, in the #MeToo movement, Milano, and others, received criticism for erasing the work and voice of Tarana Burke who had originated the movement. The primary critique being that white women co-opt what Black women create without crediting the work while also ignoring the original intent of the movement. For their article on the Person of the Year 2017 for *Time* magazine, Stephanie Zacharek, Eliana Docterman, and Haley Sweetland Edwards interviewed numerous women who made headlines during the #MeToo moment. The article contextualizes different women's experiences, reactions, and highlights their stories and use of voice to hold their perpetrator's accountable. They write, "The phrase was first used more than a decade ago by social activist Tarana Burke as part of her work building solidarity among young survivors of harassment and assault. A friend of the actor Alyssa Milano sent her a screenshot of the phrase, and Milano, almost on a whim, tweeted it out on Oct. 15." The authors attribute the original movement to Burke and interview her. However, the significance of framing Milano's tweet as "a whim" de-centers the work of Burke and centers the affluent and white Milano. Burke had created the "me too" movement in order to help those marginalized in society with less access to services. Specifically, those people who are most vulnerable to questions of credibility, isolated and marginalized for difference. However, Milano's previously cited tweet, did not give credit for the idea or context for the phrasing #MeToo. Vanya, much like Milano, acted on a whim and incidentally silenced their Black predecessor.

In the same episode when Vanya violently silences Allison, we see the moment of fear that Vanya's powers create in the father figure. A flashback shows a young Vanya being trained by Hargreeves. However, this scene shows Vanya directly resisting her father's orders. Vanya resists her training and uses sound to throw a tantrum by exploding wine glasses at will. However, during Vanya's outburst, she also breaks Hargreeves' monocle and cuts his face with a shard of glass. Vanya's power hurts the father figure and poses a threat to his authority and dominion over the child. Rather than talking to the child, the father figure chooses to create a soundproof tank in the basement, hidden away from the other children and locks her away in solitude and silence. The lesson for the young Vanya is that dissonance leads to literal marginalization—prison. The aftermath of silencing Allison is quickly felt by Vanya. In Episode 9, "Changes," written by Bob DeLaurentis and Eric W. Phillips, Vanya sits in the tub, covered in her sister's blood. The scene shows her love interest washing the blood off of her body and trying to reassure her. Vanya is quiet and staring off into middle space. Her silence reads as a person in shock especially coming from the prior scene where she violently silences her sister's voice. The scene repeats the violence committed by white people on Black bodies as Vanya has a flashback and re-remembers the trauma she inflicts. The viewer sees the scene again and is reminded of how Vanya silenced her sister. Leonard, the white man, continues to reassure her that the violence was necessary, and that he is the only one who loves her. Leonard's words of love and reassurance in order to boost Vanya's self-esteem read as a metaphor for (white) patriarchy encouraging white women to fear and ultimately to silence Black women. Vanya continues to focus on her intent rather than her guilt by telling Leonard that she did not intend to hurt Allison.

During the episode, Vanya explains that she needs to talk to her brothers and sister and explain what happened. Vanya assumes that her family can forgive her violent transgression against Allison because her intentions were not bad. Days after Milano's tweet went viral, criticism that Milano had co-opted the movement began to emerge. Although Milano began giving credit to Burke in interviews (Sobel: 2018), the damage was done. Articles contextualizing the #MeToo movement often originate in Milano and footnote Burke. Rochelle Riley discusses Burke's critiques of people ignoring the marginalized in her article "#MeToo Founder Tarana Burke Blasts the Movement for Ignoring Poor Women." She begins her article by referencing Milano, and argues, "She didn't look like Alyssa Milano. But maybe that's because Tarana Burke, founder of the #MeToo movement that has led to complaints and indictments against dozens of men—and some women—for sexual harassment and assault, is a big, bold, fierce, powerful, outspoken Black woman, who is finally being seen" (2018). The dichotomy between the Vanya and Allison is one of limiting each other's powers and silencing each other. The show often presents Vanya as silent and Allison lies and pretends. But Allison is ultimately silenced by Vanya through the cutting of her vocal cords. Vanya is dangerous not only because she resists patriarchy, but because she silences those who might also attempt to resist patriarchy. The distinction between Allison and Vanya is that Allison commits her act of complicity by being manipulated as a child. Allison does not understand, nor does she recognize why her powers are being used until she is an adult, at which point Allison tries to apologize and move forward. However, Vanya, with the power and ability to amplify dissonance and use it as a power, decides to silence her sister. She knowingly and violently attacks her sister rather than joining forces and working together. Vanya could amplify Allison's voice and her own but instead, she wants her voice to be valued above others.

In the episode "Changes," Vanya seeks to explain to her brothers what happened and be forgiven. However, her brother Luther, the new family patriarch, fears Vanya's dissonant voice and superpowers and locks her away in the silent chamber where their father figure once kept her. The scene plays out with Luther and Klaus looking at Vanya, imprisoned in the quiet room, while screaming from a window in the door. The viewer sees Vanya pounding on the window but silenced by the impenetrable door. Vanya's brothers discuss what to do with her and argue about whether they should keep Vanya imprisoned. Luther says, "She's not just a danger to us" (32:26). Vanya's dissonant voice poses a threat to the family as well as to society. Although Vanya's threat to the family is quite literal, as seen in her attack against Allison, the statement is figurative as well. Vanya now controls her power—her voice—and can make others hear her. Much like the backlash over the #MeToo movement where men reported being less likely to hire women (Bower: 2019; Oliver: 2018; Gardner: 2018), women telling their stories and being heard threatens to destabilize societal norms for men's behaviors. Unlike the autobiography that could be shelved, not read, or ignored, Vanya's dissonant voice forces others to listen to her. Imprisoning Vanya in a silent chamber becomes a metaphor for silencing the voices of women. Finally, the visual of two brothers, two men, staring at the scared screaming but silenced woman in a cell, shows their complicity in keeping her quiet.

While trapped in the cell during the same episode, Vanya hallucinates her younger self talking to her. Although, as initially discussed, the psychological effects of the dysfunctional family become a factor in how the siblings relate to each other.[12] However, when Vanya hallucinates her younger self, Number 7,[13] the viewer gets a glimpse of the trauma Vanya suffered for believing she was "ordinary." Number 7 calmly observes, "Even after all these years. Afraid of our power" (40:36). Number 7, being a resistant and defiant child, recognizes the fear her power of dissonance creates as it disrupts the authority and continues, "Our brothers and sister. They're just like dad. Driven to keep us down. A muted voice. Isolated from the group. Never in the limelight. Never the center of attention. It will never end. Not until we act" (40:56). The literal and figurative statements about their father figure, silencing her voice, and her siblings' desire to silence her drives Vanya to focus her powers and to act erratically. This crucial moment in the plot shows the destructive force of silencing women's voices out of fear for destroying the patriarchy. In this case, childhood trauma that is perpetrated again on Vanya causes her to react violently. The father figure in the show, represented by an eccentric, old-fashioned white man, indoctrinates the children into his worldview. He trains the children and authoritatively controls their lives and how they use their powers. Hargreeves is domineering, cold, and distant with the children. A representation of his domineering distance is that he numbers the children rather than naming them. The children do not merit a name because they serve his purpose. The father thus becomes a representation of patriarchal society that not only indoctrinates (super)humans into conforming to his own standards and needs, but remains unfulfilling to those who live by its rule. Therefore, if the children show any resistance, they are punished. If they resist and are a threat to his authority, they are silenced and ultimately marginalized because they can no longer serve a purpose.

Allison, however, continues to argue for Vanya and criticizes Luther's patriarchal behavior that is reminiscent of their father's doctrine. She uses a small pad of paper and a felt marker to express her thoughts. However, visually, the small pad of paper limits her voice, as does the amount she writes with the large paper. When Allison confronts her brothers for imprisoning Vanya in the silence chamber, the brothers physically remove Allison from the space and refuse to allow her to release Vanya. Allison, the Black woman, is willing to forgive and free her sister, the white woman. With Allison's voice removed, she is powerless against her brothers' voices and physicality. Allison is left with the written word which is a role reversal for her and Vanya. However, the written word does not suffice to effectively come together and fight. Again, the moment where Allison confronts her brothers about Vanya inside her silence chamber, behind the window, acts as a visual metaphor for the #MeToo movement. Allison is left with merely a few words, like #MeToo, to express what has been done. Allison uses these words to show how to move forward, but the brothers deny her to take action.

In sum, neither character contends with or deals with assault or harassment of a sexual nature. Neither is a victim like the people who share their #MeToo stories, such as Anita Hill and Christine Blasey Ford. However, as is noted in various articles about the #MeToo movement, women's stories of sexual assault and harassment center around the banal quality of the stories because of the sheer number of incidents. The commonality makes the events seem unremarkable and not pressing. In addition to the quotidian aspect, women are often not given credibility in their stories or are silenced. It is this latter aspect, the lack of credibility and silencing of women's voices, that is visually relevant to *The Umbrella Academy*. Allison and Vanya act as a visual metaphor for women's lived experiences that is simultaneously gendered and raced. One character represents the lack of credibility, in particular of Black women, and the other represents the silencing of women's voices, from outside and within. Both characters seek to share their stories, to participate fully in society and to be heard by those that matter to them. While this essay focuses on season 1 of *The Umbrella Academy*, it is worthy to note that the primary action of season 2 continues to act as a metaphor of raced and gendered experiences for the sisters. The action takes place in Dallas, Texas, in 1963 surrounding the Kennedy assassination. The siblings find themselves scattered and trapped in the past, only to confront their dysfunctional family structure in order to ultimately try to save the world from yet another apocalypse. The sisters' voices become central to their own individual lives in the season 2 arc. Allison gets involved with the American Civil Rights movement while refusing to use her superpower. And Vanya finds herself as a nanny living on a remote and secluded farm, having forgotten her powers again, but discovering her lesbian feelings for the wife and mother of her host family. Both sisters continue to act as gendered metaphors of the threat women pose on societal norms. Both Allison and Vanya play the role of the "normal" woman without superpowers and the patriarchal white man's stereotypical fear of her: Allison is a Black woman fighting for racial equality thus disrupting the power of the white man, and Vanya disrupts the patriarchal family structure by being a lesbian and thus eliminating the need for a man. The second season continues to use stereotypical images of how women's voices disrupt and create dissonance for white men. Hence, *The Umbrella Academy* visually echoes the cultural relevance of women's dissonance.

Notes

1. For more about emotional labor and the additional work women do, see: Arlie R. Hochschild, *The Managed Heart: Commercialization of Human Feeling* (Berkeley: University of California Press, 1983).
2. I refer to her as Allison throughout the essay because it is the name the character chose for herself in the show. "Number 3" is the distancing and non-identity bearing name her father-figure gave her. "Rumor" is a codename that references her superpower.
3. I refer to her as Vanya for similar reasons as I refer to Allison. Please note the order that I listed the names as a not-so-subtle reference to Vanya and her powers. Vanya was given "Number 7" by her father-figure; however, Vanya was raised believing that she was without superpowers, which turns out to be false. Vanya discovers her superpowers late and thus gets the code name after the first two names. She is "the White Violin."
4. For more information about sexual assault and violence, the National Sexual Violence Resource Center https://www.nsvrc.org/ and the Center for Disease Control https://www.cdc.gov/injury/features/sexual-violence/index.html keep statistics about sexual assault.
5. There were 18 articles designated by the *New York Times* as related to the #MeToo movement at the time of the writing of this essay.
6. For more on Black feminism critiquing racism, see: Hill Collins P., *From Black Power to Hip Hop: Racism, Nationalism, and Feminism* (Philadelphia: Temple University Press, 2006); bell hooks, *Black Looks: Race and Representation* (Boston: South End Press, 1992); Akasha G. Hull, Patricia Bell-Scott, and Barbara Smith, *All the Women Are White, All the Blacks Are Men, but Some of Us Are Brave: Black Women's Studies* (Old Westbury, NY: Feminist Press, 1982).
7. As it turns out, Allison is correct and Vanya's love interest happens to have vengeful and malicious intent towards Vanya's family.
8. Thomas, in response to Hill's allegations, during his testimony before Congress referred to the accusations of sexual harassment as a "lynching" highlighting his position as a Black man.
9. The question-and-answer sequence highlights the marginalization of Vanya within the family and her later marginalization outside the family.
10. There is not enough space or time in this essay to analyze the inherent sexism in the critique of Allison using her superpower to parent. I compare this scene to *The Incredibles*,

a Pixar movie about superheroes who are forced into hiding. The main characters have children and use their superpowers to their advantage to parent. Specifically, the father uses his super strength to parent. Further exploration of superpowers and parenting could be fruitful for analyzing sexism.

11. Coalitions are formed through similar, but differing, oppressed experiences and identities within systems of oppression. In this case, Vanya and Allison share a similar experience of being dismissed, marginalized, or doubted by their voices. I use the term "coalition" here in direct reference to Kimberlé Crenshaw's essays on the framework of intersectionality. See: Kimberlé W. Crenshaw, "Mapping the Margins." *Critical Race Theory: The Key Writings That Formed the Movement*, edited by Kimberlé Crenshaw ... [et al.]. (1995).

12. Their relationships to each other are disharmonious and create tension for the varying plot points.

13. For the ease of reading, I refer to the younger Vanya as Number 7 since she has a hallucinatory conversation with herself.

## Works Cited

@Alyssa_Milano. "If You've Been Sexually Harassed or Assaulted Write 'Me Too' as a Reply to This Tweet." *Twitter*, October 15, 2017, 1:21 p.m., twitter.com/alyssa_milano/status/919659438700670976?lang=en.

Bower, Tim. "The #MeToo Backlash." *Harvard Business Review*, September-October 2019. hbr.org/2019/09/the-metoo-backlash. Accessed December 2, 2019.

"Changes." *The Umbrella Academy*, written by Bob DeLaurentis and Eric W. Phillips, directed by Jeremy Webb, Netflix, 2019.

Gardner, Abby. "Christine Blasey Ford Reveals the Threats She's Faced Since Testifying Against Brett Kavanaugh." *Glamour*, November 26, 2018. glamour.com/story/christine-blasey-ford-reveals-the-threats-shes-faced-since- testifying-against-brett-kavanaugh. Accessed December 2, 2019.

_____. "Death Threats and Discrediting: The Treatment of Christine Blasey Ford Is a Reminder of What's at Stake for Sexual Assault Survivors." *Glamour*, September 21, 2018. glamour.com/story/christine-blasey-ford-death-threats-why-women-dont-report-sexual-assault. Accessed October 10, 2019.

_____. "During Christine Blasey Ford's Testimony, Contempt for Women Was on Full Display." *Glamour*, September 27, 2018. glamour.com/story/contempt-for-women-christine-blasey-ford-testimony. Accessed October 10, 2019.

Harris, Aisha. "She Founded Me Too. Now She Wants to Move Past the Trauma." *New York Times*, Oct 15, 2018.

"I Heard a Rumor." *The Umbrella Academy*, written by Lauren Schmidt Hissirich and Sneha Koorse, directed by Jeremy Webb, Netflix, 2019.

Katz, Celeste. "In the Age of #MeToo, Will Christine Blasey Ford's Experience Be the Same as Anita Hill's?" *Glamour*, September 17, 2018. glamour.com/story/christine-blasey-ford-anita-hill-kavanaugh-thomas-supreme-court-hearings. Accessed October 10, 2019.

Leon, Concepcion de. "Why We Still Need Anita Hill." *Glamour*, April 12, 2016. glamour.com/story/why-we-still-need-anita-hill. Accessed October 10, 2019.

"MeToo Mvmt." metoomvmt.org/about/#history. Accessed October 10, 2019.

"Number Five." *The Umbrella Academy*, written by Bob DeLaurentis, directed by Ellen Kuras, Netflix, 2019.

Oliver, John. "Workplace Sexual Harassment: Last Week Tonight with John Oliver." July 29, 2018. youtube.com/watch?v=dHiAls8loz4. Accessed October 15, 2019.

Pew Research Center. "How Social Media Users Have Discussed Sexual Harassment Since #MeToo Went Viral." pewresearch.org/fact-tank/2018/10/11/how-social-media-users-have-discussed-sexual-harassment-since-metoo-went-viral/ft_18-10-11_metooanniversary_majority-social-media-users/. Accessed November 30, 2019.

Renkle, Margaret. "The Raw Power of #MeToo: [Op-Ed]." *New York Times*, Oct 20, 2017.
Rochelle, Riley. "#MeToo Founder Tarana Burke Blasts the Movement for Ignoring Poor Women." *Detroit Free Press,* November 15, 2018. freep.com/story/news/columnists/rochelle-riley/2018/11/15/tarana-burke-metoo- movement/2010310002/. Accessed November 30, 2019.
Sehgal, Parul. "#MeToo, Fictionalized: [the Arts/Cultural Desk]." *New York Times*, May 02, 2019.
"Sexual Assault in the United States." *National Sexual Violence Resource Center.* nsvrc.org/node/4737. Accessed December 28, 2019.
"Sexual Violence Is Preventable." *Center for Disease Control,* December 19, 2019. cdc.gov/injury/features/sexual-violence/index.html. Accessed December 28, 2019.
Sobel, Ariel. "Why #MeToo Activist Alyssa Milano Will Not Speak at Next Women's March." *Advocate,* October 30, 2018. advocate.com/women/2018/10/30/metoo-activist-alyssa-milano-wont-be-stopped. Accessed December 2, 2019.
"We Only See Each Other at Weddings and Funerals." *The Umbrella Academy,* written by Jeremy Slater, directed by Peter Hoar, Netflix, 2019.
White, Jack E. "The Stereotypes of Race." *Time,* October 21, 1991.
Zacharek, Stephanie, et al. "Person of the Year 2017: Silence Breakers." *Time,* 2017. time.com/time-person-of-the-year-2017-silence-breakers/. Accessed October 10, 2019.users-have-discussed-sexual-harassment-since-metoo-went-viral/ft_18–10–11_metooanniversary_majority-social-media-users/. Accessed November 30, 2019.

# About the Contributors

Lisann **Anders** holds an MA and Ph.D. in English literature from the University of Zurich, Switzerland, and an MA in screenwriting from NUI Galway. Her research interests include Shakespeare, popular culture, and film. She has published several essays in edited volumes, including "Making Her Own Destiny: Disney's Diverse Females" and "The Normal Abnormal: Identity Formation in the Circus Space."

Dana **Fore** is a native Californian who received a Ph.D. in Victorian British literature (1798–1900) from the University of California, Davis, in 2005. His interests include disability theory, the Gothic, film studies, and the literature of fantasy and horror. His analyses of the fantasy and horror genres have discussed Gothic conventions in the *Supernatural* series and elements of the uncanny in *Doctor Who*.

Morgane A. **Ghilardi** is a research and teaching assistant at the University of Zurich. Her dissertation focuses on gender, technology, and the politics of artificiality in contemporary American media. She has been invited to speak about her research at the Swiss Digital Association, the University of St. Gallen, and Stanford University, among others, and was the recipient of the 2019 U.S. Embassy SANAS Travel Award.

J.E. **Hornsby** is a senior lecturer of French and Francophone studies at the University of Kentucky. She holds an MA in French literature and a doctorate in gender and women's studies. Her research focuses on gendered narratives and how they are visually represented in comics and/or film in France and the United States. She teaches courses in French about comics, film, and 20th- and 21st-century women's narratives.

Miranda **Johnsen** studies the portrayal of trauma in both postwar American literature and film at Gustavus Adolphus College. Her research includes the representations of existentialism, post-structuralism, and metaphor in HBO's *The Leftovers*, and comparisons of how Tove Jansson's *Moomin* novels and Hayao Miyazaki's *Studio Ghibli* films depict industrialism's effect on nature.

Fernando Gabriel **Pagnoni Berns** is a professor at the Universidad de Buenos Aires (UBA)—Facultad de Filosofía y Letras (Argentina). He teaches courses on international horror film. He has authored a book about the Spanish horror TV series *Historias para no Dormir* (2020) and has edited a book on Frankenstein bicentennial. He is editing a book on director James Wan and another on the Italian *giallo* film.

## About the Contributors

Alokparna **Sen** is a graduate of the master's program at the Department of English at Jadavpur University in Kolkata, India. Her areas of interest include postcolonial literature, postmodern literature, and speculative fiction (with a focus on fantasy fiction, superhero fiction, and horror fiction). She cotranslated *Thakurmar Jhuli*, the seminal collection of Bengali folktales, into English, as a master's project.

Kathleen **Shaughnessy** is a Ph.D. candidate at the University of Iowa. She studies science, crime, the Gothic, and medicine in 18th and 19th century British literature. Her research traces depictions of malpractice in works of Gothic fiction.

# Index

ableism 89
abuse 5, 7, 33–7, 46, 108, 111–3, 115–8, 120–5, 142
adoption 7, 12–4, 17, 19–21, 24, 33, 49–55, 57, 59, 61–7, 76, 95, 97, 115, 124
alter ego 32–41, 43, 45, 47
artifice 37, 70, 72, 79–80, 83
audience 1–2, 4, 12–3, 15, 18, 25, 29, 40, 42, 71, 73, 85, 90, 99, 108, 110, 112–3, 119, 122–4, 129, 131, 134–5, 141–2, 146–8, 152

belonging 50–2, 56–7, 67, 101–2, 133
Bildungsroman 10, 19, 22, 28, 103
body 12, 23, 35, 40–2, 46, 50, 52, 57, 60–1, 63, 65, 76, 82–3, 86, 90, 93–5, 98, 100–1, 105, 112, 124, 128, 130, 132–3, 136–48, 159; *see also* physicality

child endangerment 111–5, 122–3; *see also* abuse
civil rights 4, 75, 86, 104, 163
coalition 154, 164; *see also* unity
comics 1–8, 10–7, 19–24, 27–30, 32, 34, 47, 52, 58, 66, 70–1, 73–6, 85–7, 106, 109, 111, 123–6, 128, 141, 143–7, 151
community 52, 55, 75, 89, 103, 110, 112, 150–1
constructedness 7, 44–5, 49, 54, 70–2, 75, 80–2, 84, 96, 122, 130, 148
crystal moment 5, 127–8, 132–3, 138–45; *see also* crystal song; music; musical moment
crystal song 127–8, 131–2, 145–6; *see also* crystal moment; music; musical moment
deconstruction 6–7, 38, 44–5, 49, 54, 56, 70–3, 75–6, 78–86, 96, 98, 100, 105, 112, 115, 118, 122–3, 129–30, 148
diegesis 3, 71–5, 82–5, 127–30, 132–7, 140–2, 145–6, 151
disability 5, 88, 89, 90–7, 100, 102–6, 118
domestic violence *see* abuse; violence
drugs 16–9, 21–2, 25, 40–5, 62–3, 73, 76, 131, 135, 140, 142

estrangement 5, 7, 18–9, 49–67, 124
ethnicity 51–2, 67
eugenics 91, 97, 100

family 2–3, 5–7, 10–2, 14–8, 20–1, 23–9, 40, 50, 52, 55–9, 61–2, 64–7, 70–2, 75–8, 81–4, 86, 93, 102, 104, 110, 113, 116, 119–22, 124–5, 133–5, 148, 153, 155, 158, 160–3
femininity 86, 99
feminism 7, 149, 163; *see also* #MeToo
Ford, Christine Blasey 149, 152, 158, 162, 168
fragmentation 6, 55, 71, 77, 80–1, 84, 131, 135
freak 75, 89–90, 93, 95, 97, 103, 105

gender 2–3, 71, 76, 79–82, 84, 86, 147–9, 151, 153, 158, 162–3
genre 1–2, 5, 32, 48–9, 54, 70–4, 77–8, 83–5, 88–9, 92, 94, 103, 108–12, 122, 147
Gothic 5, 7, 10–2, 14–30, 89, 92
Grace 3, 26, 58, 71, 77–84, 86, 116, 145, 157

Hargreeves, Allison 3, 4, 23, 25–9, 34, 36–40, 45, 56–7, 60, 62–3, 65, 76, 80–2, 86, 104–5, 112–3, 116–24, 130, 132–5, 139–42, 148, 151–64
Hargreeves, Ben 3, 10, 12–3, 15, 19, 21–4, 27, 29, 41, 60, 63–4, 76, 77, 83, 105, 112–4, 118, 123–4, 136, 145
Hargreeves, Diego 15, 22, 27–9, 34, 36, 50, 52, 57–8, 60–1, 64, 66, 76, 80–3, 98, 104–5, 112–3, 115, 118–120, 124, 133–5, 140–1
Hargreeves, Five 12, 15, 20–1, 28, 46, 57–8, 60, 65–6, 76–7, 79, 83, 94, 102–5, 112–3, 118–9, 124, 133, 136–42, 144–5, 152, 164
Hargreeves, Klaus 3, 10, 12, 15, 17, 18–23, 28–30, 33, 40–7, 57–8, 60, 62, 65, 76–7, 83, 94, 104–5, 112–3, 115–6, 118–9, 124, 133–5, 140–2, 160
Hargreeves, Luther 15, 18, 23, 27, 29, 33–43, 45, 47, 57, 58, 60–3, 65, 76–7, 80, 83, 85, 93, 99, 105, 112–3, 115, 118–120, 124, 129–30, 132–5, 140–2, 160–2
Hargreeves, Reginald 3, 10, 12–3, 18, 29, 32–8, 40, 42–3, 46–7, 50, 62, 63, 76, 93, 95–6, 102–4, 112–24, 133, 135, 137, 142, 145
Hargreeves, Vanya 3, 7, 10, 15–6, 21, 23–9, 39, 50, 56–7, 61–3, 65, 76–8, 81–3, 86, 94, 100–2, 104–5, 112, 116–24, 128, 131, 133–7, 140–1, 143–6, 148, 151–64

169

# 170 Index

heterochrony 5, 139, 141
heterotopia 5, 7, 38, 127–8, 132–5, 137–9, 141–3, 145–6
Hill, Anita 150, 152–3, 158, 162, 164

Irony 17, 42, 71, 74, 77–8, 83–5, 87–8, 140, 146, 152

Jenkins, Harold 124, 142, 143; *see also* Peabody, Leonard

liminality 17, 32–47, 104

masculinity 38, 88, 99
melodrama 72, 76, 83, 86
Milano, Alyssa 149, 159–60, 164–5
musical moment 128, 130–2, 146; *see also* crystal moment; crystal song; music

nationality 2, 13, 14, 49–53, 55, 59, 62, 64–7, 75, 96, 100, 106, 163, 165
nostalgia 4, 34, 71, 74–5, 77, 85–7, 137
Number Five *see* Hargreeves, Five
Number Four *see* Hargreeves, Klaus
Number One *see* Hargreeves, Luther
Number Six *see* Hargreeves, Ben
Number Three *see* Hargreeves, Allison
Number Two *see* Hargreeves, Diego
parody 96, 100, 103
Peabody, Leonard 24–5, 27, 120–1, 124, 142–3, 146, 152, 160; *see also* Jenkins, Harold
performativity 6, 59, 72, 78–9, 81, 84, 86, 110, 129, 132–3, 136–7, 139–41, 143, 145
physicality 5, 14, 16, 20, 23, 33, 35, 38–41, 47, 75, 78–9, 89–96, 100, 105, 109–10, 113, 115–6, 118–20, 138, 133–4, 136–7, 139–43, 147–8, 158, 162; *see also* body
post-cinematic 7, 70–2, 79, 81–2, 84–5, 87

race 2–3, 50–3, 55, 59, 66–7, 71, 76, 86, 91, 124, 147–8, 151, 153, 158, 162–5

satire 89, 95, 99, 104
self-consciousness 54–5, 58–9, 64, 74, 90, 129
self-destruction 63, 141–2
self-discovery 15, 24, 141–2
self-relexivity 5, 71, 73, 78, 83–4, 127, 132, 136, 139, 145
silence 4, 7, 57, 93, 98, 101, 147–51, 154–62, 165
stigma 89, 91, 93–4, 102, 105, 113
superpowers 3, 5, 12, 15, 52, 60, 62, 93, 110, 113, 118–21, 137, 141–3, 148, 151–6, 158, 160, 163

theatricality 128–9, 132, 137, 139, 143–5

uncanny 5, 7, 16, 84, 88, 96–8, 102, 114, 125, 137, 145
unity 3, 15, 21, 29, 40, 50, 56, 58, 64–5, 76, 78, 82, 84, 127, 133–4, 145–7; *see also* coalition

violence *see* abuse; domestic violence; hyper-violence
visuality 1–2, 4, 18, 46, 74–5, 79, 82, 95, 98, 108, 127–30, 132, 139, 141, 144, 147–8, 151–5, 157–8, 161–3
voice 1, 3, 4, 7, 22, 52, 58–60, 82, 101, 104, 125, 129, 147–64

women 3, 7, 10, 13, 75, 84, 106, 147–65

www.ingramcontent.com/pod-product-compliance
Lightning Source LLC
Chambersburg PA
CBHW032047300426
44117CB00009B/1227